Tatiana

2018

Non-Governmental Public Action

Series Editor: **Jude Howell**, Professor and Director of the Centre for Civil Society, London School of Economics and Political Science, UK

Non-governmental public action (NGPA) by and for disadvantaged and marginalized people has become increasingly significant over the past two decades. This new book series is designed to make a fresh and original contribution to the understanding of NGPA. It presents the findings of innovative and policy-relevant research carried out by established and new scholars working in collaboration with researchers across the world. The series is international in scope and includes both theoretical and empirical work.

The series marks a departure from previous studies in this area in at least two important respects. First, it goes beyond a singular focus on developmental NGOs or the voluntary sector to include a range of non-governmental public actors such as advocacy networks, campaigns and coalitions, trades unions, peace groups, rights-based groups, cooperatives and social movements. Second, the series is innovative in stimulating a new approach to international comparative research that promotes comparison of the so-called developing world with the so-called developed world, thereby querying the conceptual utility and relevance of categories such as North and South.

Titles include:

Barbara Bompani and Maria Frahm-Arp (*editors*)
DEVELOPMENT AND POLITICS FROM BELOW
Exploring Religious Spaces in the African State

Brian Doherty and Timothy Doyle
Environmentalism, Resistance and Solidarity
The Politics of Friends of the Earth International

Dena Freeman (*editor*)
PENTECOSTALISM AND DEVELOPMENT
Churches, NGOs and Social Change in Africa

David Herbert
CREATING COMMUNITY COHESION
Religion, Media and Multiculturalism

Jude Howell and Jeremy Lind
COUNTER-TERRORISM, AID AND CIVIL SOCIETY
Before and After the War on Terror

Jude Howell (*editor*)
GLOBAL MATTERS FOR NON-GOVERNMENTAL PUBLIC ACTION

Jude Howell (*editor*)
NON-GOVERNMENTAL PUBLIC ACTION AND SOCIAL JUSTICE

Jenny Pearce (*editor*)
PARTICIPATION AND DEMOCRACY IN THE TWENTY-FIRST CENTURY

Tim Pringle and Simon Clarke
THE CHALLENGE OF TRANSITION
Trade Unions in Russia, China and Vietnam

Diane Stone
KNOWLEDGE ACTORS AND TRANSNATIONAL GOVERNANCE
The Private-Public Policy Nexus in the Global Agora

Andrew Wells-Dang
CIVIL SOCIETY NETWORKS IN CHINA AND VIETNAM
Informal Pathbreakers in Health and the Environment

Thomas Yarrow
DEVELOPMENT BEYOND POLITICS
Aid, Activism and NGOs in Ghana

Non-Governmental Public Action Series
Series Standing Order ISBN 978–0–230–22939–6 (hardback) and
978–0–230–22940–2 (paperback)

You can receive future titles in this series as they are published by placing a standing order. Please contact your bookseller or, in case of difficulty, write to us at the address below with your name and address, the title of the series and the ISBN quoted above.

Customer Services Department, Macmillan Distribution Ltd, Houndmills, Basingstoke, Hampshire RG21 6XS, England

Knowledge Actors and Transnational Governance

The Private–Public Policy Nexus in the Global Agora

Diane Stone

Murdoch University, Western Australia, and University of Warwick, UK

First published 2013 by
PALGRAVE MACMILLAN

Palgrave Macmillan in the UK is an imprint of Macmillan Publishers Limited, registered in England, company number 785998, of Houndmills, Basingstoke, Hampshire RG21 6XS.

Palgrave Macmillan in the US is a division of St Martin's Press LLC, 175 Fifth Avenue, New York, NY 10010.

Palgrave Macmillan is the global academic imprint of the above companies and has companies and representatives throughout the world.

Palgrave® and Macmillan® are registered trademarks in the United States, the United Kingdom, Europe and other countries.

ISBN 978–1–137–02290–5

This book is printed on paper suitable for recycling and made from fully managed and sustained forest sources. Logging, pulping and manufacturing processes are expected to conform to the environmental regulations of the country of origin.

A catalogue record for this book is available from the British Library.

A catalog record for this book is available from the Library of Congress.

Typeset by MPS Limited, Chennai, India.

For Richard

Contents

Preface and Acknowledgements

Global Agora brings together and examines perspectives on knowledge networks, global governance and the think tanks that have burgeoned around the world over the last two decades. Advice, advocacy and argumentation have become key elements in the fashioning of policy programmes and structure of governance, especially within the rapidly evolving institutions and networks of transnational governance.

The book is reflective of the growing salience of these actors and agents in transnational governance. At its broadest, the book represents what I hope readers will see as an original and systematic application of a body of emerging theory in the social and political sciences to a set of empirical case studies. If they wished, readers could also see it conversely as the development of my own theoretical thinking, evolving out of a personal narrative of experience in certain specific empirical settings. Either way, the assumption prevails that the development of theory and empirical narrative does not evolve in isolation from one another. As such, the arguments advanced in this book are best understood as part of my own intellectual evolution and the contribution that places and people have made to that process of evolution. This Preface identifies some of the debts I have incurred in that evolution.

The original idea for the book first emerged in August 2003, when I was located in Singapore for six weeks while my husband Richard Higgott was a visiting professor at the Institute of Defence and Security Studies at the Nanyang Technological University. The Institute is now known as the S. Rajaratnam School of International Studies. Here, a range of people, including Amitav Acharya, Barry Desker, Mely Cabellero Anthony and Helen Nesadurai, as well as M. Ramesh at the Lee Kuan Yew School of Public Policy, were all exceptionally kind and indeed convivial sounding-boards then and later during many other visits to Singapore, or to Malaysia, over the following decade. The Singapore sojourn provided me with the kernel of a case study for this volume – the ASEAN-ISIS group of policy research institutes. A journal article on the informal diplomacy of this network first appeared in *Minerva* (Stone, 2011). A heavily revised, extended and updated version is included as Chapter 6, and permission has been given by Springer to re-produce substantial sections of the article.

The 'global agora' idea first surfaced at Central European University's tenth anniversary conference in late 2000, and by January 2004 career-changing developments happened when I took leave from the University of Warwick to move to Budapest. The book was effectively put into storage for five years. Much thinking, if little writing, was done there during my tenure as the Marie Curie Chair and foundation Professor of Public Policy at CEU, although the 'agora' concept did eventually appear in *Policy Studies Journal* (Stone, 2008) with bits of this article to be reworked in Chapter 1. Founding a new graduate programme and department was exciting, exasperating and all consuming, but it did provide me with a further case study for the book – on the Open Society Institute (OSI) – CEU's sister institution. Along the way I gained many friends, colleagues and helpful critics of my work, including Agi Batory, Viola Zentai, Andrea Krizsán, Liviu Matei, Heni Griecs, Zsuzsa Gabor, Valentina Dimitrova, Ivona Malbasic, Nicole Lindstrom, Heather Elms, Eva Porras, Andy Cartwright, Nick Sitter, Andreas Goldthau and Uwe Puetter, of course not forgetting the late Yehuda Elkana, then Rector at CEU. In the Local Government and Public Sector Initiative of the OSI, Adrian Ionescu, Scott Abrams, Bob Ebel, Lisa Quinn, Kristof Varga and George Guess helped keep the fledgling degree programme afloat as well as provided *entré* into the foundation network. More recently, Heather Grabbe, Tom Carothers and Jacek Kucharczyk have proved to be wonderful colleagues in the Think Tank Fund. Outside of work, Karin Bryce, David Keresztes, Geoff Bennett, Virginia Proud, Mags Kiss and Katherine Ferdinandy found for me many other distractions in Budapest.

Coinciding with this time at CEU, my term on the Governing Body of the Global Development Network came to an end just as my involvement with the Researcher's Alliance for Development began. From this involvement came a further case study. Even though one network (the GDN) prospered and the Researchers Alliance for Development (RAD) floundered, the World Bank parentage of both these networks allowed me to maintain my links inside this international organisation after my sojourn at the Bank in 1999 came to an end, especially with Erik Johnson, Jean-Christophe Bas and Susan Wilder. The several workshops I convened on the World Bank, and for the Bank, over 2005–2010 led to my own joint publication with Chris Wright (2006), but this project was supported by the publication efforts among an informal but international network of colleagues, including Pascale Hatcher, Asun Lera St Clair, Susan Park, Celine Tan, Sophie Harman, Kim Maloney, Antje Vetterlein, Kate Weaver and also Ralf Leiteritz. The project stimulated my already growing interests in network theory. Those in the GDN and

RAD who also kept me involved in knowledge network practice, but who also provided gems of informal feedback for this book, include Inge Kaul, Bina Agarwal, Sujata Patel, Natalia Dinello, Joyashree Roy, Diana Tussie, Anna Kuznicka and Odd Helge Fjelstad.

From 2006, the Non-Governmental Public Action programme (NGPA), a research programme funded by the UK's Economic and Social Research Council, provided the time for me to consolidate my thinking as well as the financial wherewithal to conduct interviews and undertake fieldwork on the project. Jude Howell, Jean Grugel, Duncan Mathews, Andre Spicer, Richard Crook and Brian Doherty have been great sources of inspiration as well as real, practical support in NGPA activities. A different version of Chapter 5, using other empirical material drawn from the very diverse activities of the re-labelled Open Societies Foundation, appeared in Jude Howell's edited collection in the NGPA series, *Global Matters for Non-Governmental Public Action*. Similarly, parts of Chapter 3 are drawn from an article published in *Public Administration* (Stone, 2007) for which Wiley has allowed permission to re-use.

During the time with the NGPA team I was able to return to greater involvement in the Overseas Development Institute. Originally joining the Board of Trustees in 2001, I was enlisted by then Director, Simon Maxwell, to help launch the RAPID programme with Julius Court and John Young, which resulted in participating in numerous ODI workshops and meetings from 2001 through 2007. Out of this interaction has emerged the case study on RAPID (Chapter 4), an early version of which appeared in *Public Administration and Development* in 2009. Permission to reproduce an extended and updated version of this article has again been granted by Wiley (Stone, 2009).

Over the past decade, a group of scholars (and friends) were able to distract me frequently with other enterprises that had already started with the Warwick-led EU FP6 Network of Excellence on Globalisation, Governance and Regulation (GARNET) and the EU FP7 project on Global Re-ordering and the Evolution of Regional Networks (GR:EEN). The GARNET community – especially Denise Hewlett but also Brigitte Young, Eleni Tsingou, Shaun Breslin, Caroline Kuzemko, then later Len Seabrooke – helped considerably in getting me involved in GARNET and GR:EEN workshops in Europe, North America and Australasia. The knowledge and insights I secured from these two collaborative projects all assisted with the finalisation of this book, and the support of the European Commission Framework Programmes is duly acknowledged.

In 2008 I was called back to Budapest in 2008 to co-Chair the committee to design the new School of Public Policy which kept me there off and on for another four years. It has been over the last four years while I have been either away on secondment or sabbatical from the University of Warwick that the book has been written. I greatly appreciate the University's flexibility in allowing me the time and space to balance these competing commitments and engagements. Since late 2010 I have been resident as a Winthrop Professor at the University of Western Australia (UWA), in Perth. Here I have found the much needed time to finish this book. Even so, with UWA as a partner institution in the GR:EEN Network, my colleagues, especially Mark Beeson, Sarah Percy, Jeanette Taylor and Elena Douglas, still managed to inveigle me into various workshops, grant applications, teaching or other publication ventures. Hannah Hoffman was an able research assistant, Kelsie White kept things on track, while Barbara Evers made sure I got out occasionally. In the final phase, anonymous reviewer Sabine Selchow provided constructive feedback and Richard Higgott, at times as much of a distraction as a helper, came good with his extensive and constructive comments on the penultimate draft.

There is a fast and rapidly growing community of scholars writing on think tanks in the 21st century. I have kept in touch with many of those of us who were labouring in this field of enquiry in the early, indeed unfashionable, days of this topic in the 1990s. We have kept the lines of discussion open as we crossed paths and shared papers at conferences around the world. Andrew Denham, Heidi Ulrich, Frank Fischer, Stella Ladi, Don Abelson, Ivan Krastev, Simon Maxwell, Inderjeet Parmar, Josef Braml, Goran Buldioski and especially Kent Weaver have all been supportive and constructive at many points in time over the years. What was once dismissed as an irrelevant 'cottage industry' during my doctoral studies in the late 1980s has today become a booming industry worldwide.

List of Abbreviations

ABCDE	Annual Bank Conference on Development Economics
AGREN	Agricultural Research and Extension Network
ALNAP	Active Learning Network on Accountability and Performance in Humanitarian Action
APA	ASEAN People's Assembly
APEC	Asia Pacific Economic Cooperation
APGOOD	All Parliamentary Group on Overseas Development
APR	Asia Pacific Roundtable
ARF	ASEAN Regional Forum
ASEAN	Association of South East Asian Nations
ASEAN-ISIS	ASEAN-Institutes of Strategic and International Studies
ASEAN-PMC	ASEAN-Post Ministerial Conference
ASEAN SOM	ASEAN Senior Official Meeting
AusAid	Australian Agency for International Development
BBC	British Broadcasting Corporation
BREAD	Bureau for Research and Analysis of Development in North America
CEE	Central and Eastern Europe
CERGE-EI	Centre for Economic Research and Graduate Education-Economics Institute in Prague
CEU	Central European University
CGIAR	Consultative Group on International Agricultural Research
CIDOB	*Fundación CIDOB* (Barcelona Centre for International Affairs)
CIGI	Centre for International Governance and Innovation
CIPPEC	Centre for the Implementation of Public Policies Promoting Equity and Growth, Argentina
CSCAP	Council for Security Cooperation in the Asia Pacific

CSIS	Centre for Strategic and International Studies, Indonesia
CSPP	Civil Society Partnership Programme
DAC	Development Assistance Committee
DANIDA	Danish International Development Agency
DAWN	Development Alternatives with Women for a New Era
DEC	Development Economics Department (World Bank)
DECDG	Development Economics Department Data Group (World Bank)
DECPG	Development Economics Department Prospects Group (World Bank)
DECRG	Research Group in the Development Economics Vice Presidency
DfID	Department for International Development
DGF	Development Grant Facility of the World Bank
DRM	Dialogue and Research Monitor
EADI	European Association of Development Research and Training Institutes
EADN	East Asian Development Network
EBPDN	Evidence-Based Policy in Development Network
EITI	Extractive Industries Transparency Initiative
EngKaR	Engineering Knowledge and Research
EPIN	European Policy Institute Network
ETLA	*Elinkeinoelämäntutkimuslaitos* (Research Institute of the Finnish Economy)
EU	European Union
EUDN	European Development Network
EU-GRASP	The EU as a Global-Regional Actor in Security and Peace
FLACSO	*Facultad Latinoamericana de Ciencias Sociales* (Latin American School of Social Sciences)
fSU	former Soviet Union
G20	Group of Twenty
GATS	General Agreement on Trade in Services
GAVI	Global Alliance for Vaccines and Immunisation

GDN	Global Development Network
GONGOs	Governmentally Organised NGOs
GPGs	Global Public Goods
GPPN	Global Public Policy Network
GR:EEN	Global Re-ordering: Evolution through European Networks
Grupo Faro	Foundation for the Advance of Reforms and Opportunities, Ecuador
HPN	Humanitarian Practice Network
IDB	Inter-American Development Bank
IDRC	International Development Research Centre
IFRI	Institut Français des Relations Internationales
ILGA	International Lesbian, Gay, Bisexual, Trans and Intersex Association
IMF	International Monetary Fund
INBAR	International Network on Bamboo and Rattan
INECE	International Network on Environmental Compliance and Enforcement
INET	Institute of New Economic Thinking
IR	International Relations
ISDS	Institute for Strategic and Development Studies, Philippines
ISIS Malaysia	Institute for Strategic and International Studies, Malaysia
ISIS Thailand	Institute for Security and International Studies, Thailand
ISO	International Organization for Standardization
KNET	Knowledge Network
LACEA	Latin American and Caribbean Economic Association
LGI	Local Government and Public Service Reform Initiative
MANGOs	Manipulated NGOs
MOOCs	Massive Open Online Courses
NEAT	Network of East Asian Think Tanks
NED	National Endowment for Democracy
NGO	Non-Governmental Organisation

NGPA	Non-Governmental Public Action
NPM	New Public Management
ODC	Overseas Development Council
ODI	Overseas Development Institute
OECD	Organisation for Economic Co-operation and Development
OSF	Open Society Foundations
OSI	Open Society Institute
OSISA	Open Society Initiative for Southern Africa
OSIWA	Open Society Initiative for West Africa
PASOS	Policy Association for an Open Society
PIEN	Public Integrity Education Network
PNoB	Parliamentary Network on the Bank
PRSPs	Poverty Reduction Strategy Papers
RAD	Researchers Alliance for Development
RAND	Research and Development
RAPID	Research and Policy in Development
RDFN	Rural Development Forestry Network
REDD	Reduced Emissions from Deforestation and Forest Degradation
REDD-net	Networking for equity in forest climate policy
RiPPLE	Research-inspired Policy and Practice Learning in Ethiopia & Nile Region
SIIA	Singapore Institute for International Affairs
SPP	School of Public Policy
T1	Track One
T1 ½	Track One and a Half
T2	Track Two
T3	Track Three
TAN	Transnational Advocacy Network
TEN	Transnational Executive Network
TIRI	Transparency International Research Institute
TTF	Think Tank Fund

UK	United Kingdom
UN	United Nations
UNDP	United Nations Development Programme
UNESCO	United Nations Educational, Scientific and Cultural Organization
UNRISD	United Nations Research Institute for Social Development
USAID	United States Agency for International Development
WBI	World Bank Institute
WHO	World Health Organization
WTO	World Trade Organization

Introduction

The global agora

'Global policy' is a phrase that is nowadays seen more frequently in official reports and the political lexicon. Yet, it is still not well established as a concept. This book makes one cut into outlining and assessing the conceptualisation and praxis of global policy processes by investigating the transnational policy activities of research networks, policy institutes and think tanks. The intention of this study is to broaden our understanding of how these semi-private bodies and their quasi-public networks have gone transnational and become incorporated into governance. The networks discussed in this volume and the plethora of other knowledge networks and global policy partnerships that have proliferated in the last couple of decades are central actors in the formation of the 'global agora', that is, nascent transnational domains of public space, private policy and knowledge-based authority.

A central assumption in the chapters that follow is that one way governance emerges is from strategic interactions and partnerships of national and international bureaucracies with non-state actors in the market place and civil society. In these interfaces, the creators and distributors of policy knowledge – in the form of scientific theories, concepts and models, data sets and statistics, policy analysis and evidence-based policy recommendations – become central players in decision-making. In the weak institutional context of global and regional governance, they are arguably more influential in shaping the parameters of policy-making than within the more traditional confines of institutionally mature nation-states.

Governance as a concept is difficult to nail down given the multiple meanings it has acquired over the last quarter century. Generally, 'governance' refers to processes of governing, conditions of ordered rule or methods by which society is governed (adapted from Rhodes, 2012: 33) or the 'attempt to steer state and the economy through collective actions' (Torfing, 2012: 101). The idea of governance can be applied to concerns of internal governance of private organisations such as multi-national corporations as well as public bodies like international organisations. Alternatively, the idea can have wider external remit and relevance in understanding societal rule and ordering such as the governance processes of the European Union or other regional bodies.

By contrast, the term 'public policy' is used in this volume in a more limited sense. Public policy is understood to mean decision-making processes and courses of action brought about by laws, legislation, standards, funding and regulation promulgated by official actors and delegated entities in specific sectors leading to an outcome of formal or informal governance. *Public* policy is usually considered to be undertaken for public purposes, even if some private interests are served in the process, and subject in some degree to mechanisms of public and professional accountability. Considerably more elusive, and in some quarters contested, is the idea of 'global public policy' or 'transnational public policy'. Indeed these phrases are notable for their absence from the social science lexicon. By the end of this book, and as discussed later in this Introduction, the word 'public' is often dropped in favour of the terms 'transnational policy' or 'global policy processes'. In the global agora, groups and communities that might form a 'public' are less visible or are particularly poorly organised.

The policy networks of knowledge organisations

This book emerges from a larger research enterprise on 'Non-Governmental Public Action' funded by the United Kingdom's Economic and Social Research Council. The specific focus of this book is to examine how knowledge organisations act transnationally via networks, or 'global research-user chains', analysing knowledge utilisation practices of international organisations and global policy networks (Howell, 2012). The research objective was to ask questions about the manner in which knowledge organisations deliver conceptual understanding of policy problems, how networks set policy agendas and the effectiveness and legitimacy (or not) with which they implement and monitor (non-)governmental public action. Knowledge organisations are too diverse and too numerous for all to be dealt with in adequate empirical detail in this study. Nor can it hope to encapsulate the variety of network character and activity.

Consequently, a primary focus has been on one group of knowledge organisation directly concerned with translating science, evidence and research for policy-making and governance: that is, policy research institutes, whether they be based in universities or affiliated to other organisations like foundations and 'think tanks'. Due to their role in science translation or research brokerage, they are pivotal organisations for their dense interactions and networks with other knowledge actors such as universities, philanthropic foundations and government research entities.

The empirical backbone of the book is based on case studies of four network organisations. Each network is transnational in its operations, albeit in different degree. Each network has well-established and substantive connections with either governments, international organisations or multilateral initiatives through funding support, contractual relationships for provision of analytical services or the professional involvement of network members as expert consultants in policy deliberations. These networks are also well connected to, if not fully incorporated or co-opted into, global policy processes. That is, depending on the specific policy field and issues, these networks have at times been important players in policy debates and problem definition or in standard setting and evaluation of policy programmes. Their engagements with official public policy actors have also had a recursive impact in bolstering their reputations as credible expert organisations providing reliable policy analysis and research. The case study networks are as follows:

The Global Development Network – GDN   This 'network of networks' is an international association of development researchers and research institutes built upon several regional networks. It is devoted to ameliorating poverty through the 'creation, dissemination and application of knowledge'. Initially launched by the World Bank it is now independent with head offices based in India.

The Overseas Development Institute – ODI   Although not strictly a network, this London-based think tank operates in a highly networked mode. An independent non-profit organisation, the ODI works closely with its main benefactor, the UK Department for International Development, in a range of development programmes built on network principles.

The Open Society Foundations network – OSF   This private philanthropic foundation is focused on civil liberties and human rights concerns with offices and programmes world-wide. It is a privately funded global initiative, bank-rolled by the billionaire George Soros. An independent entity, the OSF nevertheless enters partnerships with a range of public, market-based and non-profit actors on various issues.

ASEAN-ISIS The Association of Southeast Asian Nations (ASEAN) Institutes of Strategic and International Studies (ISIS) is a regional think tank network. It was deeply involved in policy deliberations on region-building acquiring, for a time at least, significant agenda setting capacity. ASEAN-ISIS is a good example of transnational policy processes at the regional level of governance.

All four cases can be classified as forms of non-governmental public action given their stated aims of securing specific public objectives and their legal constitution as 'charitable', 'third sector' or 'independent' organisations. Second, each case has a common focus on the knowledge–policy nexus, albeit in different ways. That is, they seek to 'bridge' the research and policy worlds. Effective research communication and dissemination is central to achieving policy relevance. Third, all have a transnational dimension to their activities although they direct attention towards slightly different regions, countries and constituencies of the world. Fourth, all have a common policy interest in transition and development, especially in the context of the globalisation of the world order and economy in the early twenty-first century. Finally, each case can be characterised as an empirical example of a governance network and illustrative of broader and more general and diverse dynamics of 'network governance'.

The reasoning behind the choice of these networks is not to generalise from them regarding the nascent dynamics of transnational policy processes. Instead, they serve to illuminate the harnessing of academic enterprise and research advancement to the task of governing. Indeed, the concluding chapter introduces another nascent network – *Think20* – that is coalescing around the G20 as a putative advisory body and which suggests the dynamic and enduring nature of the subject under study.

Transnational networks and global policy

A key idea that is developed in the following chapters is that knowledge networks represent a mode of transnational governance. Although there is considerable blurring, two types of networking are the empirical focus of discussion, that is (i) knowledge networks and (ii) policy networks. However, to maintain a strict distinction between knowledge networking through intellectual exchange and research collaboration on the one hand, and policy coordination networks can be a false one.

Defining networks is a fraught endeavour, informed as it is by competing concepts and frameworks from across a burgeoning social science literature. This study falls in what is now a traditional understanding of the network logic of organisation being distinct from market modes of organisation in the private sector of exchange, competition and commodification, and the top-down chains of authority of hierarchical mode of bureaucratic organisation associated with the state. Governance can be produced by markets or by hierarchies, but so too by networks of commonly affected and related actors. A broad definition is adopted here.

> We can define *governance networks* as a horizontal articulation of interdependent, but operationally autonomous, actors from the public and/or private sector who interact with one another through ongoing negotiations that take place within a regulative, normative, cognitive, and imaginary framework; facilitate self-regulation in the shadow of hierarchy; and contribute to the production of public regulation in the broad sense of the term. (Torfing, 2012: 101)

A key idea is that network actors are mutually interdependent and need to pool their resources. Rather than interest-based bargaining, the case studies in this volume underline that the main form of interaction of knowledge networks is via deliberation, research and information exchange in the effort to produce common understandings of problems and potential solutions and thereby may come to act like policy networks.

Undoubtedly, policy networks are proliferating at the transnational level. However, it should not be assumed that network density equates with policy influence. Such impact largely depends on the type of network structure and composition. As Chapter 2 outlines, there are four main types or 'species' of policy network that are identified as functioning in transnational spheres of policy debate and delivery that give shape to the private and public spheres of regulatory activity and policy delivery in the global agora:

Global Public Policy Networks (GPPNs) are tri-sectoral and *share interests*. They are alliances of government agencies and international organisations with business (usually corporations) and civil society. Actors invest in GPPNs to pursue material or organisational interests but have in common a shared problem and enter into a policy partnership for the delivery of public policy. Their private but public character defies categorisation of these policy arrangements as either civil society or third sector organisations.

Transnational Advocacy Networks (TANs) encompass a range of non-governmental organisations and activists with *shared beliefs*. TANs seek to shape the climate of public debate and influence global policy agendas. They are much less integrated into policy-making than GPPNs. TANs are bound together by shared values, dense exchanges of information and services, and a shared normative discourse. They are called advocacy networks due to their norm orientation and location in civil society.

Transnational Executive Networks (TENs) are semi-official bureaucratic structures that *pool authority* via inter-governmental networking. The key actors in TENs are government officials acting with state authority – that is, regulators, judges, parliamentarians, national and local bureaucrats – who find routes for reconfiguring state sovereignty through networks across borders.

Knowledge Networks (KNETs) are characterised by *shared scientific understanding* as their prime motivation is to create and advance knowledge as well as to share, spread and often use that knowledge to inform policy and apply to practice. The expertise, scientific knowledge, data and method, analysis and evaluations that help constitute knowledge networks provide the experts within them with some authority to inform policy.

The sources of power and authority as well as the logic behind the organisation of these four ideal types are distinguishable respectively by material interests and shared policy problem in the case of GPPNs, normative agenda-setting ambitions in the case of TANs, politico-legal office for TENs and epistemic authority vested in KNETs. These network species are used as a heuristic for explanation only. In reality, networks exhibit a mix of these features. The intention is not to develop a new network idea or arsenal of jargon. Instead, the objective is to work with existing concepts and categories recognising that transnational policy networks take different shape and have differential impact across time, place and issue. Nor is it the objective of this volume to force a synthesis of network ideas, even though some of the concepts overlap.

This project also seeks to inform theory by criticising the dominant neo-pluralist framework of most North American writing on networks, such as TANs, and the neo-corporatist nature of European literature by focusing on elite non-governmental actors. The discussion reveals the dual dynamic of openness and closure in networks as both 'gateways' and 'gatekeepers'. In doing so, additional questions about global policy processes and how networks are helping to compose transnational public spheres arise.

Theorisation of a 'transnational public sphere' is weak. Moreover, much current thinking within the literature is characterised by teleological presumptions of cosmopolitan destinies. This realm, where such legitimacy questions and accountability issues are raised, remains poorly conceptualised. Taking the ancient Greek concept of the *agora*, and conceptually stretching it to the transnational level, Chapter 1 queries the presumed progressive potential of global civil society and non-governmental organisations (NGOs) in forging this sphere. It makes no presumption about the communicative, progressive or deliberative character of network interactions or what some international organisations refer to as 'global programmes'. The dynamics for exclusion, seclusion and division may also prevail. The global domain encompasses a wider array of political relationships inspired by liberal democracy through to coercive arrangements of strong authoritarianism as well as patterns of disorder and randomness when rational planning is not feasible or authority and responsibility unclear. The global agora may become an accessible participative domain for plural expressions of policy input. But, equally so, it might not. Hence the focus on elite transnational actors and their policy networks in subsequent chapters.

Another aim of this book is to develop the idea of 'global public policy'. Unlike some others (*inter alia* Coleman, 2012; True, 2003), this is pursued by dropping the idea of the 'public' in 'global public policy' to stress that 'global policy' is as likely to be formulated, funded, implemented or monitored by private entities as it is by states. The foci of much policy scholarship has been to address the impact of transnational dynamics impacting *upon* domestic politics (*inter alia*, Skogstad, 2011) rather than to see the locus of policy power and implementing authority *within* these transnational dynamics. Further, global public policy has been defined recently as 'policy making that takes place on the global rather than the regional or the national scale and is expected to affect, if not be part of, governance of all parts of the world' (Coleman, 2012: 673). In Coleman's definition there is a useful distinction between 'international public policy' as being distinctively limited to inter-state relations and states as the key actors, whereas global public policy actors also include NGOs, corporations, social movements and indeed, in some cases, individuals such as Bill Gates and George Soros. By contrast, 'transnational public policy' is not axiomatically on the same territorial scale as global public policy, covering only some countries or a region, although many of the same kinds or private and non-state actors are involved in the policy processes.

'Transnational' and 'global' can be used interchangeably, and the reader will find this often the case in this volume. There is a shift away from the *topos* of territorial bounded notions of policy to assess policy spaces of the global agora where the process of policy-making may well be transnational, and indeed quite localised in impact, as well as global. The policy spaces are multi-nodal and the policy processes poly-centric. As will be argued in the first two chapters, public policy has been a prisoner of the word 'state' even while the state is fast being re-configured by globalisation. New configurations of authority are emerging through global and regional policy processes that *co-exist* alongside nation-state policy processes. The study identifies new public spaces where global policies are fashioned and implemented. These global or regional spaces – such as transnational commissions and taskforces, privately initiated global policy forums like the World Economic Forum in Davos or global funds and partnerships like the Global Facility for Disaster Reduction and Recovery – reveal a higher degree of pluralisa-tion of actors, fragmentation of decision-making and multiple authority structures than is the case at national levels. Authority is more diffuse, decision-making is partially privatised and sovereignty is muddled. Public policy scholars have yet to examine fully these processes and new managerial modes of transnational public administration.

Method and organisation of the book

There is a rich literature on transnational networks and global gov-ernance that has been built by scholars of international relations and international political economy. By contrast, the policy studies tradi-tion tends to limit its foci to local and national domains (albeit with exceptions to some sub-fields such as environmental policy). The aim of this book is to shift the conceptual lens of the terrain of public policy studies away from its methodological nationalism, that is, the now often contested assumption that 'power resides in national processes and is properly studied within the locus of the state' (Neumann and Sending, 2010: vii).

   This analytical component drew upon an extensive range of published, on-line and 'grey' material generated by the four case study networks and was complemented by field work. Field work was primarily participant-observation over a period of approximately a decade. This was of an ad hoc nature rather than via a consistent presence in the case study networks. On occasion there were informal interviews with research-ers associated with or personnel of ASEAN-ISIS, GDN, OSF and ODI, but more generally, the insights of this book are buoyed by the casual conversations with staff working for these organisations. The 'grey' materials of these organisations – internal memos, emails and draft documentation – also came with engagement in some of the operations of the case study networks or participation in conferences, board meetings or other activities.

The author was a member of the secretariat within the World Bank that launched the GDN in 1999. From 2001 to 2004 she served on the GDN's governing body, and retained personal links to other members of the governing body as well as the GDN Secretariat. Until late 2012 she was a member of the Board of Directors of the ODI and has worked with ODI staff on a number of projects but most particularly the Research and Policy in Development (RAPID) programme that is discussed in Chapter 4. Teaching at the Central European University (CEU) from 2004 to the present day allowed her to establish solid professional contacts with staff members in one of the initiatives of the OSF. At the time, the offices of the Local Government and Public Sector Initiative (LGI) were housed on the same floor, indeed the same corridor, of what was then a nascent Public Policy Program at CEU. During the year 2010–11, Diane Stone was a board member of LGI and currently she serves as a sub-board member of the Think Tank Fund, both of which are discussed in following chapters. Of the case study organisations, ASEAN-ISIS was the least accessible, but fieldwork in Malaysia and Singapore – along with long-term personal and professional contacts with researchers at universities in the region who participated in ASEAN-ISIS programmes – facilitated research into this network. There is also considerably more secondary scholarly literature on ASEAN-ISIS than could be said for the other three case studies combined. Regarding the relatively short discussion in the final chapter of a putative case study network – *Think20* – the author participated in an early formative meeting in Canada in May 2010.

Participant observation helps ameliorate problems of the methodological position of the observer. Researchers on the 'outside' of organisations – whether they are based in independent think tanks or universities – tend to over-emphasise the homogeneity and unity of purpose of international organisations and networks. They often do not get inside the organisational 'black box' to appreciate internal dynamics. However, observers 'inside' organisations can over-state the rivalries, fragmentation and incoherence of their employers or funders underestimating the power differentials, policy influence or exclusivity perceived by outsiders. Participant observation can capture the insights of both camps by gaining access to the detail of organisational life without being overwhelmed by daily business or beholden to organisational rules and policy positions (Schatz, 2009). The approach contends that grounded knowledge of organisational dynamics is acquired on the basis of being a participant rather than a spectator.

However, participant observation poses some ethical considerations (Mosse, 2006). The author had access to internal documents of two of the case study organisations. Also, she was privy to personal conversations. While these conversations are not reported in the chapters that follow, or the identities of individuals revealed (except where material has already been made public on blogs, in publications or elsewhere), the discussions and email exchanges form a backdrop to the analysis that unfolds. Needless to say, the interpretations are those of the author alone and do not represent an official position of any of the networks discussed.

The book is organised in eight chapters. The first three chapters start by developing the idea of policy-making in the global agora. The main idea of Chapter 1 is that a global agora is emerging. The case study networks are a few tiny cogs in the network operations of the agora. Unlike social and political organisation within nation-states where sovereignty and public authority tend to be well-grounded principles, the global agora is characterised by the blending and meshing of market forces, public sector actors, intellectual life and public discourse in transnational policy communities and networks. This messiness and disorder, but inter-connectedness in the agora, will be considered in the final chapter in the context of 'intertwingularity'.

The second chapter focuses on network forms of governance by discussing the policy roles and functions of the four main species of network identified above. In addition, the chapter introduces additional network-driven concepts that act as frameworks for interpretation of the sources of power of networks. The four 'species' concepts above are used to identify different empirical manifestations of network. By contrast, the interpretative frameworks draw on the wider political science traditions of thought associated with (neo-)pluralism, corporatist ideas of interest intermediation, neo-Gramscian concepts of hegemony and finally rationalist epistemic community frameworks that posit an inherent power of science and consensual knowledge to shape policy.

The third chapter moves from the network focus in the preceding chapter to an organisational focus on policy research institutes. The term 'think tank' has become ubiquitous in the political lexicon. It is entrenched in scholarly discussions of public policy as well as in the 'policy wonk' of journalists, lobbyists and spin-doctors. This does not mean that there is a consensus among observers on the constitution, roles or political influence of think tanks. Indeed, the organisational structure, ambitions and policy impact of think tanks vary massively. Usually they are established legally independent or non-profit bodies, and many claim to act in the 'public interest' to inform policy debate. Think tanks conduct policy research of some kind and act as a research communication 'bridge' between production of (social) science and policy-making. This chapter argues that the notion of 'think tank' has become the amalgam of many different storylines. For the general public, the stress is on the public benefits they generate via knowledge communication and policy education. With funders it is their capacity to access and inform decision-makers, often behind closed doors. Towards government agencies and actors, they proffer a source of rationality, solutions to problems, conceptual tools and expertise to apply to policy. In relation to political parties or social movements or advocacy networks, they are creators of mobilising discourses – normative language, policy rhetoric and data to support the cause. It is their multiplicity of tailored narratives and organisational capacity to adapt quickly in different argumentative or institutional fields that makes them the 'discursive software' of choice (Fischer, 2003). Finally, many of these organisations have adapted quickly to regional and global dynamics in their research agendas and policy activities, as the following case study chapters outline.

Chapter 4 represents the first case study chapter. Sometimes a powerful force, (social) science is neither immediately nor automatically persuasive in policy debates. Numerous organisations advocate the need to 'bridge research and policy'. Philanthropic foundations, national social science funding regimes and international organisations have sought to improve knowledge utilisation. Similarly, research consumers such as NGOs and government departments often complain of research irrelevance for policy purposes. The concern of this chapter is with 'evidence-informed policy' within the field of international development. Like most think tanks, ODI operates on the basis of persuasion and consensus building via debate, research and analysis. Yet, ODI is distinctive among think tanks in being one of the first to create a communications programme called 'Research and Policy in Development', or RAPID in short form. It is a programme that other institutes have emulated or tapped into for operational support in research communication. The RAPID programme provides guidelines, mentoring and training about how research and analysis can be made relevant, responsible and, indeed, ethical as a means 'to help save lives, reduce poverty and improve the quality of life' (Young, 2005: 727). The chapter addresses how and to what effect ODI behaves as a 'knowledge broker' or 'policy entrepreneur' between bureaucracies, policy networks and international organisations. Think tanks in general, not only ODI, do not have the luxury of sitting on the academic sidelines of public debate or policy dialogue. They must engage the policy world. However, attempts to inform or influence policy often give institutes a problem-solving focus rather than a critical dynamic. The chapter is a vehicle to address 'knowledge utilisation' via the network modality.

Chapter 5 introduces a different kind of organisation – the Open Societies Foundation network – a philanthropic body. It is an operational foundation that both funds and carries out its own programmes and initiatives around the world and provides funding support to successful grant applicants. As a philanthropy that has grown to adopt global interests, it can be considered a global civil society actor. The OSF initially focused on social and economic issues of transition societies in Central and Eastern Europe and the former Soviet Union and geared to transferring Western policy norms and practices regarding market economies, educational systems, freedom of information law and so forth into these transition countries. This norm advocacy is neither apolitical nor without policy ramifications. Accordingly rather than treating OSF in too simple fashion as a civil society actor, the argument developed is that the network has been a vehicle for the 'soft' policy transfer of Western ideas and concepts about economic and political organisation. To some degree, all case study networks in this book are involved in policy transfer processes.

Chapter 6 assesses the ASEAN-ISIS network as a case study that focuses upon regional level of governance. Instead of its policy transfer capacities, the power and effectiveness of this network is assessed in terms of its role as a venue for informal diplomacy which was important in helping create an 'interpretative community' that generated new ideas of regional identity and organisation. Informal diplomacy entails sequestered discussions of an 'invitation only' grouping of academics and intellectuals, journalists, business elites and others as well as government officials and political leaders. Generally, official participants attend, as the saying goes, 'in their private capacity'. Indeed, informal diplomacy can be regarded as a very specific type of non-governmental public action. Performing this policy role as an organiser of semi-private policy dialogues in region-building processes undermines its independent and private status. Political patronage and participation in this research coalition for regional cooperation highlight the elite interconnections of this 'NGO' with governments in ASEAN and the wider Asian region.

Chapter 7 starts with an analysis of the policy discourse of the World Bank as an international organisation delivering 'global public goods'

(GPGs) and specifically knowledge as a public good. This policy discourse has allowed the organisation to represent itself as the Knowledge Bank. The network case study is the GDN which was created by the World Bank and later sponsored by a range of other public and private development agencies. Reflecting its parentage, the goals of the GDN are primarily cast in the language of economics and of development research being a 'public good'. The GDN represents a mechanism for the spread of the now waning (post-)Washington consensus and neo-liberal ideology. This dissemination occurs notwithstanding the pluralist composition of the network and the way in which the dominant ideology is diluted, to some extent at least, by other social science narratives. As a global knowledge network the evolution of GDN from a project gestated within an international organisation to then establishing itself as an NGO before becoming an international organisation in its own right demonstrates a remarkable organisational trajectory between the public to private sector and back. This case study reveals most clearly how international organisations and partner networks co-constitute a public sector of service delivery in the global agora.

Starting from ODI as the classic example of independent 'research broker' think tank, OSF as an operating foundation and policy transfer network, and ASEAN-ISIS as a regional quasi-diplomatic network, the case studies end with the GDN as a global public sector network. In other words, there are gradations of private-ness and public-ness in networks over time as well in the constitution of networks or policy partnerships. Yet, the GDN case is more than simply its movement from inside the international public sector to the outside and its transmogrification again into public status. The GDN is also highly indicative of the potential institutionalisation of the network form. This process is the reverse of privatisation. Usually, the antonym of privatisation is nationalisation. This antonym does not apply in the global agora. Other lexical contortions might include *publicisation* of non-governmental public policy or a (*re-*)*communalisation* of private regimes. None of these terms are satisfactory in capturing the many refractions of this public space. Public-ness in the global agora is of a shifting kaleidoscope character. Hence, Chapter 8 revisits the theme of the global agora as a public domain. It does not address questions of democratic accountability and representation. These questions are valid ones, and on which much headway has been made by others (see Sørenson and Torfing, 2007), but beyond the scope of this particular book. Instead, the concern here is to address how conceptions of the 'public' are negotiated and re-made in transnational policy spaces (Newman, 2005).

Chapter 8 does not compare and contrast the case study networks nor seek to generalise from them. Rather they are descriptive cases and do not point to a universal trend. They are illustrative of the compounded cultural complexity of the relatively unstable social and political formations that networks represent and through which governance can be enacted. Instead, this chapter focuses on the common context of 'intertwingling' in the global agora that these networks and others inhabit. While the abstract ideas and concepts created and communicated by knowledge networks and organisations matter and can be intrinsically important, the final chapter stresses that the power of ideas is best understood in conjunction with an appreciation of combined forces of interests and institutions as well as the information overload that has come with the internet. In contradictory tension, the public character of the global agora is in the making via a combination of these forces in what is a partial privatising of public policy.

1
The Global Agora: Privatising Policy Processes in Transnational Governance

A global agora is emerging. The global agora is partly configured by new policy actions and partnerships where the idea of 'public' and 'public sector' is remade. However, the concept of transnational or 'global public policy' is neither an institutionalised nor accepted understanding of governing beyond the nation-state. Accordingly, this chapter asks: What is global public policy? Where is it enacted? Who executes such policies? The first section sets out to delimit the discussion to transnational policy spaces where global public policies occur. These spaces are multiple in character and variety and will be collectively referred to as the 'agora'. This section also addresses what is 'global public policy' and some difficulties with the use of the term as well as the way in which some higher education institutions are responding.

The second section conceptually stretches the conventional policy cycle heuristic to the global and regional levels. This is used as an analytical device, not as a portrayal of decision-making realities. It is done to reveal the higher degree of pluralisation of actors as well as the multiple and contested modes of authority than is usually the case at national levels of policy making.

The last section asks: Who is involved in the delivery of global public policy? The activities of transnational policy communities reveal the dual dynamics of new public spaces carved out in tandem with privatising modes of decision-making. The intermeshed character of the global agora and the co-mingling of private and public actors in the delivery or financing of public goods make publicness more problematic. Governance is re-configured around various 'new architectures' that 'recreate the public either at a higher level or through a more complex network structure' (Cerny, 2010: 107).

Public spheres and private policy practice in the global agora

If global public policy is distinct and to some extent delinked from national processes of policy making, the venues in which such policy action occurs need not be tied to sovereign structures of decision-making, that is, the state. This is not to suggest a divorce between global and national policy processes. However, national public institutions no longer serve as the sole organising centre for policy. Instead, the playing field itself has been re-structured through historical and structural changes to the 'state' and 'sovereignty' (Cerny, 2010). Through the re-invention of a Greek political concept, this re-structured playing field will be referred to as the 'global agora'.

The notion of 'agora' is a familiar concept in studies of Athenian history and politics. 'Agora' means a marketplace or a public square. While it is commonplace in the contemporary era to see the 'marketplace' and the 'public square' as distinct domains, such boundaries were neither hard nor fast in the Greek agora. Importantly, the 'agora' was not only a marketplace but the heart of intellectual life and public discourse. The space could be used for an election, a dramatic performance, a religious ceremony, military drills or sports. The agora was:

> ... the natural venue for the greatest of gatherings, and business transactions would take place there as a matter of course. It was a place where people could exchange gossip and views as well as goods, and flock to hear the latest rumours. They could catch sight of those who decided the course of political events. Not least the latter could make themselves visible there and get some sense of the strength of support of their projects or of the different factions among the people. ... (The agora) was thus a public space. (Hannay, 2005: 12)

In short, the Greek agora (or equally the Roman forum) was the centre of civic activity.

The agora was a physical place as well as a social and political space in the Greek city-state (Wycherley, 1942: 21). The public landscape included landmarks such as the Mint, shrines and statuary, shops and law-courts, the market hall and the council house, and the Assembly. Artifacts from archaeological digs – public documents inscribed on stone, weight and measure standards, and jurors' identification tickets and ballots – reflect the administrative nature of the site.[1] As is apparent, the agora was a fusion of social, economic and political interaction.

Public-private boundaries were ill-defined. Political activity was as likely to take place inside private shops (cobblers, barbers) as it was in public buildings. That is, the 'commercial impinged upon the public buildings and shrines of the central agora at many points, and probably on every side' (Wycherley, 1956: 10). It could also be a heavily militarised space.

The merging and the blurring of the commercial and the public domains is nonetheless apparent in the modern global era (Touaf and Boutkhil, 2008). Today, the manner in which the commercial sector or businesses 'impinge' on global politics and recipient publics has also been called 'market-multilateralism' (Bull and McNeill, 2007).

> The agora embraces much more than the market and much more than politics. As a public space it invites exchanges of all kinds ... Although the agora is a structured space, it is wrong to attempt to sub-divide into sectors like markets, politics or media. (Nowotony et al., 2001: 209)

The idea of 'agora' identifies growing global public spaces of fluid, dynamic and intermeshed relations of politics, markets, culture and society. This public space is brought about by the interactions of its actors – that is, the sociability of multiple publics and plural institutions. Of course, some actors are more visible, persuasive or powerful than others. In these dynamics, traditional views on the role of experts, and of trust in scientific knowledge, are contextualised and challenged by the intermingling that has become intrinsic to the agora (Nowotony et al., 2001: 205 passim).

The global agora is a social and political space – an 'imaginary' generated by globalisation – rather than a physical place. Unlike the Greek agora, contemporary publics cannot flock to a civic centre. Nevertheless, some have already adopted the term to speak of the agora as an electronic or digital global commons (Arthurs, 2001: 97; Alexander and Pal, 1998). Likewise, the FutureWorld Foundation (discussed again in the Conclusion) has picked up the term and describes its information portal as a 'global agora' that 'will be a virtual town hall and community library for inhabitants of the global village' (2013). More generally, this type of 'intertwingularity' captures the idea of ease of connection and communication. The global agora is also a domain of relative disorder and uncertainty where institutions are underdeveloped and political authority unclear, and dispersed through multiplying institutions and networks. It is a challenge to the 'myth of 1648', that is, 'of a world of mutually recognizing, non-interfering sovereign state' emerging with the Peace of Westphalia (Armitage, 2013).

The 'agora' concept is useful for highlighting the 'co-mingling' of communities, and specifically in the contemporary global era, for disrupting the centrality of sovereignty. In the scene that opens Plato's *Republic*, the dialogue that ensues takes place in a *metic* household, that is, the home of a resident alien, the patriarch Cephalus and his son Polemarchus. *Metics* typically shared the burden of citizenship but with few of its privileges. Similar to Plato's Athenian agora, where political discussions took place in the dwelling of a resident foreigner, the sovereignty-challenging features of global decision-making in semi-private or quasi-public networks or public-private partnerships are increasingly apparent today. The idea of citizenship in the global agora has little or no resonance. While the global agora encompasses not only the traditional market for commercial products, but also the political market for negotiations, the public sphere for recognition and the scientific market for expert reputation, the public sector remains ill-formed and policy making limited to a few.

The concept of the global agora is normatively neutral. This is in contrast to a growing body of literature that advocates the need to democratise global governance and to enhance the legitimacy of international organisations (for example, the decade-old special edition in *Government and Opposition*, 2004). Without disavowing the value of such advocacy, nevertheless, the call for global accountabilities puts the normative cart before the conceptual and empirical horse.

Social scientists have used a series of vague metaphors to identify this realm. The vagueness is symptomatic of difficulties in finding a new vocabulary to grasp new policy structures. Well-known phrases include 'transnational public sphere' (Eckersley, 2007; Nanz and Steffek, 2004; Dryzek, 2006). With less traction, the idea of the 'transnational state' has been used to signify the 'deterritorialization' of political and economic relationships (McMichael, 2001: 201). An early analysis looked for signs of an emerging 'global polity' (Ougaard and Higgott, 2002). Likewise, the term 'global policy arena' is common place. More complicated descriptions include 'a polycentric or multi-nucleated global political system, operating with an increasingly continuous geographical space and/or overlapping spaces' (Cerny, 2010: 98), or in departure from the idea of a sovereign head in hierarchical governance, 'An acephalous ... modern global polity' (Drori, Meyer and Hwang, 2006: 14).

Some argue that the realisation of a democratic global order 'ultimately depends on the creation of an appropriate public sphere' (Nanz and Steffek, 2004: 315). Yet, the emphasis is on what is 'appropriate', that is often taken to mean a 'deliberative global politics' (Dryzek, 2006) and the presumed progressive potential of global civil society in forging this sphere whereby the transnational public sphere is conceived as a Habermasian 'communicative network' (Nanz and Steffek, 2004: 322). Others stress the growing diversity of policy actors above the nation-state as a healthy 'transnational pluralism' (Cerny, 2010; also Macdonald and Macdonald, 2010).

Unlike such normative literature, the concept of a 'global agora' as it is developed here makes no presumptions about the communicative, progressive or deliberative character of transnational public-private partnerships or network interactions. Instead, it is an open question as to 'the emancipatory potential of public spheres at the transnational level, where there is no common language or life-world, no cohesive global society and only a very weak global media' (Eckersley, 2007: 332). The prospects of private seclusion of policy deliberation to decision-making elites may well take shape. The global agora may become an accessible participative domain for plural expressions of policy input. The idea of a 'global agora' could be inspired by liberal democracy. It is equally feasible, however, that developments could be informed by coercive arrangements of authoritarianism or a reactionary anti-egalitarianism.

The Greek agora was 'patrician' (Hannay, 2005: 13) and the global agora may be no less characterised by lack of participation and by elite rule. The majority of Athenian citizenry did not participate directly in politics. Instead the Athenian agora of ancient Greece was made up of three kinds of citizen:

> ... the passive ones' who did not go to Assembly; the standing participants who went to the assembly but listened and voted, and 'did not raise their voice in discussion'; and the 'wholly active citizens' (a small group of initiative takers who proposed motions). (Hansen quoted in Urbinatti, 762–63)

It is the 'wholly active citizens' in internationally active NGOs, in international organisations, and in transnational public agencies who drive transnational policy processes. While the global agora may have dimensions of 'publicness', the capacity for, and character of, public action is much more varied.

In the Athenian agora, the Mint, religious building, shops and lawcourts, the market hall and the council house, and the Assembly were all in physical proximity even if women, slaves or resident foreigners had little participation in these forums. Even so, the agora was a site for the exchange of information or sharing of gossip. In the global agora, the international institutions are dispersed between Washington DC., The Hague, Geneva and Paris. The nodes of global finance are found in exclusive venues in New York, London, Tokyo and a few other global venues such as Basle or Davos. There is no centre. Instead, there are multiple dis-connected arenas for policy making. The agora is acephalous, that is, without a sovereign head. And the flow of information is more uni-directional downwards to the masses.

The idea of agora accords with the 'epistemological position that borders around global policy are variable and are being created and recreated in response to globalizing processes and global problems' (Coleman, 2012: 680). The concept is 'not infected with an unhealthy dualism in state/market, and global/national terms' (McMichael, 2001: 201). As discussed in the next chapter, policy networks and private regulatory standard setting have the outcome to privatise or, at the very least, qualify the publicness of decision-making. As noted elsewhere, governments have delegated extensive regulatory authority to international private-sector organisations. The internationalisation and privatisation of rule-making surrounding bodies like the International Accounting Standards Body or the International Organization for Standardization (ISO) has been motivated not only by the economic benefits of common rules for global markets, but also by the realisation that government regulators often lack the expertise and resources to deal with increasingly complex and urgent regulatory tasks (Büthe and Mattli, 2011). Consequently, the institutional locations are dispersed and the boundaries of the global agora are indeterminate and opaque. Policy activity is as likely to take place inside private associations among non-state actors as in inter-governmental conferences. The vast majority of citizens of nation-states are uninformed about these policy venues and, even if interested, face significant obstacles 'to raise their voice'. Only recently has policy studies started to adjust to these new realities by interrogating the idea of 'global public policy'.

Global public policy

In the last decade, there has been increasing use of the term 'global public policy' (Coleman, 2012). Books have emerged under this title (Reinicke, 1999; Ronit, 2006) or in the related field of 'global social policy' (Deacon, 2007). University courses in development studies or political science have been launched with this label. Yet the term remains under-specified. Generally, 'global public policy' has little resonance among policy elites and the general public. The same applies to academic journals in policy studies. As late as 2011, a group of Asian scholars (Hou et al., 2011) were exhorting for a more global perspective in the persistently American-centric and state-focused *Journal of Public Administration Research and Theory*. Only recently, the new journal *Global Policy* complements the three decades of interest of *Global Governance* in themes of 'international civil service' and transnational administration. The editorial statement of *Global Policy* (2012) explains global policy as a process:

> The field of global policy focuses on the global as a process (or set of processes) which creates transcontinental or interregional flows and networks of activity and interaction, and the new framework of multi-level policymaking by public and private actors, which involves and transcends national, international and transnational policy regimes.

Instead of 'global policy', other terms and concepts are better established in the lexicon. One of the most current terms derived from International Relations (IR) is 'global governance'. At other times, 'global policy' is equated with the financing and delivery of global public goods (Kaul, 2005). Another synonym is the idea of global 'public-private partnerships' (Bull and McNeill, 2007) or the 'global programs' sponsored by the World Bank (2004). 'Transnational constitutionalism' is a phrase rarely encountered; indeed, these constitutional processes have emerged only in the European Union (EU) (Arthurs, 2001: 107).

In classical political science, public policy occurs inside nation-states. In IR theory, a 'realist' perspective has always and still holds that states are the dominant actor in the international system and that international policies are made between states. With its strong tendency to 'methodological nationalism' (Armitage, 2013), traditional comparative public policy has compounded this standpoint (Coleman, 2012: 685). Scholars in the field usually compare policy development within and between states where states remain the key policy-making unit. To a large extent, public policy has been a prisoner of the word 'state'.

As a political space, the world is defined and divided between states as pre-eminent sources of public authority. Consequently, traditional IR still struggles to move out of the conceptual shadow of classical geopolitics (Kleinschmidt and Strandsbjerg, 2010). Traditional approaches to policy studies occupy the same Westphalian conceptual cage albeit constrained in a different fashion. The nation-state is a 'spatial "protective cocoon"' for making social and economic policy (McMichael, 2001: 2005). Nevertheless, both IR and public policy as fields of inquiry tend to portray states as being socially exclusive 'containers' with a sharp segmentation of territorial units in a cartographic understanding of global politics (Kleinschmidt and Strandsbjerg, 2010).

Moving beyond minimalist interpretations of a realist-rationalist variety that limits analysis to comprehending the capacity of public sector hierarchies to globalise national policies does not entail jumping to maximalist positions of an idealist-cosmopolitan character that speak of deliberative world government. A complex range of state capacities, public action and democratic deliberation fall in between these two extremes. Scholars and practitioners alike are arguing that new forms of authority are emerging through global and regional policy processes that co-exist alongside nation-state processes. Governance can be informal and emerge from strategic interactions and partnerships of national and international bureaucracies with non-state actors operating from the marketplace and civil society.

However, economic globalisation and regional integration are proceeding at a much faster pace in the agora than transnational policy processes. One outcome of this disjuncture is that the power of the nation-states has been reduced or reconfigured without a corresponding development of international institutional co-operation. This is one of the major causes of a deficiency of public goods at global levels. For example, the regulation of financial flows, environmental protection or intellectual property safe-guards are inadequately provided. Bodies such as the United Nations Development Program (UNDP) and other specialised UN agencies have become central in researching and articulating dimensions of 'publicness' in the global sphere and how international organisations and non-state actors create global public goods or seek to regulate the adverse effects of global public bads (Kaul, 2005).

Policy practice is moving faster than, and beyond, the paradigmatic understanding of a Westphalian cartographic nation-state system. Multi-level polycentric forms of public policy in which a plethora of institutions and networks negotiate within and between international agreements and private regimes have emerged as pragmatic responses in the absence of formal global governance. If 'public policy' is 'whatever governments choose to do or not to do' (Dye, 1984: 2), then some governments are devolving policy-making. This is a double devolution: first, beyond the nation-state to global and regional domains and, second, a delegation of authority to semi-private networks and non-state actors.

But this notion of public policy is too limited for this book on two counts. Indeed, the underlying premise is to contest the idea that public policy is whatever *governments* do. Instead, the key idea is that while many policies are public in their targeted audiences, or in delivering public goods, the instigators or financiers of such policy can be private. From this vantage, global public-private partnerships are a 'hybrid type of governance, in which non-state actors co-govern along with state actors for the provision of collective goods, and thereby adopt governance functions that have formerly been the sole authority of sovereign states' (Schäferhoff et al., 2009: 451). Second, instead of tying politics and policy making to physical space where we think of geographical nation-state space as a container for society, we are better served by thinking of space as a relationship with the environment. This 'forces us to think of space not as a given entity but as something that is constructed – not only as a human construction – but exactly in the encounter between *humans* and *non-humans*' (for example, fish, cars or the detritus of natural disasters) (Kleinschmidt and Strandsbjerg, 2010). Disaster management policies or standards for sustainable fisheries or pollution programmes have emerged as transnational policy processes because fish swim through and pass legal spaces of territorial waters, or effective policy implementation in reducing car exhaust emissions into the atmosphere requires collective cross-national public and private commitments.

One indicator of the growth of transnational modes of public policy is the extent to which it is becoming a distinct domain of teaching. Graduate programmes in 'global public policy' were very rare in the 1990s, but were burgeoning by the second decade of the twenty-first century. These initiatives provide insight into attempts to conceptualise and operationalise for educational purposes, this space of policy practice and scholarship. The Master of Global Policy Studies degree at the Lyndon B. Johnson School of Public Affairs claims to consider 'the full range of influences on contemporary global policy – governments, private industry, and non-governmental organizations' in order 'to equip professionals with the tools and knowledge necessary to be leaders in an increasingly interdependent world'.[2] University College London delivers a Master of Science in International Policy that 'brings together the academic study of IR with analysis of public policy formulation and governance beyond the nation-state',[3] while the School of Public Policy at Central European University (CEU) aspires to be 'a new kind of global institution dealing with global problems'.[4] The educational programmes at CEU have been criticised for creating an elite cadre who conforms to 'the ideology of globalization ... and tends to be compliant with its requisites'. That is, CEU is 'training the administrators of globalization' (Guilhot, 2007; also Stubbs and Wedel, 2013). Many other examples could be given. The point is that universities are adapting to their changing environment to provide education and training for young professionals who need the skills and knowledge to traverse transnational policy processes. By building these programmes, universities and their graduates give tangible meaning and sense to the idea of global policy. As 'expanding globalized institutions of science and expertise', universities, their scholars and their students are drawn into, and structure, the global agora (Drori, Meyer and Hwang, 2006: 12). One way of interrogating this is to ask if the traditional policy cycle concept of policy studies can be stretched to accommodate dynamics in the global agora.

A global policy cycle?

The global agora is expanding and diversifying. The state is not necessarily retreating or in decline. However, it is re-configuring with the dynamics of globalisation and remains an important and key agent in the agora. Yet the constitution of the agora – its values, discourses, symbols, norms, institutions and practices (Arthurs, 2001: 89) – are also created by other non-state actors that have acquired or appropriated public authority when responding unilaterally or in partnership to global problems. Transnational policy processes appear in several different ways; that is:

- Problems are transboundary, arising from crime, diseases, pollution or drug trafficking, or problems emerge from new supra-territorial methods of decision-making;
- Problems relate to management of the global commons, that is, stewardship of outer-space, the oceans or Antarctica;
- Problems experienced simultaneously within nation-state but which contain elements of cross-national concern due to character of actors or financing involved, for instance, tobacco control, slum management or pollution from cars (see Coleman, 2012: 681–82).

Grappling with these problems have led to new forms of 'soft' authority or 'soft law' (Arthurs, 2001), which complements the traditional 'hard' or formal authority of states and international organisations. 'Soft' authority is seen in the emergence of private regimes, global standard setting and transnational policy communities. The exercise of public and private authority through policy networks and law-like arrangements, such as codes of practice, creates transnational policy processes. Unlike the title of this section, the phrase 'transnational policy processes' will be used hereafter as not all processes are global in either design or impact. Nevertheless, these processes, whether regional or limited to a few countries, form part of the global agora.

Adapting traditional concepts from policy studies highlights some of the difficulties in capturing analytically the idea of public policy in the global agora. The standard idea of the policy cycle is to divide it into four stages (Rushton and Williams, 2012):

1. agenda-setting,
2. decision-making,
3. implementation,
4. monitoring and evaluation.

One advantage is that this heuristic with its focus on process brings into sight the central role of non-state actors and modes of self-regulation.

Problem definition and agenda setting

There is no global decision-making process, at least not in the sense understood in policy studies where there is an authoritative, sovereign decision maker. Consequently, at the global level, the 'ownership' of public problems is often characterised by a policy vacuum. Which countries or what institutions have responsibility for dealing with issues is not automatically apparent, and if public goods are insufficient, those who take responsibility for their financing and provision are not self-evident. Contemporary social and civic regimes in the policy sectors of health, labour standards and social inclusion are sectors where non-state activists have been prominent (Keck and Sikkink, 1998; True, 2003). Agenda-setting is more contested, externalised beyond the nation-state and open to the input and disruption of a variety of political agents.

Some see this diversity of interests and institutions as a sign of a healthy and vibrant global civil society (Keck and Sikkink, 1998). That is, indicative of a pluralistic set of political pressures and countervailing power in the global agora where the anti- and alter-globalisation movements voice their causes in the same domain as multi-national companies, the media, states and international organisations. The World Social Forum, for example, reacted to the agenda-setting or 'opinion-forming' aspirations of the World Economic Forum in Davos. Agenda-setting is characterised by cacophonic sets of debates and demands where it is unclear who, or what institution, has the authority or legitimacy to mediate. There are not only significant problems of negotiation and compromise but also uncertainty concerning in which forums it is appropriate to advance issues. This has consequences for policy co-ordination and policy coherence alongside continuing conflict and power battles of who gets to set global agendas.

Decision-making

Transnational policy processes complicate decision-making with a greater propensity for policy transfers. Policy transfer is a process whereby knowledge about policies, administrative arrangements or institutions in one place is used across time or space in the development of policy elsewhere (Evans, 2009) but which are transformed and translated in the transnational process of transfer (Prince, 2011). Many governments and international organisations become proactive in promoting cross-border policy harmonisation (especially in regional arrangements) or in exporting policy lessons. The spread of the Ombudsman institution (Ladi, 2011b), freedom of information laws, tobacco control approaches (Rushton and Williams, 2012), gender mainstreaming (True, 2007) or the OECD's guidelines on budgetary best practices are examples of policy transfer and standard setting (Brütsch and Lehmkuhl, 2007).

There is no 'world parliament' or 'global state', nor is there likely to be such a singular forum. Even so, international commissions such as those headed by Brandt, Palme and Brundtland often function as venues for the official discussion of global policies. The G20 is the most recent incarnation of international summitry. The standard toolkits available for nations willing to co-operate on global issues are international treaties and conventions. These are difficult to secure in the first place, and effectiveness is problematically reliant on compliance and a culture of good international citizenship. Too often there is an implicit assumption that states will act 'rationally' and recognise that collective action is to their long-term interests.

The transnational dimensions of public policy and decision-making is usually seen as the responsibility of international organisations such as the Bretton Woods institutions or other bodies such as the World Trade Organisation (WTO), Global Environment Facility and International Telecommunication Union. They have the scope and delegated powers to deal with specified common property and transboundary problems. These organisations do not have a global remit but are restricted by their charters to limited domains of responsibilities. These are disaggregated regimes that collectively create a complicated architecture of institutions, laws and instruments.

Looking towards these organisations for coherent responses to global policy problems, one finds serious unresolved co-ordination issues and overlapping responsibilities. This can lead to co-operation among international organisations, but it also leads to 'turf battles' where authority is contested. Similarly, in the absence of enforcement capabilities and use of sanctions, non-compliance remains high. It provides incentive for international organisations to look to partners in civil society or the business sector that may be better able to co-finance and deliver public goods as well as to exert influence and cajole compliance.

For example, international organisations do develop policies to deliver global public goods, (as discussed in Chapter 7). The World Bank is a good example. The World Bank defines 'global and regional programs' as programmatic partnerships having the following characteristics:

- The partners contribute and pool resources (financial, technical, staff, and reputational) towards achieving agreed-upon objectives over time.
- The activities of the programme are global, regional or multi-country (not single-country) in scope.
- The partners establish a new organisation with a governance structure and management unit to deliver these activities (IEG, 2007: xvi).

Through its Development Grant Facility, the Bank has funded issue-specific programmes such as the Global Invasive Species Program, the Global Forum for Health Research, and the Consultative Group for International Agricultural Research (CGIAR), amongst numerous other initiatives. These examples are a snapshot of considerably more diverse activity of public policy being 'spun-off' to semi-autonomous networks and partnerships to which we return in Chapter Two. Moreover, it is not restricted to international organisation. Business plays a role in multilateral initiatives: for example the Global Road Safety Partnership and the Global Business Coalition on HIV/AIDS. These global programmes are sector or issue specific, executed through multiple public and private venues rather than a single executive authority.

Policy implementation and international co-ordination

There are major analytical problems when addressing public policy implementation in a global context. International organisations generally lack both the authority and the means to enforce policy compliance. Implementation is dependent on international co-operation and states behaving as responsible 'international citizens' to keep their commitments as well as educating electorates and convincing them of the real impact of global problems on local communities. There are few sanctions that can be employed against recalcitrant states except for engineering consensus, moral pressure from other states, trade sanctions and at the extreme, military intervention. From senior officials in both international organisations and bilateral development agencies, there are numerous pronouncements about the need for joint commitment, co-financing or aid harmonisation, all of which represent pleas for policy co-ordination. Time consuming processes of consensus building, the diplomatic pressures for compromise, the sources of opposition, and the resource implications of developing global policy programmes significantly delay state co-ordinated international action.

Notwithstanding these difficulties, on issues ranging from organised crime and terrorism to human rights, the environment, finance and trade, it is increasingly evident that government officials are exchanging information, coordinating policies, enforcing laws and regulating markets through increasingly elaborate informal inter-governmental channels. Public policy is enacted in the decentralised and technocratic activities of judges, regulators and legislators working with foreign counterparts on specific issues (Slaughter, 2004; Büthe and Mattli, 2011). Similarly, there are partnerships of business, NGOs and other civil society actors, governments and international organisations. Examples include the Global Alliance for Vaccines and Immunisation, now known simply as GAVI,[5] and the Global Water Partnership.[6] These 'global public policy networks' (sometimes called 'transnational public-private partnerships', Bull and McNeill, 2007) are quasi-public or semi-private and will be discussed in greater detail in the next chapter. They can be contrasted with private regimes. For instance, the bond-rating agencies such as Moody's and Ffitch (Sinclair, 2005) and the ISO are different types of private actors that perform global roles of accreditation and co-ordination, respectively. The vast diversity of arrangements have led another set of observers to describe the trend of private engagement in policy combined with some regulatory authority as 'experimentalist governance' (Sabel and Zeitlin, 2012) that leads to 'global rule making' (Büthe and Mattli, 2011).

Generally, the emergence and spread of legal and law-like arrangements mean that states cooperate in more or less precise, more or less binding and quasi-independent regimes, but also that non-state actors can engage in the framing, definition, implementation and enforcement of these norms and rules (Brütsch and Lehmkuhl, 2007). It is a process of constant tinkering with, and adjustment of, rules or standards. However, global standards and best practices that may be adopted in bureaucratically mature OECD countries are far less likely to be seen in poor developing countries or states in conflict; consequently, the pattern of implementation is also highly uneven and contingent. At the same time, there may be on-going shifts in the balance of power between different international organisations, and continual contests and 'forum switching' of global issues and responsibilities. For instance, global health issues are addressed by the World Health Organisation but increasingly also in a number of World Bank initiatives or via public-private partnerships like the Global Fund to Fight AIDS, Tuberculosis and Malaria.

Transnational monitoring and evaluation

Reflection on both success and failure may promote efficiency, innovation and learning in policy. At the national level, evaluation is usually undertaken 'in-house' by national bureaucracies, commissions of inquiry or audit agencies. In global spheres, evaluation comes from various sources. The international financial institutions often have an in-house capacity for research and evaluation that bolsters their sovereignty-challenging policies. For instance, the intellectual homogeneity and professional strength of the economists within the international financial and trade institutions is well recognised. The reports from the World Bank Independent Evaluation Group, or the International Monetary Fund's (IMF) Independent Evaluation Office, feed back into the refinement and management of global programmes and also represent a *de-facto* template and set of standards for other initiatives regarding governance and oversight.

Often, evaluation is contracted out to private-sector experts and advisers while unsolicited advice and evaluation comes from NGOs and social movements. The sheer volume of knowledge, expertise and advice cannot all be incorporated and potentially creates incoherence, conflict and gridlock. There is a need for translators and interpreters of analysis and for 'knowledge management' systems. Such experts who edit and vouch the credibility of information and analysis acquire some power as 'editors' in determining what meets international standards and best practice. Rather than operating independently, they are often to be found in transnational networks of think tanks, consultants, university policy centres, professional bodies and consultancy firms. 'The opening up of international governance to greater deliberations among a wider array of actors has contributed, perhaps not surprisingly, to an increasing preoccupation with struggles over the truth status of knowledge claims and the resources for making those claims more or less believable to diverse publics' (Miller, 2007: 330). In the weak institutional context of the global agora, these policy actors are arguably more influential in shaping the parameters of policy making, defining problems and specifying what constitutes 'global public goods' and selling their 'expert evaluation' services than they are within the confines of the nation-state.

Order and chaos in the global agora

The model of the policy cycle depicts a linear model of policy, moving from one stage to the next. In reality, policy making is messy. It is more accurate to conceptualise the policy process as a chaotic and constantly changing set of aspirations and accidents. This is apparent at national levels, but even more so beyond the authority structures of 'sovereign' nation-states. Complexity is accelerated by (i) the growing diversity of institutions and actors; (ii) interdependence and porous boundaries between organisations; (iii) ambiguity, in part due to an information overload, and (iv) flux, where change has a changing character (Steger, Amann and Maznevski, 2012: 4). This 'complexity' poses significant management challenges for transnational organisations that the positive connotations of 'intertwingularity' do not convey.

A major theme in the conceptual literature on public policy is a prescriptive one of making the policy process more rational. However, to search for signs of an orderly or stable transnational policy process is at least fruitless, and at worst, misguided. In the absence of global government, transnational policy processes are more fluid and fragmented than might be found in the mostly stable political systems of the OECD nations. Instead, disorder and unpredictability is the norm. Due to the vast differences in policy style, structure, institutional set-up, powers and resources of transnational policy arrangements and regulatory frameworks, there is no consistent pattern to transnational policy processes. On the contrary, the bewildering array of public action is complicated by its often semi-private composition. The absence of, or constantly contested, authority structures within the global agora mean far greater time and effort is also spent convening, debating and negotiating in arenas created by interlocutors to promote compliance rather than exert enforcement.

These disjointed transnational policy processes are further compromised by the 'new public management' with its ethos of contracting out, 'freeing' managers and providing market incentives for efficiency and effectiveness. However, where this state-centric managerial paradigm for the public sector focusing on the downward devolution to subnational units of governance, policy scholars have missed the equally apparent upward devolution to supra-national and inter-governmental models of governance. The public domain is not under threat; instead, it is 'state-ness' that is under duress (Drache, 2001: 40). Just as the 'myth of 1648' is undermined by 'the recognition that empires, federations and other kinds of layered or divided sovereignty were more characteristic of political authority than any alleged "Westphalian" sovereignty' (Armitage, 2013), so too new transnational forms of authority and policy responsibility emerge and overlay state-guided processes. As a corollary, publicness is expanding as the global agora takes shape.

However, 'global public policy' is not necessarily as 'public' as a dispassionate observation of the public-sector organisations found in liberal democracies or established through inter-governmental treaty arrangements would confirm. Instead, transnational policy processes can be considerably more exclusive, temporary, *ad hoc* and privatised, hence more immune, opaque and unaccountable to sovereign authorities or civic critique. The gestation of the global agora, of which transnational policy processes are one large part, is also part of a more general reordering of the private and the public and the greater fluidity between market and non-market activities that necessitates a re-conceptualisation of basic categories. Yet, orthodoxies are often well entrenched: 'An attachment to the notion of the public sphere as a nation-centred arena is one reason for critics' delayed recognition of the importance of understanding transnational public spaces' (McLaughlin, 2004: 162). These spaces are entwined in complexity. Unlike the implication of their book title (Ougaard and Higgott, 2002), rather than moving *Towards a Global Polity* in a singular sense, instead we are witnessing many miniature polities and global programmes emerging in plural shape and form. In these spaces arise diverse groupings of transnational policy professionals.

Transnational policy communities

Investigation of those who execute or implement global public policies has long been underdeveloped. Attention is now being paid to individual agents of policy making with attempts to get inside the 'black box' of international organisations (Xu and Weller, 2008: 37) to address the roles, powers and impacts of what has been variously described as 'international civil servants' (Weiss, 1982) or 'supranational bureaucrats' (Bauer, 2012). They might also be described as the 'wholly active citizens' in the global agora, those who are proposing and implementing global public policy. It is useful to dis-aggregate these actors into three general types. The umbrella term 'transnational policy community' will be used for all three types. They are the drivers of global policy, directly involved in the diffusion of ideas, standards and policy practice.

First is the 'internationalised public sector official'. This is the type of individual to be found in 'transnational executive networks' (Slaughter, 2004). Due to the cross-boundary character of contemporary policy problems, whether it be related to crime, disease or pollution, collaborative and information-sharing networks have developed from high-level bureaucrats and legislators directly involved in national political process through to lower level national regulators. These state officials operate in inter-governmental networks and often interact with their colleagues in international organisations.

Second, 'international civil servants' are employed by an international organisation to staff its secretariat and institute operations. They are not state delegates. The conventional paradigm of international civil service includes impartiality, objectivity and international loyalty, rather than national particularism (Weiss, 1982: 288–92). Yet, the reality of international administration is more complex, where national interests continue to be pursued. Inside international organisations, civil servants have considerable capacity to shape (or delay) policies due to their expertise, routines and positions of power (Xu and Weller, 2008). The relative lack of analysis of these actors, or a tendency to treat them as a conforming to the conventional paradigm, combined with the lack of transparency of most international organisations, means their roles as policy implementers in the global agora and their contributions to policy innovation are rarely open to public scrutiny.

'Transnational policy professionals' are the third type of policy actor. This is a diverse but growing community of consultants, foundation officers, business leaders, scientific experts, think tank pundits and NGO executives who are increasingly notable for their global policy reach and professionalism. Their status as either public or private agents is not always clear-cut. Private consultants are contracted by public bodies, and private experts are co-opted into official advisory bodies. Rather than acting individually, they are usually found in a network or association that is often in receipt of public support or official patronage.

All three categories of actors interact in varying degree with each other to facilitate multilateral co-operation and the delivery of global public goods. It is increasingly evident to see individuals building careers across all three categories. Their sources of power and influence vary. In general, however, they hold power as a result of their (semi-)official position; their control of information and other organisational resources; their technical expertise or epistemic authority; or their often lengthy international experience as career officials and consultants. Transnational policy communities are professional spaces that widen opportunities for international career mobility as well as facilitate information sharing, policy coordination and network interactions. But they do so in increasingly complex environments: 'executives must manage an (internationalizing) human resources pool; more variety in the management systems; more variety in the means and ends, ranging from simple financial goals to a more comprehensive view; different business models for different business units ... differing cultural values; a plethora of stakeholders with different claims (investors, customers, employees, regulators, etc.); various political, legal and economic environments ...' (Steger, Amann and Maznevski, 2012: 4).

Networks, coalitions and public-private partnerships create diverse spaces of assembly in the global agora. Many could become a means for civic engagement and a vehicle for expanding participation for civil society and social movement activists. Coalitions of NGOs convening around a common cause are often called 'transnational advocacy networks'. However, the 'agora' is also an economic sphere of commerce and market exchange. Networks can be a force for 'market deepening' (Reinicke, Deng et al., 2000) or for the promotion of ideals of corporate social responsibility. Industry-related networks such as the International Council on Mining and Metals provide guidelines for member companies to work towards sustainable development goals, while business associations like the International Chamber of Commerce performs an advocacy function, championing the global economy as a force for economic growth, job creation and prosperity. They operate more as 'insider groups' given their closer connections with governments. Along with the notion of 'knowledge networks', these species of network are discussed in detail in the next chapter. Suffice to say it here, these structures have become increasingly numerous and are cogs constituting the global agora.

The different varieties of networks that intersect and help compose public spaces can be a force for democratisation by creating a venue for representation of 'stakeholder' interests, a means for wider participation in modes of global governance and a venue for societal voices. In short, networks are 'gateways'. However, policy debate in the agora need not be democratic. Instead, as in the Athenian agora (Urbinati, 2000), the global agora is invariably managed by elite transnational policy communities. Many developing countries, and most ordinary citizens, have limited resources to devote to national policy deliberations and simply do not figure in global dialogues. Despite widening internet 'connectivity', at present they remain 'passive' or 'standing' citizens in the agora. At best, the digital agora allows groups to track and observe the activities of the 'wholly active' citizens who have acquired privileged vantage in transnational policy communities.

Transnational networks and policy processes create new pressures on national leaders and call forth new forms of leadership and public management. Policy making and administration of global nature means understanding the fast-changing venues and dynamics of nascent decision-making milieu, greater cross-cultural sensitivity and different behaviours on the part of policy actors. This is not limited to diplomats but has widened and applies to the more diverse 'transnational policy communities'. Similarly, there are greater pressures on, and opportunities for, parliamentarians and political party officials to engage with counterparts. Indeed, the World Bank seed funded the development of the Parliamentary Network on the Bank (PNoB) to germinate such collaboration. Leadership skills required in the global agora mean functioning in several languages, comprehending the legal and political context of many policy venues (for example, the EU, neighbouring countries, WTO) and mastering different modes of communication and policy deliberation.

The geographical dispersion of transnational policy communities means that policy actors meet irregularly, are highly reliant on information technology and travel all the time. It may be the case that many adopt a globalised identity and outlook. In other words, the values guiding the behaviour of bureaucrats are increasingly shaped by the imperatives of the global economy and constraints on sovereign control of policy that prompt new modes of collaboration. Whether or not transnational policy communities are becoming a class apart, that is, delinked from national identities and loyalty to state-defined interests as opposed to having a paramount commitment to global or regional concerns, is something that is yet to be subject to in-depth anthropological and ethnographic work.

Transnational policy professionals are not directly comparable to traditional bureaucrats. Their hybrid character as often being both private and public actors at the same time suggests that they could present difficulties of management and accountability for nationally constituted citizenries or parliaments. The networks, partnerships and global or regional programmes they work in are 'radically decentralized'; that is, 'they are not organizationally connected within any overarching constitutional structure allocating complementary roles and responsibilities in relation to a shared democratic public, as are the multiple public agencies within the state' (Macdonald and Macdonald, 2010: 24). This is largely due to their duties and responsibilities being more privatised or less public. Networks tend to behave like regulated organisations rather than extensions of administrative agencies under legislative control. Hybrid entities – given their private, informal and 'delegated authority' status – are intrinsically less responsive to the political preferences of their political masters and publics. Moreover, global programmes and networks are sometimes temporary arrangements, networks are re-named and yet other programmes can be unpacked and re-assembled into different entities. This makes enforcing accountability difficult. It is more than simply an issue of strengthening bureaucratic control as the nature of networked transnational policy communities implies that public authority has been semi-privatised.

The requirements of a transnational network executive or officer of a philanthropic entity (such as the Gates, Ford or Aga Khan Foundations) may require management skills and bureaucratic knowledge that differ from counterparts in national or local governments. Consequently, the types of graduate programmes referred to earlier may well spread as pressures increase for innovation and creativity in how national leaders as well as non-state executives project their organisational and commu-nity interests in the global agora. More young elites will be encouraged to undertake international education and training. Already, dual degree programmes and international consortiums of graduate education such as the Global Public Policy Network aim 'to prepare some of the world's most able graduate students to assume global leadership roles in the coming decades'.[7] Such programmes provide graduate training for administrative positions in internationalised public sectors. These programmes also cater for international organisations (which appear to be growing in number and policy ambit) as well as for new generations of policy entrepreneurs who see their future careers in transnational networks and regimes. For too long, the scholar of public policy and administration has assumed an insulated sovereign domain of policy making. What happened beyond these borders was the stuff of foreign policy and diplomacy. Such assumptions are no longer tenable in policy studies in either theory or practice.

Conclusion: Exclusionary participation in the global agora

A global agora is evolving with inter-connecting tangles of networks, global public-private partnerships and multilateral initiatives. These transnational policy processes are distinguishable from national and inter-governmental processes, but remain co-mingled, not detached (Kennett, 2010: 21). Consequently, this book is much more than an account about 'how states govern at a distance' (Neumann and Sending,

2010: vii). Instead, the agora is portrayed in its network character, managed by business and policy elites in transnational policy communities. The agora is presented as likely to be more exclusionary than participatory. The objective has been to shift the focus from institutions, actors and policies at the nation-state level, to address how policy making has transnational dimensions. This is not to deny the continuing power and impact of nation-states. The domestic politics of nation-states will continue to ensure difference and diversity. States will remain important mediators of globalisation, but their capacities to react and respond will differ dramatically. Transnational actors and networks will not only continue to by-pass national and inter-governmental policy-making processes to influence or partner with international organisations but also seek to create private regimes of standard setting or new modes of experimentalist governance.

The global agora is a public space, although it is one where authority is diffuse, decision-making is dispersed and semi-privatised, and sovereignty is muddled by recognition of joint responsibility and collective action. Public space is generated not by physical sites of policy deliberation but by the social or network interactions that emerge in response to material changes in the world, whether that be the common property problem of declining fish stocks or trans-boundary problems of drug trafficking. As discussed in the next chapter, transnational policy networks – whether they go by the label 'partnership', 'alliance', 'facility' or 'forum' – are an increasingly visible mechanism of global public policy. For the scholar, these developments presage the need to overcome the methodological nationalism and agoraphobia of mainstream public policy scholarship to examine transnational policy processes and communities.

2
Knowledge Networks/Policy Networks

Ideas matter. Although a cliché, access to and control over, knowledge is one key in determining the way power is constituted and used. As authority over political, social and economic activity is diffused globally among a variety of public and private actors, knowledge networks (KNETs) become crucial arbiters and coordinators in policy formulation. Yet, there remain considerable shortcomings in our conceptual and empirical understanding of how knowledge organisations have become transnational, densely networked and interactive with policy communities.

This chapter explores the *transnational* features of knowledge agencies. The specific focus is upon the *policy-related* roles of researchers and other experts who may be based in universities, consultancy firms, philanthropic foundations, independent research institutes and think tanks and who interact in KNETs. The discussion is based on the assumption that there is a dynamic relationship between (global) governance and knowledge. The EU, the World Bank, the WTO, the OECD and the World Health Organisation (WHO) are just some of the international organisations that have become important funders and consumers of research and policy analysis. For organisations that have global or regional remit, networks provide connections between knowledge producers and decision makers for evidence-informed policy. In post-modernist perspectives, such networks have become one form of 'governmentality' (Sending and Neumann, 2010; Ilcan and Philips, 2008), that is, symptomatic of a 'capillary' character of power relations (Walters, 2012: 9).

The following section introduces the idea of 'global knowledge networks' and how they connect to, but are different from, related concepts such as 'transnational advocacy networks', 'transnational executive networks' and 'global public policy networks'. Rather than forcing a synthesis, each of these network types offer different perspectives on why networks emerge and the principles and/or interests around which collective action occurs. In short, these are different 'species' of networks.

The second section addresses global knowledge networks as a contemporary manifestation of long-standing debates about the link between ideas and politics. If ideas matter, how do they matter and why? Knowledge networks are one mechanism to make ideas matter. However, to provide an explanation of why networks make ideas matter requires recourse to some of the theoretical literature on networks. The epistemic community, discourse coalition and neo-Gramscian network approaches provide different foci of analysis – science, discourse and ideology – for the interpretation of the sources of power of knowledge networks.

The final section discusses networks as policy processes and governance structures. As a social technology, the network can be regarded as both organising structures for governance and agents or vehicles for activism and policy advocacy. As will be argued, transnational networks are creating new public spaces in the global agora.

Networks in the global agora

KNETs – as well as other kinds of network – contribute to the shape, diversity and (in)equality of the global agora. Networks can be thought of as a form of assembly and public action. Networks are potentially a means for civic engagement and a vehicle for expanding participation. This is neatly captured in the social movement character of 'transnational advocacy networks' (Keck and Sikkink, 1998; Diani and McAdam, 2003). TANs have become a popular concept within the IR literature, especially on environmental issues and gender studies (see *inter alia*, Huelshoff and Kiel, 2012; True, 2003), but there are also other network concepts to allow us to identify four main species or types.

- Global public policy network – GPPN
- Transnational executive network – TEN
- Knowledge network – KNET and
- Transnational advocacy network – TAN

By no means is this an exhaustive list of social science thinking on networks. Older concepts from public policy have been 'stretched' to keep pace with supra-national and sovereignty-challenging developments of global governance and transnational regulation. For instance, the concepts of 'policy community' and 'advocacy coalitions' have sometimes been used to identify transnational action (see the network literature reviews undertaken by Holten, 2008 and by Thompson, 2003).

Notwithstanding the diversity of network ideas, this chapter selects four of the better established network concepts for detailed discussion. Each is sufficiently distinct in terms of explaining the composition, sources of power and authority as well as causal impact of networks on policy. Nevertheless, these four concepts are ideal types. Table 2.1 summarises the features of each type. In reality, there can be significant blurring or overlap rather than hard and fast conceptual boundaries between each species.

Transnational advocacy networks

The first species is 'transnational advocacy networks' (TAN – Keck and Sikkink, 1998). TANs are similar to, but more issue focused than social movements. Characteristically, they accommodate a range of NGOs and activists. They are bound together by shared values or 'principled beliefs' and a shared discourse where the dominant modality is information exchange. They are called advocacy networks because 'advocates plead the causes of others or defend a cause or proposition' (Keck and Sikkink, 1998: 8). In other words, these networks are norm based and mission oriented in seeking to have their values recognised in policy. Examples include the transnational campaigns surrounding issues like anti-slavery and debt relief. In response to women's transnational advocacy networking, 'the United Nations has opened spaces for their global influence' (True, 2007: 378). This has sometimes had a 'boomerang effect' back into national policy contexts with re-definitions of state interests and identities as a result of transnational pressures.

A TAN emerged around the theme of 'blood diamonds' or 'conflict diamonds' in part as a response to the covert 'dark network' mode of operation of arms traffickers (Raab and Milward, 2003). Other examples include the Cluster Munition Coalition or Development Alternatives with Women for a New Era (DAWN) operating in the 'Global South'. At a regional level, there are civil liberties advocacy bodies like ILGA-Europe, the International Lesbian, Gay, Bisexual, Trans and Intersex Association.

TANs usually have a strong normative basis for any moral judgements they make in seeking to shape the climate of public debate and influence global policy agendas. However, compared to other network species, they are not well integrated into policy making and operate more like 'outsider groups'. They exercise 'voice' and seek to sway public opinion. The growth and relatively high degree of public exposure of

Table 2.1 Network Species

	Transnational Advocacy Networks (TANs)	Global Public Policy Networks (GPPNs)	Transnational Executive Networks (TENs)	Knowledge Networks (KNETS)
Alternative Terms	Global civil society networks	Global programmes, global public private partnerships	Governmental networks, transnational constitutionalism	Epistemic community
Participants	True believers Purposive actors	Stakeholders specific to a policy issue or problem, tri-sectoral	Judges, politicians, regulators, officers of the state	Scientists, experts
Authority	Normative, value based	Partnership principles of shared decision-making	Politico-legal office, sovereign authority	Episteme
Capacities	Convening power, persuasive narratives of change, advocacy	Force for market deepening, delegated decision-making, implementation efficiencies	International coordination, state interests extended and internationalised	Evidence providers, interpreters, theorisation and conceptualisation
Theorisation	Neo-pluralist	Neo-corporatist	Power sharing, inter-state regulation, 'transnational state'	Neo-Gramscian or post-positivist perspectives
Policy Change	Agenda-setting	Agenda-setting, resource mobilisation, interest mediation	Collaborative regulation	Paradigm shift or (in case of *doxic* communities) paradigm maintenance
Locus	Civil society	Between market and state	Public sector, state based.	Cross-cutting civil society, market and state differentially according to issue

Policy transfer modalities	Spreads values and norms	Develop best practices and standards	Peer review, harmonisation	Modes of evaluation, assessment frameworks, methods of (social) scientific inquiry
Accessing networks	Open to those subscribing to the principles	Limited to stakeholders with vested interest and sharing the common policy project	Limited to state authorised actors	Limited to those with recognised education, training and mastery of 'communication codes'
Network coherence and coordination	Common cause, shared ideas and values, reform-oriented	Shared interests, resource interdependencies and shared policy responsibilities	Allegiance to the state, pooled sovereignty or inter-governmental decision-making authority	Consensual knowledge, scientific protocols, peer review and standards of professional expertise
Public Action	Overtly in public sphere, generally outsiders to policy process	Creating issue-specific public space via network, global public goods provision	Extension of state policy responsibilities via networks of government officials	Global knowledge, public goods production
Policy outputs and outcomes	Voice, alternative vision	Soft law, policy coordination, shared implementation responsibilities	Rules, harmonised regulation, common standards and information sharing	Codified knowledge, expert advice and analysis for policy formulation and review

TANs has been propelled by technological advances in transport and communications (Waddell, 2011).

Global public policy networks

The second kind of network is the 'global public policy network' (GPPN) (Reinicke and Deng, 2000). Sometimes called 'transnational public-private partnerships' these networks are tri-sectoral in character. That is, they are alliances of government agencies alongside international organisations as well as corporations and elements of civil society. Official involvement of public actors bestowing governmental patronage or development assistance gives some 'insider' status to official decision-making for these networks. Stakeholders invest in these communities to pursue material interests but have in common a shared problem. Their interactions are shaped by resource dependencies and bargaining. They tend to cohere around the international organisations and governments that have entered into a policy partnership for the delivery of global public goods.

The transnational character of policy problems establishes rationales for co-operation. Examples include the Global Gas Flaring Initiative, the Global Environment Facility, and one of the oldest, CGIAR. Although technically an inter-governmental organisation, the International Network on Bamboo and Rattan (INBAR) connects a global network of partners from the government, private and not-for-profit sectors in over 50 countries to define and implement a global agenda for sustainable development for bamboo and rattan producers.

Over time a network may become institutionalised with the creation of formal arrangements such as advisory committees, consultation procedures and recognition by state and multilateral agencies in the implementation of policies. GPPNs are different in their publicness and sources of authority. Although the term 'corporatism' has fallen out of fashion and the 'operative word today is partnership' (Ottaway, 2001: 266), a neo-corporatist framework of interpretation has considerable applicability in that groups settle problems through negotiation and joint agreement. While official actors from governments or international organisations are partners in these networks, they are not 'inter-governmental' in the manner of the next type of network species. Instead, GPPNs are quasi-public or semi-private.

Transnational executive network

The third kind of networks is not based in civil society as is the case with TANs, or overlapping into it as do GPPNs. Instead, 'transnational executive networks' are strategic devices for states to extend their public authority beyond borders. These networks are almost exclusively composed of 'internationalised public sector officials'. In this perspective, the state is not disappearing but it is becoming disaggregated and penetrated by horizontal networks existing between 'high level officials directly responsive to the national political process – the ministerial level – as well as between lower level national regulators' (Slaughter, 2004: 19). These networks of, for example, judges, legislators or regulators such as utilities commissioners are inter-governmental in character, and the state remains core as a sovereign actor. The actors who compose TENs are formally designated power holders and rule makers who derive their authority from their official positions within their nation-state. Examples of such networks include the International Association of Insurance Supervisors and the International Network on Environmental Compliance and Enforcement (INECE).

Terrorists, arms dealers, money launderers, drug cartels and human traffickers operate through global networks. In this context, an underlying logic of some TENs is that networked threats require networked responses (Kahler, 2009). For example, the Financial Action Task Force (FATF) was created as a response to cross-border money laundering. Networks become tools for the maintenance of sovereignty where global problems are solved by 'networked government' collaboration. As mechanisms for the state to re-invent itself, TENs offer a system of 'checks and balances' to ensure accountability and public responsiveness (Slaughter, 2004: 29). TENs are the most public type of network discussed in this book. They operate at the behest of national polities who delegate state representatives to develop coordinated responses to shared international policy concerns. The concept also 'falls back on a Neorealist notion of power based on "state capacities"' (Scott-Smith and Baumgärtel, 2011: 274) and is considerably more state-centric than the other concepts.

Knowledge networks

A KNET is a fourth type of network, a system of coordinated research, results dissemination and publication, intellectual exchange, and financing across national boundaries. These networks create and advance knowledge as well as disseminate that knowledge to inform policy and practice (Parmar, 2002). Another definition:

> Global knowledge networks create and transfer knowledge – scientific, community based and policy relevant – as well as the necessary hardware and finances to support knowledge acquisition and

implementation. ... such knowledge networks operate within a globally shared system of knowledge creation and transmission, while the practices of individual members are informed by the histories, politics and ecologies of the national and local places in which they work ... (Gross Stein et al., 2001: 6–7)

KNETs take quite different shape and many are impermanent entities. For example, the 'networks of excellence' funded by the European Commission differ on criteria of legal status, membership, degree of institutionalisation and issue focus when compared to more permanent scientific bodies like CGIAR.

KNETs incorporate professional bodies, academic research groups and scientific communities that organise around a special subject matter or issue. Individual or institutional inclusion in such networks is based upon professional or official recognition of expertise such as commitment to certain journals, conferences or other gatherings and organs that help bestow scholarly, ideological and scientific credibility. KNETs are often also practically engaged in 'capacity building', that is, mobilising funds and other resources for scholarships and training, supporting institutional consolidation that facilitates both network regeneration and knowledge construction. The primary motivation of such networks is to create and advance knowledge as well as to share, spread and, in some cases, use that knowledge to inform policy and apply it to practice.

KNETs are essential for the international spread of research results, scientific practice and what is deemed international 'best practice' on matters such as banking standards, gender mainstreaming or corporate social responsibility. International organisations and other multilateral initiatives require policy analysis and research to support problem definition, outline policy solutions, monitor and evaluate existing policy as well as to provide scholarly legitimacy for policy development. In other words, knowledge is a key resource in global public policy development. KNETs are often represented as a form of 'governmentality'.

... one of the key issues of global knowledge networks concerns how the production, collection and movement of knowledge are linked to the technologies of government. From a governmentality approach, technologies of government are not simply mechanical devices; they are assemblages of forms of practical knowledge, with practices of calculation and types of authority and judgements... (Ilcan and Phillips, 2008: 713)

From this theoretical vantage, governance is regarded as a widespread phenomenon and not one limited to the sphere of the state (Walters, 2012: 11). In other words, practical knowledge is mobilised to govern a domain (such as development or security policy), but is linked to theories, programmes and expertise that supply it with policy objectives and which can be viewed as an apparatus of rule. Recognising the techniques by which knowledge organisations seek to shape their own conduct (such as via peer review, rigorous methodologies and international standard setting), or that of other groups or organisations, provides insight into the 'forms of reason' and 'regimes of truth' that operate within institutions and at specific historical junctures (Walters, 2012: 11).

Many KNETs are engaged in the so-called 'disinterested pursuit and exchange of knowledge', and this is a key feature distinguishing them from 'transnational advocacy networks' and 'global public policy networks'. However, knowledge production is not divorced from the social and political worlds of the policy process. Whilst at one level this may be obvious, the social practices within KNETs give their product – ideas, publications, analysis – a patina of scientific objectivity and technocratic neutrality. Sophisticated computer modelling, positive economic theories or scientific papers published in refereed professional journals create 'communication codes' that construct some knowledge as more persuasive or reliable. These codes are not only expensive to reproduce but difficult to access. Another distinction to be made is the degree of policy relevance of these networks. Some are focused primarily on knowledge creation and sharing, for example, the academic 'networks of excellence' sponsored by the European Commission. Others like the Asian Fisheries Social Science Research Network operate with an agenda of using knowledge to inform policy and practice in their field of food security, fisheries and rural development.

Reprise

An important distinction needs to be made between policy networks and KNETs. Knowledge networks are composed of organisations with shared perspectives, joint interests and common scholarly agendas where members are 'homogeneous rather than heterogeneous in their fundamental views' (Struyk, 2007: 83). By contrast, policy networks are more heterogeneous and designed to mediate between participants with differing interests. Nevertheless, KNETs can be drawn into policy development, business-related advocacy and civil society activism. KNETs are not a pure type. Instead, these networks blur and blend with other network types in a 'web' of interactions. Consequently, DAWN has not only the features of both a KNET in sponsoring research and various publications but also the character of a TAN given its advocacy of women's rights. It is also the case with CGIAR having the character both of a GPPN with long standing support and policy input from governments and international organisations, and a KNET that conducts agricultural research and funds scientific laboratories.

Some TENs are strongly focused on information sharing and draw upon research and professional expertise to support their deliberations. Consequently, these network species are fluid conceptual categories. In policy practice, KNETs do not operate in isolation or hermetically sealed from other networks. Moreover, policy-engaged networks are always founded on some form of 'taken-for-granted' knowledge and expertise entrenched in the way it approaches economic, political and social issues.

Of the four network species, TENs have greatest executive authority where government officials have a dual domestic and international function. Networks become tools for the maintenance of sovereignty where global problems are confronted by governmentally organised networks. What makes TENs 'public' is that actors who compose them are formally designated power holders and rule makers who derive their authority from their official positions within their nation-state. Compared to TANS, which tend to be generated by 'bottom-up' strategic initiatives with solid foundations in civil society or connected to wider social movements, GPPNs have greater official standing and public authority as they tend to be initiated or convened by international organisations.

Despite the blurring that occurs in reality, the power bases and logic of organisation of these species as 'ideal types' are distinguishable. GPPNs are defined by shared material interests and partnership principles in delivering public goods; TANS by their normative ambitions and advocacy orientation; TENS by their political–legal character as intergovernmental networks; and KNETs by their claim to knowledge creation and epistemic authority. All species are to be found in the global agora.

Explaining networks

Just as there are quite different types of networks in operation in the global agora, so too there are competing explanations as to how knowledge influences political thinking, if at all. Where the preceding section identified overlapping *types* of network that are traversing the global agora – TANs, GPPNs, TENs and KNETs – this section draws on an additional set of network concepts but to a different purpose, that is, to provide varying conceptions of *how* the knowledge and norms, the ideas and values of networks might exert influence.

Three distinct schools of network interpretation are outlined by discussing first, the 'epistemic community'; second, post-positivist concepts of 'discourse coalitions' or interpretive communities and third neo-marxist and Gramscian thinking on 'embedded' or 'subaltern' knowledge networks. 'Ideas do matter', and while these frameworks share the position that ideas, research and knowledge are endemic to the policy process, they do so from quite different epistemological standpoints. Respectively, the network models posit first, science, objectivity and rationalism as a compelling force that can drive policy; second, the influence of discourse and subjectivity; and third, the role of hegemony and material interests as the sources of power in the global agora.

Epistemic communities

These communities are 'scientific' in composition, founded on 'codified' forms of knowledge. Researchers and scientists seek privileged access to decision-making forums on the basis of their expertise and scholarly insight. Yet, epistemic communities also assert their independence from government and other societal interests on the basis of their commitment to expert knowledge. These communities are identifiable by:

1. shared normative and principled beliefs which provide the value-based rationales for their action;
2. shared causal beliefs or professional judgements;
3. common notions of validity based on inter-subjective, internally defined criteria for validating knowledge;
4. a common policy enterprise (Haas, 1992).

The status and prestige associated with the expertise of epistemic community members and their high professional training and authoritative knowledge regarding a particular problem is politically empowering and provides some communities limited access to the political system. This is especially the case in conditions of 'uncertainty' – for example, persistent societal problems such as urban decay or poverty, natural disaster or rapid technological advancement – where policy makers cannot make decisions on the basis of existing knowledge or past experience and approach expert groups for assistance.

An epistemic community of cetologists experienced policy influence in circumstances where governments around the world were uncertain regarding whale populations and species, and the impact of the whaling industry on this ecology. The scientific knowledge made available by this community during international debates played an important role in the decision of most nations to support the 1982 adoption of a moratorium on commercial whaling (Peterson, 1992). Their scientific consensus also bolstered the TANs agitating to 'Save The Whales'.

An epistemic community is one kind of KNET. But the approach has a specific representation of the role of knowledge or science as being based on facts and empirically discernible realities. Consensual knowledge takes the form of concrete knowledge of the physical world, objectively beholden by an epistemically privileged Cartesian observer (and collectively the epistemic community) who then turns into a dispassionate advisor to the powerful. It is rationalist, technocratic approach to decision-making. Analysis from this network perspective considers that solutions to problems can be found by utilising the correct knowledge and evidence. The utility of this approach for understanding the power of KNETs is that knowledge in the form of scientific consensus represents a source of policy change. 'Truth speaks to power', so goes the famous phrase coined by Aaron Wildavsky (1987). However, as the discussion below outlines, rarely is knowledge or expertise uncontested; KNETs, or the individuals and organisations within them, are better regarded 'as "competitive definers" engaged in a contest to define the truth' (McKewon, 2012: 279).

Discourse coalitions and interpretative communities

The assumption of a universal and factual body of knowledge grounded in the natural world from which epistemic communities and other bodies of experts can draw from in order to devise directions for policy makers on 'what to do next' has been challenged by different perspectives of knowledge as being contextually constructed, situational and always bound up with particular practices and powers. Post-positivist and post-modern scholarship on networks is diverse and occasionally dense. The literature is replete with jargon and over-lapping terms that nevertheless signify different assumptions and categories. The lesser known 'transnational discourse community' approach developed by Danish public administration scholars identifies symbols, language and policy narrative as a source of power. The framework puts emphasis on the transnational qualities of professional groups, and secondly, the role of discourse. Networks are interactive venues where the national identities of researchers, donors and international civil servants are complicated by the professional commitment to questions of international development assistance, financial crisis or trade reform that are increasingly less questions of national determination under the forces of globalisation.

> Public sector professionals, traditionally expected to represent a specific national view on any issues in their international activities, no longer only do that. In fact, by foregrounding their professional identity, they transcend the power of the nation-state system to impose its categories of identity upon them. They also tend to assume a global or regional rather than a national outlook on key issues ... (Krause Hansen et al., 2002: 109)

Transnational identities are further enhanced by face-to-face communication at international meetings. This frame provides a social constructivist view of how transnational policy communities (outlined in the previous chapter) cohere.

Second, drawing upon the ideas of social theorist Michel Foucault, the discourse community concept locates discourse at the interface of power and knowledge. Discourses generate 'effects of truth', that is, naturalising specific ways of thinking and normalising certain ways of doing things. Discourse is a system that, through language or text, or a set of statements or social interactions, structures the way we perceive reality. Our discourse constrains perceptions. It shapes how groups respond to particular situations and how some things come to be regarded as normal or legitimate – the 'taken-for-granted' features of a social order. Discourse institutionalism (Kjaer and Pedersen, 2001; Schmidt, 2008) and the interpretive turn in policy studies (Fischer, 2003) regard processes of meaning-making – deliberation and argumentation – as prior to, and informing, interest formation and institutionalisation.

Transnational discourse communities construct identifiable policy narratives which serve to establish the goals of reform, justify the necessity of change, describe the means to achieve better results and predict outcomes. This approach is very similar to the idea of 'interpretive communities' arising from socio-legal studies. An interpretive community rests upon 'professional interpreters': think tank directors, research fellows, legal experts, scholars and others.

> All professional interpreters ... are situated within an institutional context, and interpretative activity makes sense only in terms of the purposes of the enterprise in which the interpreter is participating. Furthermore, a given text is always encountered in a situation or

field of practice, and therefore can only be understood in light of the position it occupies in that enterprise. ... Thus, interpretation is constrained ... by the 'cultural assumptions within which both texts and contexts take shape for situated agents'. Meaning is produced neither by the text nor by the reader but by the interpretative community in which both are situated. (Johnstone 2005: 189, quoting Stanley Fish)

'Texts' is an umbrella term for the web-sites, meetings, publications and policy commentary (briefs, speech writing, etc.) produced by the interpreters. The situations and 'field of practice' are constituted through networks that function as forums where new social realities can be constructed, debated and interpreted as individuals came into contact and interact. Discourse contributes to the formation of inter-subjective understandings operating as the social glue of networks/coalitions/communities.

Power and knowledge also operate through the social and institutional practices of the network and the 'boundary drawing discourses' that create distinction between experts and lay people, between good and bad professionals, and thus who is inside or outside the community. 'The specific vocabulary and jargon, the speech and meeting rituals etc. create possibilities for the professionals who master them' (Krause Hansen et al., 2002: 111). Boundary-drawing helps a community to canonise certain viewpoints at the cost of others, elevating them to unquestioned status and superior position. In this perspective, multiple truths are constructed by persuasive or credible expert narratives about social and economic realities. Truth is created.

A related concept developed by a Dutch environmental policy scholar is of discourse coalitions (or network), which makes useful distinctions between different stages of discursive influence starting with the formation of coalitions, then the extent to which a coalition shapes public understanding of a problem and, finally, governmental responses in the form of public policy and law (Hajer, 1993: 47). Discourse coalitions seek to impose their 'discourse' in policy domains. If their discourse shapes the way in which society conceptualises the world or a particular problem, then the coalition has achieved 'discourse structuration' and agendas are likely to be restricted to a limited spectrum of possibilities. If a discourse becomes entrenched in the minds of many as the dominant mode of perception, it can become distilled in institutions and organisational practices as the conventional mode of reasoning or 'global space characterised by regimes of truth' (Prügl, 2004: 72). This latter process is 'discourse institutionalisation'. The framework captures how discourses are transformed, or discarded, in their articulation through the policy cycle. There is a greater degree of indeterminacy compared to rationalist epistemic community approaches that regard evidence and scientific consensus as implacable and stable truths.

The classic example of a discourse coalition is the manner in which airborne pollutants were re-cast as 'acid rain' (Hajer, 1993). Another example of the power of narratives shaping public and political consciousness is the shift in terminology from 'female circumcision', which implies a minor surgical procedure, compared to the emotionally loaded term of 'female genital mutilation', which has strong connotations of human rights abuse. Likewise, the TANs concerned with illegal trading of diamonds found power in the portrayal of their cause with emotive terms such as 'blood diamonds' or 'dirty diamonds'. In this latter case, the discourse community, or coalition, achieved discourse structuration in popular imagination with Hollywood films starring Leonardo DiCaprio, and extensive media coverage, as well as discourse institutionalisation with the creation of the Kimberley process of diamond certification.

The substantive content of policy discourses is important, but so too is the interactive processes by which ideas are spread. The mode of discourse can be 'coordinative' or 'communicative'. Coordinative discourse refers to the creation, elaboration and justification of policy and programmatic ideas among transnational policy communities. By contrast, communicative discourse is concerned with the relationship between policy makers and the public (Schmidt, 2008: 310).

In general, discourse approaches allow scope for ideas to have independent force and inherent power in policy. Even so, discourses are not stable or uncontested and can be transformed by the institutional context into which they are propelled. Discourse coalitions and communities stress agency; by contrast discourse institutionalism has greater recognition of pre-existing structural constraints regarding how any discourse is received in society or politics. To understand the politics of discourse is to understand a key element of how knowledge in the form of research, professional codes and expert advice gets translated into policy and then moulded by that context (Schmidt, 2008). But, meaning-making has structural consequences in shaping or limiting the frame of reference for policy making or what is considered politically viable. Power and capacity for change comes from the idea itself, irrespective of who, or what, articulates that discourse.

This set of concepts with post-modernist or social constructivist sensibilities are in distinction from both the epistemic community framework and neo-marxist instrumentalist accounts of the next section which portray ideas, norms or expert knowledge as a resource utilised by an agent. Power or change capabilities are seen to reside in the individual or institutional agent that advocates on behalf of state, communal or corporate interests. Both the first and the next approach presuppose agents who create shared identities and common interests through instrumental actions and coalition building. This is not to negate the role of those actors or institutions that articulate the ideas. But representing KNETs as one important interpretative mechanism in the global agora provides a structural explanation of the power of ideas. Over time and through multiple discourses and venues, specific policy ideas become an organising logic or coordinative paradigm. As discussed in later chapters, expert discourses, such as the 'ASEAN Way', become a structuring force.

(Dis)Embedded knowledge and subaltern networks

The 'embedded knowledge network' framework stresses the role of ideas being connected and subsidiary to interests (Sinclair, 2000). This perspective is crystallised in the oft-quoted phrase: 'theory is always for someone, and for some purpose' (Cox, 1981: 128). From this theoretical vantage, KNETs represent a means for sustaining the neo-liberal capitalist order through the reproduction of ideas supportive of it. That is, scientific expertise is used for ideological purposes of 'paradigm maintenance' and the normalisation of dominant discourses of power (Bull and McNeill, 2007). For instance, within the World Bank, the researchers in the Development Economics Research Group and the other academic and professional economists with whom they interact created, disseminated and broadcast the neo-liberal market principles of the (post-)Washington Consensus: privatisation, deregulation and liberalisation (Broad, 2006). Consequently, policy becomes a battle of ideas, networks the battlegrounds and knowledge a weapon in the service of material interests.

Not dissimilar to institutionalised discourses, 'embedded knowledge networks' are 'ostensibly private institutions that possess authority because of their publicly acknowledged track records for solving problems, often acting as disinterested 'technical' parties in high-value, high-risk transactions, or in validating sets of norms and practices for a variety of service-provision activities' (Sinclair, 2000: 488). The approach emphasises the importance of authoritative judgement making, built and sustained through trade journals, professional associations and research departments (of investment banks) or consultancies. Credit-rating agencies such as Moody's or Standard and Poor are one example.

This approach treats knowledge, discourses or ideas as a tool of power used by dominant interests in maintaining the capitalist order. Knowledge networks are viewed as part of the micro-politics of contemporary hegemony and symptomatic of the 'war of position'. Think tanks, foundations, consultants and research institutes are one component of globalising elites, that is, a 'directive strategic element within globalising capitalism' (Stephen Gill quoted in Sinclair, 2000: 494). Ideas do not have independent power (as implied in discourses approaches) but are tied, and usually subservient to, social and political interests.

What becomes considered to be the truth involves gaining control over material resources such as the media. This includes gaining control of knowledge networks. The emphasis is on 'organic intellectuals', playing a central role in hegemonic projects where specific sets of ideas are funded, generated and disseminated by foundations, think tanks, publishing houses and NGOs. Consequently, global knowledge networks can be viewed as an evolving contemporary social mechanism to make certain ideas – put in league with particular social forces – more powerful and hegemonic. Instead of truth speaking to power, power decides what is true. Analysis of the role of American philanthropic foundations funding educational programmes, think tanks and international exchange to promote the idea of US global power and sustain ideological hegemony is indicative of this school (Parmar, 2002).

However, it is often evident that networks are often composed of contradictory knowledge or reflect discursive competition. Hegemony is incomplete and partial. Neo-Gramscian approaches posit a degree of intentionality or purposive strategy to knowledge agents and networks that is not necessarily the case. A grid-like complex of ideas shaping consciousness and dominating the global order gives little credence to alternative world-views and sites of intellectual resistance.

A further approach drawing upon subaltern studies and the critical feminist literature sees knowledge-makers not only as elite actors occupying command posts of capitalism, but also as 'those in defiance of dominant epistemological flows of power' (Rai, 2005: 124). Subaltern studies loosen the hegemonic grid-like power of the neo-Gramscian approach but continues to ask how knowledge networks legitimise and/or challenge flows of power. The expansion of knowledge networks as 'sites of authority' potentially accelerates the 'normalisation of the dominant discourses of power'. Nevertheless, it also brings some new opportunities as networks give activists, critics and feminists some access to expert communities and increased attention within the institutions of global governance (Prügl, 2004: 79).

Network disaggregation

The different understandings of networks outlined above provide quite different conceptual tools to address the policy relevance of empirical examples of KNETs and their influence (or not) with other policy institutions. To summarise, the 'embedded knowledge network' framework stresses the role of ideas being connected and subsidiary to interests. KNETs represent a means for sustaining the neo-liberal capitalist order through the reproduction of ideas supportive of it. Consequently, policy becomes a battle of ideas and knowledge is a weapon in this battle. By contrast, the 'transnational discourse community' perspective posits that ideas have independent force and inherent power. Presenting science or consensual knowledge as objective truths, epistemic communities claim the power of 'evidence' and represent a technical rationality with a bias towards technocratic policy making.

Of the KNETs discussed in later chapters, some can be described as having epistemic-like characteristics or aspiring to be perceived as epistemic communities. The label has some caché. The Global Development Network has epistemic community characteristics; however, it is a very broad and loose coalition of social scientists. Although the development discourse of economists is dominant, other expert narratives are audible. In another frame of analysis, given the nature of its sponsorship and political support from the World Bank and other significant international organisations in the field of development, GDN might be considered as embedded.

The ASEAN-Institutes of International and Strategic Studies is an epistemic-like network given its orientation towards regional cooperation and institutionally embedded given the nature of its official patronage. Over more than two decades, ASEAN-ISIS developed a relationship of trust with governments of the region through the processes of 'track two diplomacy'. The Open Society Foundations has the features of a TAN with its discourse on the 'open society' and direct funding of policy advocacy and civil liberties groups in transition states as well as international NGOs like International Crisis Group. Yet, it also has the character of a KNET given its sponsorship of academic research, scholarship programmes, scientific research and strong organisational orientation towards policy research and analysis. Yet, the capacities to set policy agendas and structure public discourse are highly unstable and mediated by the considerable scientific competition within these networks as well as outside them.

None of the case study networks of later chapters could be described as 'disembedded' or subaltern. The case studies organisations are all engaged with the political mainstream and interact with policy makers. While the Overseas Development Institute (ODI) and GDN are synchronised with the bureaucratic interests of UK Department for International Development (DfID) and the World Bank, respectively, it must be said that these network organisations are neither puppets nor unthinking mouthpieces for their funders and patrons.

Networks such as DAWN are subaltern KNETs or TANs choosing to challenge dominant policy discourses. Notwithstanding their lack of policy or political influence, these networks perform wider societal roles of knowledge creation and capacity building. Their 'struggles' – the 'underside in the play of dominations' – helps explain the normalisation of 'winners in history' (Walters, 2012: 113–34). Networks that appear to have little policy impact or to be espousing unorthodox policy perspectives are neither completely ineffectual nor hopelessly marginalised. Instead, subaltern KNETs, and the TANs they interact with, are symptomatic of how dominated groups 'representing counter-discourses and oppositional constituencies' form identities through common language and understanding. These TANs mobilise resources around alternative definitions of reality, potentially to create 'competing public spheres' (Eckersley, 2007: 333).

By drawing the above analytical distinctions it is possible to better understand the ways in which power relations are disturbed and then reconstituted at different governance levels. Networks are political spaces to re-invent the processes of policy design, implementation and evaluation. Coordination and regulation of the global agora via networks represents regime adaptation. But no one network is alike. Where certain networks perpetuate power constellations, other types can help confront and sometimes undermine it. There is a dual dynamic of counter-public spheres.

Noting network power

Three further points on network power are worth consideration. First, there is normative and ideational power of networks as convenors of sets of actors who create and broadcast the ideas that inform problem perception and set policy agendas. The content of policy knowledge, and its credibility, is also an important consideration in networks becoming a site of authority.

Second, networks function as structures that can either exclude/include, co-opt/induct, legitimise/revoke or accept/deny various perspectives and participants. That is, networks create boundaries.

Third, networks become a new locus or a 'site' for the enactment of public authority, albeit a locus disaggregated from the traditional Weberian understanding of a public sector bureaucracy in sovereign states. Instead, public authority is re-invented in semi-private or quasi-official policy networks in a part privatisation of governance in the global agora.

KNETS as expert agents and authority structures

Governments as well as international organisations require the creation and widespread acceptance of persuasive accounts of 'public policy problems' as the foundations for making legitimate policy and just laws. KNETs not only provide expert interpretations and scientific narratives, they also create self-supporting structures of authority to incarnate as 'neutral' research brokers and advisors. The legitimacy and credibility of a KNET's expertise is drawn through a circular process between the knowledge it produces and the audiences that use and thereby legitimise that knowledge. In sum, KNETs do not simply revolve around centres of power waiting for their products to be used by more powerful actors; instead, the network is itself one site and form of power with capacities, of varying degree, to (re)produce dominant knowledge and discourses that define fields of action.

Think tanks, law firms and university institutes are recognized as centres for expert, scientific and authoritative advice not simply because of the scholarly credentials of these organisations (and their self-referential habits). It also occurs because of the relationships with policy makers and donor groups that a network structure facilitates. Through their club-like tendencies, networks both accrue and accredit authority through the collective policy entrepreneurship of their members.

KNETs draw together their power and policy influence strategically by combining epistemic, discursive and ideological practices. Networks are not mechanically linking knowledge and governance arenas, that is, 'bridging research and policy'. Instead, the interaction of knowledge and policy is one of mutual construction. As will be discussed in Chapters 3 and 4, the routine activities of research and analysis within the ODI and in the Open Society Foundations network are recursive in a dialogue with governmental consumers and patrons.

Inclusion and exclusion in the privatisation and pluralisation of policy

Unlike most liberal and pluralist analyses which see the rise of networks of non-state actors as a progressive contribution to a global civil society, this book is more cautious. Organisational density and diversity can disrupt hierarchies and disperse power, but networks can also represent new constellations of privatised power. Instead of being civil society manifestations of bottom-up, non-statist globalisation, some networks are better viewed as mutually imbricated in the affairs of states and international organisations. This is clearly the case with not only TENs, but also GPPNs given the neo-corporatist inclusion of either international organisations or governments as sponsors who also delegate representatives as decision-making participants. For example, as a global network of environmental compliance and enforcement practitioners, INECE was launched in 1989 by the Netherlands Ministry of Housing, Spatial Planning and the Environment and the US Environmental Protection Agency to link more than 4,000 practitioners – inspectors, prosecutors, regulators, parliamentarians, judges, international organisations and NGOs from 120 countries.[1] The parentage of the INECE network is within government.

By contrast, the governance functions of KNETs and TANs are obscured by their non-governmental status and often by their critical or adversary stance. Nevertheless, their policy advocacy, agenda-setting efforts and expert commentary on transnational problems embed them in a variety of relationships with official decision-making forums (Sending and Neumann, 2010: 110-31).

Consider, for instance, the Evian Group. Founded in 1995, the Group is a coalition of opinion leaders from academic, corporate and government opinion leaders committed to fostering an open global market economy and a rules-based multi-lateral framework. It has a strong research identity given the calibre of its members as leading trade economists and lawyers, and its role in higher education and professional training, and is hosted at IMD Business School in Lausanne. It also operates like a TAN in its advocacy of trade liberalisation to achieve growth and sustain the momentum of globalisation. But this kind of advocacy closely concords with the policy agendas of the WTO, the G20 and many governments, whereby Evian claims that has played a key role preparing decision makers for international meetings.[2]

Such networks can be a force for democratisation by creating a venue for representation of 'stakeholder' interests, a means for wider participation in modes of global governance and a venue for societal voices. In this sense, networks are 'gateways' to new policy spaces. This entails new arenas for alternative politics, new actors and audiences, and new kinds of strategising. However, these same networks can also be exclusive, elite and closed to deliberative decision-making. But networks can also be 'gatekeepers'. 'Gate-keeping' can occur in policy networks that operate on the basis of specialised technical knowledge or privatise decision-making to stakeholders.

As has already been noted, networks systematise the knowledge generated by diverse individual and organisational knowledge actors and impose a rationality that gives precedence to a particular conception of knowledge – usually of a codified, technocratic, secular, Westernised and gendered variety. The exclusionary expert language of scientific technique, economic modelling or professional standards enhances the status of KNETs as 'sites of authority' with particular 'communication codes'. Once mastering such 'codes', inclusion into such networks can be a double-edged sword for those seeking policy reform. They run the risk of absorption into dominant practices and co-option into network 'truths', as well as the cost of some estrangement with grassroots groups and activists not so well versed in the 'communication codes' and jargonised argot of, for instance, neo-liberal agendas and acronyms on matters as varied as TRIPS, PRSPS, GATS or GPGs.[3] The participants in the Evian Group are well versed in the professional language of the WTO. Indeed, some of the leading Evian members could be argued to be epistemic creators of the codes and jargon of neo-liberal trade theory (Higgott and Erman, 2010: 463).

In their professional context, specific groups of knowledge producers – whether they are economists, anthropologists or statisticians – have a cognitive interest in the selective use of their mode of problem definition, methodological approaches and policy solutions. It becomes a self-reinforcing dynamic that encourages resistance to other perspectives or disciplinary approaches. Consequently, a network can develop a carapace, sometimes in the interests of internal network cohesion and unity but also to exclude those who do not speak the same specialised language. Policy debate is not taken out of the public domain, but it is cordoned off from those not deemed to be so-called 'stakeholders' or those without mastery of the communication code.

The barriers to participation in policy networks are not restricted to expert credentials or professional conformity to the norms or ideology of its community. Sustaining a presence in, or monitoring a myriad of, transnational regulatory 'coalitions' or 'policy alliances' is highly resource intensive for individuals or their organisations. Accessing participation in GPPNs requires time, commitment and funds. Many developing countries, and most ordinary citizens, do not have sufficient resources to devote time to following international policy deliberations. When developing countries are stretched significantly to deliver adequate representation in official venues such as WTO negotiations or treaty discussions, developing effective strategies for their engagement with the more informal transnational policy processes of networks may remain elusive. The dominance of OECD and G20 actors in regional and global policy debates is notable. Accordingly, 'openness' and 'closure' is not an evenly balanced dynamic across networks. Instead, access and exclusiveness varies considerably across networks, over time and according to issue area or policy field.

Networks as public places and public actors

A third point on the power of networks revolves around their often ambiguous public or private status. The networks that populate the international political economy often have fluid and interchangeable characteristics, private but undertaking public action and *vice versa*. The re-creation of the 'public' in the global agora is fundamentally different from the public spaces associated within sovereign states. There is no equivalent of public institutions such as the ministries, executive agencies and other public bodies with legal remit to deliver public services or impose sanctions. It is less feasible to oppose one category of the public against the other category of the private realm when governance becomes a partnership (McLaughlin, 2004: 163), that is, a mix of private and public.

In the interests of legitimacy or to secure resources and official patronage, network executives sometimes stress their public orientation. The discourse of 'public goods' provides one. For example, KNETs represent a means to protect and preserve the public status of knowledge, that is, a means to deliver a public good as will be discussed in Chapter 7 on the GDN (Stiglitz, 2000). The web-sites, publications and data of knowledge groups and networks provide a wealth of information. More tangible training programmes, public events, mentoring and fellowships also represent a public service.

Whether it be actively or reluctantly, governments are devolving public responsibilities and authority. This is a double devolution: first, to domains beyond the nation-state in global and regional domains, and second, a devolution of authority to private networks and non-state actors. Nevertheless, global or regional networks are not public entities – that is, accountable to formally elected representatives of the public or a sovereign authority. A network may be accountable to network members, but these member organisations and individuals cannot be considered as representatives of the 'global public'. Notwithstanding their public sources of support from governments, or their production of public goods, these (semi-) private networks are not subject to the usual reporting and accountability requirements of public bodies in liberal democracies.

The public, even the well-informed OECD countries, are still largely unaware of the roles, reach and influence of global networks. Newspapers and the electronic media do not carry news reports on the Evian Group or INECE. Combined with the technocratic character of many such networks, the potential dynamic is for the public, or the citizenry of nations, to become passive and thereby become excluded and political responsibility to be undermined. As a consequence of the lack of transparency and mechanisms for public representation, and lack of knowledge about them, these networks operate with relative autonomy and in some anonymity. In any event, they are more able to thwart challenges to their activities or call for transparency by emphasising their non-state, private status or delegated authority. This tendency is compounded in KNETs that also stress their disinterested, scientific and politically neutral endeavours.

Consequently, this chapter ends on a cautionary note regarding the democratic potential and deliberative capacity of global (knowledge) networks. They may well be sites of stakeholder engagements, collective action and joint deliberation, but globalisation does not deliver a level-playing field for networks. It is characterised by an uneven distribution of resources and a hierarchy of discourses where 'subaltern knowledge networks see the spaces for negotiations and deliberations leading to radical outcomes decreasing' (Rai, 2005: 127). The encroachment into policy making and policy delivery by policy networks and their increasing complexity and autonomy make it difficult, particularly for developing economies, marginalised communities and local activists, to become fully embedded in these transnational policy processes. That is, 'global spaces and places are increasingly integrated and deterritorialized, even as they remain stratified' (McLaughlin, 2004: 166). The global agora is composed of public spaces, but these are spaces where relatively few can be public actors. The extent to which global and regional networks become a focal point of public affairs has meaning primarily, or only, for those who have the resources, patronage or expertise to enter and traverse the agora.

Conclusion

Global policy networks set in motion a structural dynamic that both excludes and opens up policy making to certain groups. In principle, and in popular mythology, the evolution of policy networks offers a flatter and more horizontal structure (compared to public sector hierarchies) for policy coordination and public service delivery that are porous to participation of private and civil society actors. Yet, networks also privatise decision-making.

It is now well accepted that networks provide governance support: networks are viewed as more flexible than the often rule-bound and more rigid bureaucracies; they can promote wider policy participation and build additional routes to decision makers; they can draw together the multiple resources, skills, expertise of actors in corporations and civil society; they perform aggregative and brokerage functions to negotiate and build compromises or boost coordination and compliance around rules, as well as performing a socialisation role (Börzel and Heard-Lauréote, 2009). Yet, as this and the previous chapter have suggested, a further critical role of networks is knowledge creation and policy definition. A seventh role, building on all the above, is that authority construction is undertaken via the professional relations within the network that create networks as a new social technology of legitimate and credible governance, that is, a new policy space.

Networks are becoming a mode of governance whereby the patterns of linkages and interaction are the means through which joint policy is organised. In short, there is a functional interdependence between public and private actors so that networks allow resources to be mobilised towards common policy objectives in domains delegated or delinked from the more traditional hierarchical control of governments. Furthermore, the network logic itself is being diffused by international organisations with their advocacy of partnership and multi-stakeholder policy coalitions as a method to deal with global problems. Networks become platforms of 'interoperability' (Walters, 2012: 112). This logic and social technology can promote flexibility and efficiency in dealing with relatively intractable cross-border policy issues. Although these arrangements can become effective mechanisms of transnational policy coordination and partnership, they can also fracture and fragment. These quasi-public policy networks can be 'under the radar' of public interest and public scrutiny and represent multiple nodes of policy autonomy and mutated authority that makes them difficult to track, monitor, engage and reform.

3
Think Tank Thinking

Chapter 1 focused on the broad governance context of the global agora where knowledge organisations and experts become bound with transnational policy making. Chapter 2 narrowed the focus to the networks within which these actors interact. The next step, pursued in this chapter, is a more specific focus on one set of knowledge organisation – think tanks. The following discussion addresses three themes in the traditions and transitions of think tanks over time, across countries and in scholarly analysis. The first theme concerns the increasing number of meanings endowed in the term 'think tank'. Today, the term is applied haphazardly to bodies as diverse as the IMF, the in-house research arms of multi-national corporations, research-oriented consultancy firms and NGOs, as well as university research institutes. The chapter will argue that it is no longer feasible to regard all think tanks as legally independent, scholarly-like, autonomous free-thinking bodies. Nor is it the case that all think tanks are private organisations grounded in civil society, or operating freely in the market place of ideas that is said to be symptomatic of pluralist liberal democracies. This bundle of assumptions has often been behind policy thinking when the Anglo-American think tank model was exported overseas by bilateral donor agencies and private foundations (Krastev, 2000).

The second theme concerns think tank transnationalisation. This is occurring alongside higher education internationalisation and the globalisation of research communities helping to create a worldwide 'invisible college'. Windows of opportunities for knowledge organisations have opened with the forces of regionalisation and globalisation. Without well-defined institutions of authority beyond the nation-state, they become editors of knowledge(s) and arbiters of research quality. In the global agora, the 'argumentative field' (Fischer, 2003: 90) is radically

different, allowing think tanks to acquire some authority as reputational intermediaries. Think tank transnational activities and analytical
work also help constitute the agora.

A third theme is the multiple identities articulated by think tanks.
The same think tank can speak different stories at different times and
places. The notion of 'think tank' has become the amalgam of many
different story lines. For the general public the stress is on their public
representation. With funders it is their capacity to access and inform
decision makers, often behind closed doors. Towards government agencies and actors, they proffer a source of rationality, solutions to problems, conceptual tools and expertise to apply to policy problems. In
relation to political parties or social movements or advocacy networks,
they are creators of mobilising discourses – normative language, policy
rhetoric and data to support the cause. It is their multiplicity of tailored
narratives and capacity to adapt quickly in different argumentative and
institutional fields that makes them the 'discursive software' of choice.

Traditions of thinking on think tanks

Following World War II, there used to be a straightforward response
to the question: What is a 'think tank'? They were often described as
non-profit policy research institutes independent of government and
other interests usually based in civil society. These institutes were concentrated in large numbers in the USA with more limited institutional
development in continental Europe, the UK and its dominions, notably
Canada and Australia. The term 'think tank' is American slang which
was used to describe the US Department of Defense-funded RAND
Corporation. The acronym stands for 'research and development'. By
the 1960s, the term was entrenched in the Anglo-American lexicon of
policy analysis and was being applied to independent research institutes throughout the English-speaking world. As a result, social science
analysis of think tanks has been shaped by Anglo-American experience
(*inter alia*, Weaver, 1989; Smith, 1991; Ricci, 1993; Denham, 1996; Stone
1996; Abelson, 2006; Weidenbaum, 2011; Medvetz, 2012). The dominance of Anglo-American perspectives of what constitutes a think tank
clouds the very great diversity and hybrid forms of think tank readily
apparent in the early years of the third millennium.

The type of constitutional architecture, historical circumstances of war
or stability, the political culture and legal traditions alongside the character of the regime in power determine the shape and extent of think
tank development in any given country. They vary considerably in size,

legal form, policy ambit, longevity, organisational structure, standard of inquiry and political significance. There is considerable scholarly debate, and competition, over how to identify these organisations, symptomatic in the competing typologies (Abelson, 2006; Boucher, 2004; McGann, 2007; Zhu, 2009). This book eschews developing a tight typology or definition for two reasons. The first reason rests on the recognition that evolving think tank diversity defies exact definition. Moreover, if there is a consensus in the literature, it is that there is no consensus on definition (McGann, 2007). Additionally, think tank directories are regularly updated on web-sites such as the ones provided in Appendix One and point to the rapidly evolving ecologies of think tanks. Second, categorising different types of think tank, or mapping their development, has become a scholarly fetish that has detracted attention from more sophisticated analysis of the sources of power of these organisations and how they garner and wield societal and policy influence.

A broad but flexible definition is adopted: *think tanks do research, analysis and communication for policy development within local communities, national government and global institutions in both the public and the private domains.* Some organisations claim to adopt a scientific and disinterested approach to social and economic problems, that is, academic in style of analytical activity and geared towards publication of books and reports. Others are overtly partisan or ideologically motivated. The libertarian institutes such as Timbro in Sweden or the Atlas Economic Research Foundation can be juxtaposed to the 'progressive' TransNational Institute in the Netherlands. Many institutes are disciplinary based – economic policy think tanks such as the Institute for International Economics in Washington DC., foreign policy institutes such as Institute Français des Relations Internationales (IFRI) in Paris, social policy units like the Centre for Civil Society in New Delhi and so forth. Specialisation is a contemporary phenomenon: There are now numerous environmental think tanks – Resources for the Future in Washington DC being one of the first – but this policy sector and the 'climate science wars' have seen think tanks as a primary source of 'contrarian 'experts''' (McKewon, 2012: 279). In addition, there are regionally focussed operations, including very many addressing EU affairs; urban policy and health policy think tanks; and those institutes that reflect the communal interests of ethnic groups or business interests. While most display a high level of social scientific expertise or familiarity with governmental structures and policy processes, the more academic institutes like the highly respected 'grand-daddy' of the think tank industry, the Brookings Institution in Washington DC., can be counter-poised against the activist 'think-and-do tank'. In the

Internet age, virtually all think tanks are routinely engaged in intellectual brokerage and the marketing of ideas, whether in simplified policy briefs or in sound bites for the media.

However, the matter of 'independence' is a vexed one. The Western view that a think tank requires independence or autonomy from the state, corporate or other interests in order to be free-thinking does not accord with experiences in other cultures. In many countries, the line between policy intellectuals and the state is blurred to such an extent that to talk of independence as a defining characteristic of think tanks makes little sense. Some think tanks 'have become a permanent part of the political landscape in many different countries', notwithstanding their legal constitution as NGOs, 'so much so that they are now an integral part of the policy process' (Barani and Sciortino, 2011: 3).

Many organisations now called 'think tanks' operate within government. A well-known example is Clingendael (the Netherlands Institute of International Relations) sponsored by the Dutch Government since 1980s. Some institutes have been incubated in government and subsequently made independent. In other circumstances research institutes are attached to corporations as is evident in Japan, South Korea and Taiwan. Some political parties have created in-house think tanks in the form of party institutes or foundations. This is particularly noticeable in Germany with bodies like the Konrad Adenauer Stiftung (linked to the Christlich Demokratische Union) but which also funds policy research by other bodies. Other German foundations have been established by political parties or have ties to the *Länder* (Braml, 2004).

Given that the primary – but not exclusive – targets of think tanks are legislatures and executives, bureaucrats and politicians, independence is variable. Think tanks are often in resource-dependent relationships with these organisations and actors. Notwithstanding funding dependence or political affiliation, high-quality research and analysis along with critical advice is feasible. It is the balance of attributes that is the important consideration:

- *Financial independence* can be construed as developing an endowment or having numerous sponsors and a diverse funding base, so that an organisation is not dependent on any *one* benefactor or specific set of patrons.
- *Scholarly and cognitive independence* is reliant upon certain practices within an institute: the processes of peer review and a commitment to open inquiry rather than directed research, that is, 'not sweeping inconvenient data under the carpet …' (Weiss, 1991).

- *Legal or administrative* independence comes from constitution as a private organisation. Administrative and financial independence may be a facade under authoritarian or illiberal regimes where censorship and control prevail. Alternatively, some institutes may exhibit a high degree of research freedom despite being found within the state architecture. Appreciation of the political culture of a nation is essential to interpreting think tank independence and the scope for intellectual leverage.

- *Political independence* is derived from the freedom to develop agendas and produce material that is not constrained by political party ideology or dictated by political powers.

Funding may come from government sources, but institutes attempt to maintain their freedom in the conduct of their policy research and usually claim not to be beholden to specific interests. Other organisations are overtly partisan (connected as they may be to political parties or government) or ideologically motivated. They may trend a fine line between political access and cooption (Acharya, 2011). Nevertheless, think tank managers and staff tend to be motivated by internalised professional standards similar to those of the university setting. When they attempt to either influence or inform policy, they do so through intellectual argument, fact-finding and dispassionate analysis rather than direct lobbying or groundless opinion. To be 'nonpartisan' has value in being regarded as a trustworthy source of analysis (Hird, 2005: 101). While this discourse of neutrality has been comprehensively criticised (Ladi, 2011a), the discourse remains integral to the public image of think tanks.

Today, 'think tank' is a very elastic term. It has been applied to NGOs that have built in-house research capacity. The term is a moniker for the OECD, as well as applied to government research bureaux or units attached to political parties. Organisations that once would not have been thought of as think tanks are now all too ready to adopt the label. The label 'think tank' has symbolic power or capital (Rich, 2005: 13). That so many groups around the world wish to cast themselves as 'think tanks' is symptomatic of the effectiveness of the label in the public imagination as well as in policy circles. The label is a useful designation for approaching international donors and philanthropic foundations. Yet the brand name has been so widely used, its meaning is becoming opaque, and provides yet another reason for steering clear of hard and fast definitions developed in the early Anglo-American literature on think tanks.

Early research focused on the organisational form. Observers were interested in explaining why and how think tanks have emerged and why some think tanks are influential. They mapped the growth of this new organisation form. They distinguished independent public-policy institutes from university research centres, government research units, NGOs or lobbyists (Weaver, 1989; McGann, 2007; Rich, 2004; Smith, 1991). They focused on the organisational ingredients of what makes a think tank successful, how think tanks are managed, who funds them, who quotes them and whom they try to influence (*inter alia* Struyk, 2007; Weaver, 1989). Initially, the growth and increasing diversity was represented as sign of a healthy pluralist democracy where think tanks contributed to a 'market place of ideas' (Weidenbaum, 2011).

Fifty years ago, it was possible to argue that the practice of 'bridging research and policy' or the function of connecting (social) science with governance was undertaken by independent think tanks. Today, the convergence of think tank activities with other organisations makes their distinctive role less plausible. Today, policy analysis, monitoring and evaluation is a function undertaken by a wide range of organisations that were not so directly engaged with policy issues and processes.

Interest groups are usually portrayed as promoting an interest that is sectional or promotional in an advocacy-oriented manner. By contrast think tanks have been portrayed as neutral and engaged in independent research, not unlike epistemic communities. However, with a long-term trend of professionalisation in NGOs, groups like Greenpeace, Transparency International and Oxfam have created their own sophisticated research centres. The policy analysis conducted by bodies such as these is not greatly different from what might be done in a well-known think tank like the conservative Heritage Foundation. Likewise, some large professional associations have developed a research capacity or have drawn upon the expertise of their membership. Acting as 'reputational intermediaries' the big accounting firms, investment banks, law firms, bond-rating agencies and stock analysts perform a powerful independent role monitoring firms and enforcing regulatory standards. Outsourcing of research, under the logic of the New Public Management (NPM), has favoured not only think tanks but also consultancy firms (Sturdy et al., 2008), creating incentives to establish public sector consulting divisions in these organisations.

Occasionally cast as 'universities without students' (Weaver, 1989: 564), think tanks today face stiff competition from them for funding and policy access. Despite a few exceptions (notably RAND in the USA or Fundação Getulio Vargas and FLACSO in Latin America), think tanks are not degree-granting institutions and education is not their core business. But as universities encounter greater expectations from governments to demonstrate their social and economic relevance, many have established policy institutes inside the academy that also do think tank things – that is, policy briefings, networking, government advising etc. – attempting to bridge the academic and policy realms.

The blurring of boundaries and the overlap of objectives mean that traditional 'think tanks' are losing their organisational distinctiveness (Boucher, 2004: 97). Think tanks are competing for staff as well as for official patronage and funding from new policy-analytic actors invading their argumentative field. The general public as well as the politician can readily find policy analysis among a plethora of 'free advice' organisations pushing their intellectual wares on the Internet. The cacophony of advice and analysis raises questions about power and influence in these more competitive and complex conditions.

Notwithstanding their extensive growth, or the political patronage that some enjoy, think tanks do not enjoy automatic political access or unhindered bureaucratic routes to decision makers. Think tank observers have had to confront a major methodological problem. Proof of influence is elusive. There is no clear causal chain between policy research or an idea espoused by an institute, a political decision and policy change. There are numerous intermediary forces: political parties, interest groups and the media also shape the content and reception of ideas. This hiatus is compounded as the political stature of many institutes waxes and wanes over time. Sceptics have suggested that think tanks try to manage this hiatus by 'faking influence' (Krastev, 2000).

Instead, it is fruitful to think of influence in the longer term. Paradigmatic change usually occurs over generations. Rather than influence resting in the scientific work of one or more significant scholars, it rests in the aggregate contributions of research or epistemic communities as whole, and in which think tanks are just one knowledge actor. It is the collective weight and longer-term structural impact of scientific consensus or orthodoxies that institutionally embeds certain knowledge as dominant or hegemonic within international organisations, government programmes and other evolving architectures of governance or what has been described as a 'knowledge regime' (Campbell and Pedersen, 2011). The influence of knowledge in governance is incremental and 'atmospheric'. Knowledge utilisation is 'increasingly seen as nourishing a political process rather than a single client' (Hird, 2005: 86).

Critical studies that analyse think tanks from a neo-Marxist or Gramscian perspective (Bohle and Nuenhöffer, 2005; Plehwe, 2007) argue that policy research is free neither of ideological content nor of material or class interests. Rather than a pluralist marketplace of equal exchange, a 'battlefield of ideas' emerges with policy debate marked by power plays as well as winners and losers. These studies share some common territory with elite theory critiques that identified the personal and inter-organisational ties of American think tanks with corporate and financial power (Dye, 1978).

Criticising these latter studies for their tendency to treat think tanks as passive instruments in the hands of wealthy and powerful sponsors, a post-positivist field analysis (drawing on Pierre Bourdieu's ideas) has been used to argue that the professional inter-relationships between think tanks, and the content of what they do to create what is now an international think tank industry, are also important in understanding their social and political roles (Medvetz, 2012). That is, think tanks collectively create their own professional ecology within which organisational status and influence also needs to be considered. Discourse analysis has sought to unveil the argumentative power of research and analysis, and the capacity of ideas to shape public and policy maker perceptions of reality (Fischer, 2003). These studies treated think tanks and related organisations offering policy advice as a vehicle for broader questions about the policy process and the role of ideas and expertise in governance (*inter alia* Abelson, 2006; Campbell and Pedersen, 2011; Stone and Maxwell, 2005). They employed network concepts like the interpretative community framework or discourse coalition approaches to explain why ideas matter (Acharya, 2011; Pautz, 2011). In doing so, they also chartered the international spread and transnationalisation of think tanks. Where neo-Gramscians see them as carriers of neo-liberal capitalist hegemony (Parmar, 2002; Bohle and Nuenhöffer, 2005), constructivists see them as creators of new regional identities (Acharya, 2011), and then again, institutionalists (discursive and historical) often treat think tanks as mechanisms for transnational policy transfer (Ladi, 2011a and 2011b).

Transnational think tanks

In the last two decades of the twentieth century, the number of think tanks proliferated. Estimates vary along the lines of definition, but 6,000+ think tanks worldwide is not an unrealistic figure (Seiler and Wohlrabe, 2010). Growth in the large emerging economies like India and China is extensive (see respectively, Zonana and Nayyar, 2009; Zhu, 2011). Countries where think tanks were already present such as the USA, Britain, Sweden, Canada, Japan, Austria and Germany witnessed further organisational growth. A recent phenomenon has been the internationalisation of some of the larger American institutes establishing offices in transition economies or close to regional power centres. For example, the Carnegie Endowment for International Peace has a presence in Beijing, Beirut, Brussels and Moscow, while the Center for Global Development has its 'think tank "plus"' located in London. Democratic consolidation and economic development in Latin America, the Indian sub-continent and Asia provided fertile conditions for think tank development, particularly as higher education systems expanded in these regions, creating new generations of educated professionals and opinion leaders. Even in a communist political system, the People's Republic of China, there has been a dramatic growth of both government-sponsored and private think tanks (Zhu, 2009). The demise of the Soviet Union, the colour revolutions and the Arab spring opened new political spaces for donor agencies to support think tanks as both a driver and a product of civil society capacity building.

On the one hand, the global think tank boom has been prompted by philanthropic foundations, corporations and other non-state actors demanding high-quality research, policy analysis and ideological argumentation as advisory input within their organisations. On the other hand, growth has been propelled by grants, gifts and funding from governments and international organisations seeking to extend policy-analytipc capacities or promote evidence-based policy formulation in developing and transition countries.

Well-known programmes include the Open Society Foundation's Think Tank Fund that supports new institutes across Central and South Eastern Europe and the southern Caucasus. UNDP's regional office in Bratislava held a think tank capacity-building conference in 2003 to help improve the quality of governance in Central and South Eastern Europe. Agencies such as USAID, the World Bank and Freedom House, amongst many others, have convened similar activities.

The lens through which these donor organisations often regard think tanks is very much what we might call a 'Western prism' that favours an NGO organisational template. It is often accompanied by an implicit notion that think tanks will be entrepreneurs for the promotion of civil society development. Similarly, think tanks are also often viewed by donors as agents of democratisation and vehicles for public participation in policy debate (Scott, 1999). However, think tanks are an elite and relatively technocratic organisational expression of civil society even when constituted as NGOs. The legitimacy for their input into policy making is claimed on the basis of their expert status and epistemic authority. This basis for policy engagement is in tension with

donor rationales of think tanks being a mode of democratic deliberation or representing a pluralistic counterweight to state monopoly of
decision-making.

The think tank model has been exported around the world. The
Anglo-American term and institutional template of 'think tank', with
all its cultural connotations as independent policy-analytic units outside government, has penetrated the political systems of developing
and transition countries, via overseas development assistance to support civil society. Yet, developing countries with weak bureaucracies or
experiencing state failure or (semi-) authoritarian systems distort the
manner in which such transplanted organisations operate. While the
term is ubiquitous, its translation into quite different socio-political
environments has been varied. In political cultures unfamiliar with
independent policy analysis, and under-developed civil societies or
intellectual cultures to support such institutions, alternatives have
emerged. Some South Eastern European think tanks responded to
the shortage of funding by becoming hybrid consultancy companies
(Struyk and Miller, 2004). During the early years of transition in Central
and Eastern Europe, donor-funded think tanks sometimes supported
uncritically many of the market liberal policy priorities emerging from
the power centres of Brussels and Washington DC. Detractors of these
organisations portrayed them 'as "Western institutes" in the past and
"EU driven researchers" at present ... providing support structures for
foreign experts ... and are perceived as appliers and adapters of external
paradigms' (Barani and Sciortino, 2011: 14). Nevertheless, throughout
CEE as well as the former Soviet Union, think tank initiation remains a
popular start-up option for young professionals.

It is also the case that there are development fads and phases. Donor
interest in the former transition economies was strong for two decades
from 1989 onwards. But donor attention shifted elsewhere following
the events of 9/11, as well as the continuing prevalence of poverty
and lack of governmental capacity in many parts of sub-Saharan Africa
or elsewhere in the world. Launched by the Canadian Government's
International Development Research Centre, the William and Flora
Hewlett Foundation and the Bill and Melinda Gates Foundation in
2008, Think Tank Initiative is a capacity-building programme designed
to aid developing-country think tanks 'to better provide sound research
that informs and influences policy' (IDRC, 2012). This joint initiative is
symptomatic not only of the transfer of management protocols for think
tanks and the transfer of principles of evidence-based policy research
but implicitly a vehicle for the promotion of Western democratic

values. This initiative now exists alongside other older think tank support schemes such as the GDN and various regional initiatives such as Policy Association for an Open Society (PASOS) (a network of 30+ think tanks from the former Soviet Union and Central and Eastern Europe). Collectively, they help sustain nationally based institutes but induct their fellows in international standards of research, and provide opportunity for their incorporation into transnational policy forums and networks.

International organisations such as the UN agencies, the World Bank, the IMF and the WTO have drawn think tanks into their ambit via conferences, joint research and fellowship programmes (for example, UNDP, 2003). As discussed in Chapter 7, the World Bank launched the GDN to promote think tanks in developing countries (Plehwe, 2007). The European Commission provides yet another institutional forum for think tank activity with the emergence of EU-wide think tanks, such as Notre Europe or the Centre for European Policy Studies, seeking to transcend national settings with research and policy proposals for regional integration. Likewise, the Council of Europe called its first 'Meeting of European Think Tanks' in December 2012. The very fast growth of European think tanks has led to suggestions that they have become pre-eminent 'articulators of the European public sphere' (Barani and Sciortino, 2011).

There are also unofficial global forums, such as the World Economic Forum in Davos, that make substantial use of experts for punditry as well as for more rigorous analysis. Furthermore, with on-going advances in information and communication technology, policy research disconnected from specific organisational settings has become increasingly feasible and fashionable. It has also made international research exchange and collaboration between think tanks commonplace, fuelled by the growth of knowledge networks (Stone and Maxwell, 2005).

Networking ranges from the very informal, socialising or the 'thin' element of a virtual network through to formal international associations with a secretariat and large membership. Connected by shared ideological values, the Atlas Economic Research Foundation ties together a global network of more than 400 free-market organisations in over 80 countries to the ideas and resources needed to advance the cause of liberty, providing start-up funds and technical assistance. In the development field, the Evidence-Based Policy in Development Network is a virtual platform for sharing techniques and strategies for think tanks to bridge research and policy. The National Endowment for Democracy similarly provides support services democracy-related institutes. Although now languishing, since 1997, the Japan Centre for International Exchange convened 'Global ThinkNet' meetings to promote policy-oriented dialogues within

Asia and between Asia and other regions. Europe now has numerous networks. The European Policy Institute Network (EPIN) was established in 2002 as an exchange platform and collaboration mechanism on EU issues for think tanks in member and candidate countries. In 2012, the Council on Foreign Relations (CFR) launched an international initiative – the Council of Councils – to connect leading foreign policy institutes from around the world in a common conversation on issues of global governance and multilateral cooperation. As noted elsewhere of think tank networks, they 'illustrate not only a set of flows and a connectedness in relation to policy ideas but also an exclusivity and closedness, as a limited set of ideas and "authors" circulate and reiterate' (Ball and Exley, 2010: 151).

A recent development, and one that reflects think tank institutional embedding in the policy milieu, is the rise of support services for think tanks. A cottage industry of advisors and consultants has emerged, providing toolkits and guidebooks or management expertise on how to manage a think tank (Struyk, 2007), how to network a think tank (Weyrauch, 2007) or how to engage in best-practice research (Buldioski, 2009). PASOS has produced a 'think-tank code of good governance' (Pajas, 2011) and another booklet outlining 'principles for effective quality controls in the work of independent think tanks' (Lovitt and Pajas, 2011). The Atlas Foundation offers programmes such as a Think Tank MBA and Think Tank Leadership Training.

Since 2001, *Prospect* magazine has organised an annual competition, now described as 'the Oscars of the think tank world' by the BBC, to recognise important and influential work done by think tanks across the globe. Based in France, the 'Observatoire des think tanks' also has its 'cérémonie des trophées des think tanks'. The Global Go-To Think Tank ranking has also attracted attention by think tanks using their rank as a form of publicity and self-promotion, but it has also been criticised substantively for its flawed methodology (Seiler and Wohlrabe, 2010; Buldioski, 2010). There is a Facebook community – On Think Tanks. An international NGO, One World Trust, has developed guidelines and a toolkit of 'Accountability Principles for Research Organisations'. A 'Think Tank Funders Forum' was organised by IDRC in December 2012, 'to develop a common agenda for strengthening the support' funders offer for think tanks in developing countries (Taylor, 2012). These initiatives and actors orbiting think tanks (many listed in Appendix 1) testify to the strength and tenacity of the think tank in contemporary policy processes, but also to the professional concern about the standards and accountability of institutes within their ecosystems.

Think tank tales

The previous discussion has sought to outline the rise of the think tank phenomenon as well as recount how they overlap with and compete with other organisations seeking to play a policy-analytic role. To distinguish themselves, as well as to construct their legitimacy to inform policy, think tanks engage in discursive strategies of self-reification. Only three narratives of their public value will be discussed here: first, think tanks acting in the interests of the public; second, think tanks performing a public service 'bridging research and policy'; and third, think tanks as independent thinkers.

Acting in the public interest

The mission of the think tank is often to 'serve the public interest' (McGann, 2007) and their role in society to educate the community with their policy analysis, that is, to provide 'communicative discourses'. Indeed, many think tanks have legal status as charitable organisations for educational purposes and are obligated to pursue public objectives as third sector organisations based in civil society. Echoes of publicly motivated aspirations resonate through the mission statements or home pages of many think tanks. For example:

- The Grattan Institute in Australia depicts itself as 'independent, taking the perspective of the public interest rather than any interest group, and it avoids commissioned work to ensure this independence'.[1]
- The vision of CIDOB in Barcelona is to promote 'good global governance based on democratic practices at the local, national and supranational level in order to ensure people's basic needs for freedom and a life without fear'.[2]
- The mission of the Institute of Public Affairs in Warsaw is 'to contribute to informed public debate on key Polish, European and global policy issues'.[3]
- The Egyptian Center for Economic Studies carries out research 'in the spirit of public interest'.[4]

The examples are illustrative but common. Institutes play a self-proclaimed role in representing the public interest. Rarely do think tanks seek to demonstrate that public debate has been 'informed'. Instead, 'enlightenment' is presumed to 'trickle down' and have 'atmospheric influence' on the culture of debate.

Other institutes are rather more modest about their engagement with the public and do not express a desire for public education. Instead, their strategic focus is on policy communities and decision-making elites. In other words, they seek to provide 'coordinative discourses'. For example:

- The London-based Centre for European Reform brings together people from the worlds of politics and business, as well as other opinion-formers. Most of our events are by invitation only and off the record, to ensure a high level of debate.[5]
- The C.D. Howe Institute commands the attention and respect of Canada's top opinion leaders and policy makers. The quality and pertinence of the Institute's research, and its capacity to pull together decision makers for off-the-record discussions, is unequalled.[6]
- ETLA, the Research Institute of the Finnish Economy describes its mission to 'facilitate financial and economic policy decision making in the organisations sponsoring the Institute, Finnish companies and the entire economy'.[7]
- The mission of the Center for Global Development is to reduce global poverty and inequality through rigorous research and active engagement with the policy community to make the world a more prosperous, just and safe place for us all.[8]
- The Chung-Hua Institution for Economic Research is 'an international policy think-tank for economic and industry-related research as its goal ... serving as a policy think-tank for the (Republic of China) ROC government'.[9]

Such web-site statements can be aspirational rather than an accurate reflection of policy realities. Nevertheless, objectives to 'promote understanding' or 'research in the public interest' beg the question: Understanding for whom? The narrative reveals a three-fold hierarchy with 'the public' at the bottom.

The 'public realm' is an 'audience' to which policy analysis is transmitted downwards – as a subject to be educated and wherein to raise awareness – rather than the public treated as a source of ideas and knowledge. In OECD countries people are used to seeing institute reports covered in the quality press like *Le Monde Diplomatique* and *The Economist* or a think tank expert debating topical matters on a news programme. This route to the public (or the electorate) is in reality a one-way, top-down process, interpolated by the media. Few think tanks have mechanisms for feedback from society. Those that do might use devices such as e-discussions, focus groups, Open Days, meeting series and sometimes research partnerships with NGOs and community groups. When practised, these are the deliberative elements of think tank activity, emphasising communicative discourses of public participation, the public accessibility of knowledge and the importance of experiential knowledge (Hajer and Wagenaar, 2003). However, they are resource-intensive, time-consuming activities and do not provide reliable indicators of impact.

By contrast, the 'policy community' is the realm of the think tank where more horizontal relationships pertain. Think tanks interact with other stakeholders to policy issues – the media, leading NGOs, political parties, industry representatives and bureaucrats. It is in these realms where think tanks play brokerage and gate-keeping roles that constantly redefine science/policy boundaries (Halffman and Hoppe, 2004).

At the other end of the spectrum, think tanks operate more as supplicants towards decision makers, pushing ideas and analysis upwards into official decision-making venues. This is particularly so in political systems characterised by high degree of state control, such as Vietnam, Belarus or China. Organisational survival can require an acute respect of political realities in authoritarian political cultures.

Rather than promoting the public interest, think tanks can be engaged in empire-building. This is most evident when winning grants or contracts becomes an end in itself. The corporate interest in expanding programmes, raising funds, publishing more books, securing media coverage and political patronage, and so forth are essential to organisational sustainability and growth. The fund-raising treadmill and the day-to-day concerns of management are immediate pressures that compete with longer-term, more intangible objectives to influence the climate of debate. Organisational insecurity, competitive pressures and fiscal uncertainty are becoming increasingly common. Market pressures increase the likelihood of opportunistic behaviour, or push think tanks towards consultancy to become more like firms.

This is not to suggest that there is no interaction with the public. However, it is not a strong dynamic. Very few think tanks are membership organisations. It is unusual to see think tank officials representing their organisations in schools and colleges. A high proportion of organisations are located in the central business district of the national capital. They rarely venture outside the national parallels to the Washington 'beltway' or 'le Boulevard périphérique de Paris'. The organisational cultures of think tanks are not as open and accessible for the interested citizen as their web-sites might suggest. The elite venues, dress codes, the jargon and scientific debates serve to keep the general public at bay as well as demarcate boundaries of the policy community. An unstated but real role of certain think tanks is to cordon public debate to safe sites of discussion where only those with mastery of policy and social scientific communication codes can participate. It is the opposite of 'bridging' state and society.

Public service: Bridge building

One common view of the public function of think tanks is that they act as a 'conveyor belt' between the arcane world of science, scholarship and knowledge creation and the practical world of policy making. Another common metaphor to describe the think tank role is that they are 'bridges'. The UNDP definition of think tank is indicative:

> Think tanks – organisations engaged on a regular basis in research and advocacy on any matter related to public policy. They are the bridge between knowledge and power in modern democracies. (UNDP, 2003: 6, emphasis in original)

The UNDP definition captures the belief that think tanks are an interlocutor between knowledge and power, science and the state. UNDP's choice of metaphor is not unique. As a simple Google search reveals, the discourse 'bridging', 'linking' or 'connecting' the policy and research worlds reverberates throughout the web-sites, mission statements and publications of think tanks. Think tank networks can be thought as a series of interconnecting bridges.

However, bridges are built because communities are cut off or the trade in ideas is incapacitated by lack of infrastructure. The impediments to travel or communication reveals that bridges do not transport everyone. Moreover, they can represent 'choke points'. Bridges can be obstructed. They can also become congested due to narrow avenues of passage.

Interactions of international organisations with think tanks are a case in point. In May 1999 the Secretary-General of the United Nations, Kofi Annan, convened a closed meeting of think tanks to ask their assistance in providing analyses to help guide UN policy making (ODC, 1999). Think tanks were portrayed as organisations that could screen, channel and interpret NGO analysis and advocacy directed at the United Nations and adjudicate between competing claims. Think tanks were implicitly placed in the role of 'gate-keepers' to the UN, WTO or other international organisations, potentially becoming a barrier to NGOs seeking more direct access to UN personnel and procedures.

Think tanks cater primarily to the economically and politically literate and are at some distance from the rest of society. The people who establish and work in these institutes are usually highly educated, middle-class, Westernised professionals, often from privileged backgrounds. The organisational mandates – to inform and/or influence public policy – drive them to engage with other usually more powerful elites in society. Those sponsored and funded by international organisations and donor groups tend to be well-institutionalised, mainstream institutes whose research agendas concur in considerable degree with the policy interests of their funding source. The US National Endowment for Democracy (NED) supports institutes that share its norms and values concerning liberal democracy. World Bank sponsorship of the GDN has seen a bias towards economic think tanks staffed by development economists (Bøås and McNeill, 2004; Plehwe, 2007). In other contexts, it is apparent that donors and governments prefer to interact with think tanks and expert organisations as their civil society partners rather than less professional or more radical groups (Andjelkovic, 2003: 95). Some NGOs may there-fore view the 'research community' negatively: as elite, exclusive and with insubstantial connections to the general public.

The other danger that think tanks run, especially in liberal democ-racies characterised by a system of political appointment, is 'hollow-ing out' (Denham and Garnett, 2004: 242–43). Think tank personnel are obvious recruits for newly elected governments. Electoral turnover of governments can sap the strength of some think tanks, should their staff be appointed as part of the new administration. To mix metaphors, this phenomenon is the so-called 'revolving door' phe-nomenon first noted in the USA. However, the politicisation of think tanks that usually comes with a close affinity with particular administration or political party has been identified as having a more subtle and detrimental impact on the scientific integrity and schol-arly credibility of think tanks. In the words of two British observers, think tanks:

> ... foster the impression that power in Britain is concentrated within a charmed circle, where policy wonks rub shoulders with politi-cians and businesspeople in a kind of corporatism without the trade unions. ... The existence of people who have never worked outside the policy sphere ... lends support to the impression of the increas-ing distance between government and the governed. (Denham and Garnett, 2004: 243)

A growing disjuncture between the public rhetoric of think tanks to promote an educated society in the face of the political apathy of the citizenry of many democracies throws into high relief the exclusivity of the policy communities in which think tanks prefer to circulate.

The 'vanity tank' phenomenon crystallises the tendency where personal interest outweighs public motivation. Otherwise known as 'candidate tanks' (or legacy think tanks in the aftermath of a political career), they rarely possess an extensive institutional infrastructure but are established to promote (aspirant) political leaders to lend political credibility to their political platforms (Abelson, 2006). Such institutes are not noted for their scientific protocols.

Returning to the UNDP quote, think tanks have been portrayed as a *bridge between* knowledge and power. This image rests on conceptions of science and politics as being two essentially different fields of human endeavour. To portray think tanks as a 'bridge' is to maintain the distinctions and to invite a perception of these organisations as neutral publicly motivated intermediaries between the world of science and the separate world of politics and policy. The bridge metaphor establishes a false ontological divide between theory and practice or between the 'ivory tower' and the so-called 'real world' (Stone, 1996). The boundaries between the two domains remain unchanged but are linked by think tank bridges where think tanks also play a role in both policing and mediating the boundaries. The bridge metaphor implies linearity with think tanks, editing or re-shaping knowledge in uni-directional movements from basic to applied science, from problem to solution, from theorists to 'enlightened' policy makers, a progression also underlying the epistemic community concept.

The 'bridge' metaphor, and more generally the idea of clear boundaries between science and policy, has been contested (Ladi, 2011a; Halffman and Hoppe, 2004). Think tanks are not expert organisations situated outside of or above decision processes, transmitting research from their scientifically independent position into policy. Instead, as later chapters discuss, many think tanks help provide the conceptual language, the ruling paradigms, the empirical examples that then become the accepted assumptions for those making policy. The operation of 'decoding', interpreting and reformulating socio-economic realities is where research and policy are symbiotic and interdependent. Far from standing between knowledge and power, think tanks are a crystallisation of the knowledge–power nexus.

Thinking: Creating public goods

As self-designated knowledge organisations, think tanks produce a public good, that is, data collection, theory development, policy analysis.

As mentioned, 'think-and-do tanks' can be involved in public service delivery through community programmes or policy trials. Some institutes also are engaged in ethics training, delivering in-service courses, producing TV documentaries or capacity building. These are all public goods (or more often club goods) as is research communication, which can take different formats:

1. recycling, editing and synthesis;
2. 'garbage can' policy entrepreneurship; and
3. scientific validation.

The 'garbage can' metaphor is not used as a criticism of think tanks but is adopted to stress not only how agenda-setting is a complex process, but that think tanks are embedded within shifting political dynamics. While the garbage can metaphor provides a more realistic picture of policy making as a chaotic or opportunistic process, nevertheless, the bridging metaphor is a more powerful narrative of how policy research is presumed to be incorporated into decision-making and more effective in maintaining the boundaries between knowledge and power.

Recycling bins: Recycling ideas, synthesising ideas and re-interpreting scholarly work into a more accessible format are of benefit to busy bureaucrats and electorate conscious politicians. The daily pressures of governance generally mean that decision makers function with a short attention span and rely upon their staff for the collection of relevant research and data. Think tanks strive to provide it for them. Much academic research that has policy relevance is not in a format suitable for government use. Think tanks are very effective organisations for translating dense ideas or abstract theory into sound bites for the media; blue prints for decision makers; and understandable pamphlets and publications for the educated public. Many academics disdain this kind of work, while universities and colleges do not provide the institutional or career incentives to do it.

Think tanks are a vehicle to incorporate the perspectives of former military personnel, government officials or NGO leaders who would not easily qualify for appointment to a university. The recycling of professional experience is one of the more intangible modes of bridging. It enriches policy analysis and in the eyes of many decision makers enhances the credibility and likely practicality of think tank reports.

Part of 'recycling' involves repetition. The constant restatement of policy message via different formats and products – seminars, conferences, workshops, policy briefs and web-sites, books – broadcasts and amplifies policy research. While this might be considered as duplication, repetition is necessary to raise consciousness amongst the media and the minds of policy makers to embed a particular policy discourse.

Think tanks also act as editors. International organisations and governments require knowledge organisations and reputable professionals to sift and vouch the welter of information and analysis pressed upon them by NGOs, other governments, corporations and others. Think tanks deal with the 'paradox of plenty': A 'plenitude of information' creates a 'poverty of attention' unless there are 'editors, filters, interpreters' who can validate what is good or rigorous knowledge. 'Brand names and the ability to bestow an international seal of approval' (Keohane and Nye, 1998: 89) become a source of power. Think tanks have a brand name that symbolises expertise. They are generally seen as legitimate organisations to make sense of the conflicting evidence and information overload. However, the editing, synthesis and repetition of policy research and analysis is usually not sufficient to influence policy. Instead, most think tanks aspire to become policy entrepreneurs (Mintrom, 2006: 544) and seek direct engagement with the policy process.

Garbage cans: In contrast to theories of the policy process that portray decision makers seeking rational inputs of information into policy, the 'garbage can' concept from organisation theory suggests that policy making is a chaotic process influenced by chance and uncertainty. Actors define goals and choose means as they go along. Organisations such as national ministries and executives do not have predetermined and firm goals, but define them in the process of attaching problems to solutions. In this perspective, think tanks can be thought of as:

> ... collections of choices looking for problems, issues and feelings looking for decision situations in which they might be aired, solutions looking for issues to which they might be an answer, and decision makers looking for work. (Cohen, March and Olsen, 1972: 1)

Problems are constructed in order to justify solutions that think tanks have been working on for years. Think tank solutions are on the look-out for problems. Solutions, political issues and problems are all mixed up in the organisational garbage can rather than there being a sequential process where a problem emerges, a solution is sought and decisions are made.

The 'garbage can' concept was modified and stretched beyond organisations to the wider political system to model political decisions emerging from the interaction of three streams: political events, problem recognition and policy proposals (Kingdon, 1995). The balance of importance between these three streams, and how they interact, varies from one policy setting to another. Within the US legislative context, these streams are largely independent of each other, each developing with its own dynamics and decisions. Notwithstanding the assumptions of a pluralist political context, it has been an important theory of agenda setting. In transnational policy processes, the interactions and strength of flow of the different streams can be quite different to that at national levels.

Elected or (self) appointed officials in the political stream are publicly visible actors in agenda setting. By contrast, think tanks are less visible in the policy stream, but playing a significant role in (re-)formulating policy alternatives alongside other actors. Since the agenda is always crowded and resources limited, think tanks as policy entrepreneurs are critical in keeping their 'pet' policy proposals alive.

Think tanks market policy ideas that have had long cultivation in the 'garbage can'. Policy entrepreneurs in the think tank lift from their 'garbage can' policy recommendations, problem definitions and explanations for policy dilemmas as new problems arise. Think tank policy analysis often represents sets of solutions waiting for their 'window of opportunity'. In conjunction with other 'garbage cans' they build coalitions of support via expert networks. In short, they channel the policy and political streams, to promote a convergence and seize opportunities (such as regime change, elections, policy crises) to change laws and policy.

Policy entrepreneurship takes many diverse forms, and is both organisational and individual. It rests on a strategic blend of 'softening-up' actors in the political and policy stream through use of personal contacts, networking, media strategies and the creation of powerful policy narratives that simplify complex technical issues into manageable items of public policy. It is the management of expert discourse rather than the production of research findings *per se* that empowers think tanks in agenda setting. Equally important is the scholarly credibility and intellectual authority of think tanks. This means attracting top research staff. The most successful institutes are those with staff who could as easily be found within a good university. The authority of think tank has been cultivated and groomed through various management practices and intellectual activities.

Scientific and scholarly credibility: The knowledge credentials of think tank scholars (PhDs, career profile in university or government research agency, service on blue ribbon commissions or expert advisory groups) bestow credibility and status in policy debates that gives weight to their recommendations. However, neither knowledge production nor knowledge exchange is apolitical. As argued in previous chapters, social practices associated with intellectual autonomy give their product – ideas, publications, analysis – a patina of scientific objectivity and technocratic neutrality. Practices such as peer review and professional accreditation are exclusionary processes in which only those with the relevant credentials and mastery of scientific protocols can participate but which also serve to construct think tank research and expertise as reliable.

Issues of quality and rigour are paramount. The worst fate for a think tank is to be seen as delivering unreliable or sloppy analysis. With the emphasis on policy entrepreneurship and communication of easily digestible nuggets of policy information – in the form of policy blogs, tweets and power point pitches – the products of think tanks may oversimplify complex and technical issues. There is a tension in entrepreneurial demands for timeliness and informing the right people that can compromise research processes requiring rigorous methodologies and peer review (Boucher and Hobbs, 2004: 22). Management strategies such as creating an Academic Advisory Council, encouraging university sabbatical or adjunct teaching for think tank fellows, building postdoctoral programmes and fellowships or editing scholarly journals help paper over the tension. A steadfast commitment to intellectual independence and scholarly enterprise bestows authority. Think tanks individually, and collectively, need to protect their social status as expert, research-based organisations. Initiatives like the Council of Councils are the latest tactic to preserve brand name reputation via select and selective international associations of 'leading' institutes.

Think tanks do think. Furthermore, they can play an important role in setting the standard for policy research and independent analysis. Doing so, once again, they help draw the boundary between the policy-relevant 'expert' and the non-expert advocate. Think tanks are not only an organisational manifestation of this social boundary, they become adjudicators of it by constructing narratives, routines and standards concerning their own roles between science and the state or society along with their claim to independence and intellectual autonomy.

Recognition of think tanks as independent centres for expert, scientific and authoritative advice occurs because of the scholarly credentials of these organisations. It also happens because of the relationship with policy institutions, donor groups and other patrons that have a vested interest in the widely accepted narrative that think tanks think. Commissioning and funding studies, donor interests want independent, rational, rigorous analysis that is associated with the brand name. Similarly, legitimacy for support to think tanks – and the willingness of the media to use think tank experts – rests in the belief they serve the public interest. More often than not, the think tank is represented as a neutral non-profit transmission belt of research, scientific ideas and policy analysis playing the 'independent' role of communication between state and society.

This ontological division in the portrayal of think tanks continues to be perpetuated because it serves a purpose in policy discourses. The 'bridge' metaphor has more public power, media resonance and policy attraction than does the more 'messy' modelling of 'garbage cans', complex interactions of streams or of an intermeshed knowledge–policy nexus. A diffuse and pervasive 'nexus' cannot be operationalised into a policy tool in the same way as a compelling but simplistic narrative can be built of think tanks 'bridging' or 'linking' the scholarly/political, the national/global, the state/society divides.

Conclusion

The first three chapters have a common theme addressing 'the public' as it relates to the global agora, networks and think tanks. They set the scene for the following four case study chapters as to 'how' ideas are made to matter. The next four chapters look at the Overseas Development Institute, the Open Society Foundations network, the ASEAN network of Institutes of International and Strategic Studies and finally the Global Development Network. In doing so, the book interrogates practices of knowledge utilisation within the context of social science debates on the role of ideas in policy. This literature has been criticised for assumptions that paradigmatic shifts or policy learning occurs as ideas are 'diffused' into the policy atmosphere but without a sufficient explanation of the mechanisms and agents through which diffusion occurs (Campbell, 2008). Regarding the knowledge–policy nexus, the following case studies serve three purposes: First, the cases are a way to pay attention to the organisational and individual actors who generate and advocate policy ideas on matters such as international development or regional economic and security cooperation. Second, the cases draw attention to the mechanisms by which they informed policy – the dialogues sustained over the long term, policy entrepreneurship and networks. Third, through their proactive insertion into policy networks – such as processes of 'informal diplomacy' or 'bridging research and policy' – the case study organisations became informally institutionalised in governance.

4
RAPID Knowledge

In 2007, the Overseas Development Institute was named 'Think Tank of the Year' by *Public Affairs News*, the European political information, public affairs and policy communication magazine. On receiving the award, then Director, Simon Maxwell, said the Institute's 'research, policy advice and public affairs are all directed at a single aim: to inspire and inform policy and practice …' (ODI, 2007). The Institute is only one among many organisations that seek to 'bridge research and policy'. Philanthropic foundations, national social science funding regimes, development agencies and international organisations have long sought to improve the use of development research in policy. Similarly, research consumers – such as NGOs and government departments – have bemoaned the lack of relevance of research disseminated by (social) scientists. As a consequence, some universities, think tanks and scholarly societies have initiated programmes to go beyond research communication to promote knowledge utilisation in policy processes.

This chapter continues with the theme on 'bridging research and policy' introduced in the previous chapter but with a more specific focus on the mechanics of 'evidence informed policy' within the field of international development. This is done by investigating the innovative bridging activities of one think tank in the field. Established in 1960, ODI is one of the largest and oldest think tanks in the UK. Although London-based, much of its work is conducted in developing countries. In addition, staff members of the Institute have extensive involvement in policy networks beyond the UK in transnational policy communities. The Institute has been a front-runner organisation in developing organisational strategies of policy entrepreneurship and impact assessment.

ODI has been entrepreneurial within the think tank industry by developing a dedicated programme on 'Research and Policy in Development', better known as RAPID. The objective of RAPID is to improve the communication and utilisation of ODI research. For RAPID, research communication is about organisational strategies of policy entrepreneurship that start with immediate political agendas but extend to longer-term influence through creating human capital, building networks and close engagement within policy communities.

The first section provides an overview of knowledge utilisation. Rather than separate the worlds of (social) science research and that of politics and policy making, the discussion continues with the argument that knowledge production and utilisation is intimately bound with governance. Unlike universities, think tanks do not have the luxury of standing on the 'academic sidelines' to ask questions 'whether we can or should engage directly in the policy world or remain at a critical distance from it' (Tickner, 2006: 383). They must engage in dissemination and policy recommendation. For these organisations, it is a question of how to maintain a critical position *within* their engagements with the policy world.

The second section focuses on how ODI has translated its organisational mission to inform international development policy into tools and practices of individual and organisational entrepreneurship. Staff are expected to communicate research in ways that have social and political relevance:

> We expect researchers to be policy relevant in their work and to make sure that their findings reach policy makers in a form that is accessible and useful. (Maxwell, 2005a: ix)

The Institute has also evolved towards seeking policy influence in global domains of decision making. The third section concentrates on RAPID and the various activities and services it has developed over the programme's first decade of existence.

Thus, this chapter is also about boundary-drawing discourses between 'science' and 'politics'. The central theme is to conceptualise 'the process of policy making as situated at the intersection of forces deemed "political" and those apparatuses that shape and manage individual conduct in relations to norms and objectives that are deemed "non-political", such as science or education' (Gottweiss quoted in Fischer, 2003: 81). In light of contemporary policy discourses of governments and development agencies of the need for 'evidence based policy', ODI (and think tanks in general) must manage in a creative tension their often politicised policy utility at the same time as their image of scientific independence.

The 'parallel universes' of research and policy

In common with other think tanks, ODI operates in a policy environment where donors want to see returns from their investment in development research. For decades, bilateral donor agencies such as DfID as well as international organisations and agencies like UNDP have poured large amounts of funding into research into the causes and consequences of poverty and under-development. Although figures were tentative, ODI estimated that over the decade from 1995, 'Northern and international sources provided around US$3 billion for international development research' per annum (Court et al., 2005: 3). Given such an investment, donor and development agencies not only want high-quality research, they also want to evaluate and document the effectiveness of that research (Struyk and Haddaway, 2011). The World Bank commissioned an independent evaluation of its own research relevance (Banerjee et al., 2006) while UNESCO (2008) has sponsored a long-term programme on the transfer of social sciences research findings and data to decision makers (Anon, 2004). Other reports have been produced by national development agencies such as Danida (2001), the International Development Research Council in Canada (Neilson, 2001) and the Swiss Commission for Research Partnerships with Developing Countries (Maselli et al., 2004) and the Gates Foundation in India (Zonana and Nayyar, 2009).

Alongside these developments there has been a mushrooming of research programmes and capacity building. In 2002, the GDN initiated a five-year Bridging Research and Policy project. Other think tanks like the International Food Policy Research Institute (Ryan and Garrett, 2004), which has a dedicated impact assessment unit, place considerable emphasis on research-policy linkages. These initiatives attest to a concern about inadequate communication between researchers and policy makers. The Danish Commission on Development-Related Research summarised the perceptions of the two communities: '... one group feels nobody listens, the other feels their opposite numbers have little to say' (Danida, 2001: 9). This sentiment is echoed at ODI:

> Researchers find it hard, often impossible, to abstract sufficiently from their case material to be useful, and to avoid equivocation. Policy makers find it hard, often impossible, either to read research or make it count in the political cauldron of policy information. Both sides struggle with a shortage of time, under-funding, information overload, poor channels of communication and competing priorities. (Maxwell, 2005a: iv)

Researchers and policy makers operate with different values, language, time-frames, reward systems and professional ties to such an extent that they live in separate worlds (Neilson, 2001:5). As the then director of RAPID, John Young (2005: 727), put it: 'they live in parallel universes'.

Supply and demand

RAPID researchers have identified different explanations as to why research is or is not utilised in policy making (Court and Maxwell, 2006). These perspectives are organised into three general categories of explanation, that is, (i) supply-side, (ii) demand-led and (iii) political explanations.

The first set of explanations identifies problems in the flow of data, analysis and information into the policy makers' world. Supply-side explanations to 'push' research into policy domains exhibit at least three strands of argument:

1. The *public goods* approach argues that there is insufficient research and researchers for policy planning because of inadequate incentives to fund the production of research. This logic is used to justify public support to education and knowledge production. In the field of development research, the concept has been used by the World Bank to make its claim as the 'natural candidate for taking the lead in providing these intellectual public goods' (Banerjee et al., 2006: 15).
2. Rather than a lack of trained researchers, another explanation emphasises a *lack of access* to research, data and analysis for both researchers and policy makers. Although there is a wealth of research and analysis available, there is differential or inequitable access to knowledge. Developing-country scholars often complain of the difficulties in gaining access to research resources such as data bases, libraries and participation in international conferences or research projects.
3. The supply of research can also be flawed due to the *limited policy awareness of researchers* about the policy process. Researchers can be *poor communicators* or disdain a relationship to government. Policy recommendations from researchers can be impossible to implement because political realities (such as cost-effectiveness) are not addressed.

The first two points are commonly recognised dilemmas. The third point is more about communication capacities of individuals or institutes.

A particular response by ODI has been to create 'Stories of Change', written in accessible style and disseminated via multiple media, to highlight how ODI has made a difference in international development and humanitarian issues with its research. ODI has focused specifically on *research communication* which senior management regarded as needing an overhaul for its 50th anniversary milestone in its organisational development. It has meant:

> ... a further shift from quantity, such as the number of media hits, to quality: where and how ODI is cited. A new Twitter account, for example, offers updates on ODI's online activities, with Twitter users re-posting links to ODI event streams, blogs and media hits. Facebook is lowering the barriers to interaction, so a wider audience can comment on our work, while a new flickr.com photo gallery shares images worldwide. Always well-attended by development practitioners in London, live web streaming of ODI events has taken them worldwide, with viewers logging in from Uruguay to Sri Lanka. (ODI, 2011)

The careful packaging of research results and materials is crucial to ODI's research uptake, its public image and visibility with key clients such as DfID.

Improved research communication will amount to nought without a receptive political audience that 'pulls' in research. There needs to be absorptive capacity within the state architecture and other policy-making venues. A further set of explanations outline why demand is weak.

4. Research uptake is thwarted by the *ignorance of politicians* or over-stretched bureaucrats. Research is a lengthy process requiring observance or correct methodological processes and other scientific protocols. By contrast, political problems usually require immediate attention. Politicians are driven by immediate political concerns and often employ information from trusted sources – usually in-house or close to the centre of power. They often cannot wait for scientifically rigorous 'evidence' to arrive.
5. There can be a tendency for *anti-intellectualism in government*. That is, 'too many policy makers still think of research as the opposite of action rather than of ignorance' (Ahmed, 2005: 768). Albeit varying from one country or regime to the next, anti-intellectualism can undermine research use when the policy process itself is riddled with a fear of the critical power of ideas. Censorship and oppression of

researchers are not uncommon in some developing or authoritarian states.

6. Another demand side problem arises from the *politicisation of research*. Through selective use, de-contextualisation or misquotation, research findings are easy to abuse. Decision makers face incentives to do this to reinforce their policy positions or prejudices. In terms of think tank influence, it suggests that 'the more powerful the sponsors of ideas, the more powerful the ideas' (Jacobsen, 1995: 295). Small spaces of uncertainty and nuance, such as that concerning the causes and consequences of climate change, also provide opportunity for unorthodox perspectives to be given much greater media airplay and public debate than warrants the weight of scientific understanding. (McKewon, 2012)

Political apathy or hostility towards research may also be encountered in some fragile states or other development contexts where ODI researchers operate, that dampen demand for research. In the UK and on the European and international stage, a highly competitive think tank industry can also distort demand. Awash in policy advice from numerous sources, the 'plenitude of information' in the global agora identified in earlier chapters can encourage, either selectivity or conversely, disinterest in research and analysis amongst politicians and policy makers. In all these sets of situations where demand is low, ODI encourages personal links, networking and critical engagements of its staff with decision makers to overcome misconceptions and heighten awareness of the relevance of research.

Presented in binary terms of supply and demand, the difficulties encountered by researchers (as producers) and policy makers (as consumers) contribute to the making of the 'bridge' metaphor. Communication gaps can be resolved by building bridges between the policy and research worlds. Implicitly, there is a linearity assumed in the policy process. That is, that 'evidence' is immutable and can be moved sequentially through the cycle of agenda-setting, decision-making, implementation and evaluation.

However, the social and political context is important to understanding the windows of opportunity for the uptake of research. Institutional arrangements, the political character of the regime in power and the culture of public debate (or lack of it) impinge on what is considered relevant or useful knowledge. Consequently, a third set of perspectives on knowledge utilisation complicate the simple notion of building bridges as a solution to poor use of research in policy making. Referred to as 'political models' (Neilson, 2001) or as 'social epistemology' (Jacobson, 2007), these explanations emphasise the embedded character of knowledge in policy.

7. There is a *societal disconnection* of both researchers and decision makers from those for whom the research is about or intended. In some scenarios, 'group think' may result in government and an 'ivory tower' culture in research communities. Even where there is a constructive dialogue between decision makers and experts, there may be joint technocratic distance from the general public. Counterintuitively, 'good social science' is 'both social and scientific' (Anon, 2004: 7) in this explanation.

8. Rather than influencing government, there are wider *domains of research relevance*. Researchers may have huge impact on the media or among non-governmental organisations but little or no input to policy. Likewise, 'new institutional developments associated with networking, alliances, partnerships, "knowledge agencies" and organisational learning' mean that international agencies associated with the UN engage with research communities in different modes and via transnational policy communities (UNRISD, 2005). And in more gradual processes called 'enlightenment' (Weiss, 1991), 'one should not just think about how to influence the current generation of politicians, but also how one creates another generation of politicians who have a commitment to research and policy rigour embedded in them' (Taylor, 2005: 755).

9. Building research to policy bridges does not necessarily resolve conflict over policy choices. Instead, the improved flow of knowledge can highlight the *contested validity of knowledge(s)*. Researchers disagree (Kanbur, 2001). There is scientific competition. Evidence is not value-free (Jones et al., 2012: 4–5). Reference to 'research' does not signify a single body of thinking, data or literature that is consensually recognised and accepted. To the contrary, there are struggles between different 'knowledges' or what are often described as 'discourses', 'worldviews' and 'regimes of truth'. There are also deeper questions about epistemologies and what is knowable. (Leach et al., 2005)

These latter three perspectives point to the 'argumentative field', determining what is deemed socially and politically as evidence or research that is relevant. This third set of explanation sees knowledge and power as organically related, and policy as a form of argumentation. Informed by post-positivist literature (*inter alia*, Fischer, 2003; Halfmann and Hoppe, 2004; Jacobson, 2007), policy scholars have deconstructed the authority claims of experts and scientists to emphasise the contestability of knowledge.

Bridging research and policy

How research-policy dynamics are interpreted has implications for the methods adopted to improve the relationship. If the problem is located on the supply side, then approaches to improve research communication and dissemination are adopted, for instance, the establishment of research-reporting services (on web-sites and traditional media) and training activities for researchers such as media workshops and exercises in public speaking; how to write policy briefs and so forth. The product of the researcher is not usually in a format that can be used by policy makers. An intermediary – a 'research broker' or 'policy entrepreneur' – with a flair for interpreting and communicating the technical or theoretical work is needed. This is usually an individual but sometimes an organisation like ODI carries out this function. ODI, and its staff, lay in wait in the policy stream for 'windows of opportunity' to open so that they can advance Institute analysis on say, humanitarian relief in disaster scenarios such as an event like a Tsunami or the Rwandan crisis (the problem stream), and capture the attention of those decision makers (the political stream) who need to react to such events.

A common position in 'supply-side' perspectives is that initiative and action come from the research end in efforts to customise research for policy uses. The consumers tend to be portrayed as relatively passive absorbers of research. The first GDN motto – 'better research\better policy\better world' – is indicative of this linear rationalistic thinking. The focus on making researchers better communicators has seen the creation of numerous guides, tool kits and capacity-building workshops that are 'rather prescriptive and cookbook-like in form and content' (Jacobson, 2007: 120).

If the problem of research uptake is located on the demand side then strategies focus on improved awareness and absorption of research inside government, expanding research management expertise and developing an organisational culture of policy learning. Measures that encourage official agencies to become 'intelligent consumers' of research include establishment of in-house policy evaluation units, research sabbaticals for civil servants, visiting fellows programmes in international organisations, the creation of civil service colleges or in-house training on evidence-based policy. Such measures often assume that knowledge utilisation is a technical problem that can be solved with improved knowledge management and staff training.

Political models stress the need for long-term engagement of researchers with policy makers that create common understandings and identities. It takes researchers beyond brokering research in a one-way direction to develop a more productive shared exchange on what does and does not work in the transition from theory to practice. Mechanisms that bring researchers into government, such as through internships, co-option onto advisory committees and official patronage of policy research networks, are promoted. The emphasis is on shared problem definition among researchers, policy makers and stakeholders, that is, shared learning within policy communities. Importantly, political models recognise the so-called 'dark side' of knowledge management which is 'not only about remembering and sharing knowledge but also about actively marginalizing, discarding, and forgetting knowledge that is not deemed relevant or legitimate' (Ferguson et al., 2010: 1799). These approaches do not separate the world of research and the world of policy making but see knowledge and power as inter-related discourses. The very idea of 'bridging research and policy' is considered a false one as it presents a biased view of two autonomous communities. There is less agonising about the 'weak link between research and policy'. Instead, research and policy are viewed as mutually constitutive in the sense that knowledge is power (Leach et al., 2005).

There is, however, a conundrum, noted at the end of the last chapter. An organisation like ODI needs to reconcile *internal* organisational understandings of the third set of political explanations and social epistemology that inform the Institute's operational work with the management of its *external* relations that rest predominantly on simpler narrative of the first two sets of supply and demand explanations. The political symbolism of positing a divide between policy and research communities is considerably more manageable in terms of project activity for think tanks and in their public relations with partners and stakeholders. The perception of a 'divide' or 'parallel universes' establishes an agenda that can be translated into concrete capacity-building initiatives, consultancy work, network initiatives or research communication projects – that is, building bridges.

The Overseas Development Institute

The Overseas Development Institute was created in 1960 with support from the Ford Foundation, and in 1963 its Fellowship programme was launched with support from the Nuffield Foundation. ODI addresses international development and humanitarian issues. For its 50th anniversary in 2010, the Institute introduced its new strapline: *advancing knowledge, shaping policy, inspiring practice.*

> Our mission is to inspire and inform policy and practice which lead to the reduction of poverty, the alleviation of suffering and the achievement of sustainable livelihoods in developing countries. We do this by locking together high-quality applied research, practical policy advice, and policy-focused dissemination and debate. (ODI, 2012)

This mission statement is very much one of knowledge utilisation. But the Institute is a knowledge producer in its own right as well as a consumer and synthesiser of academic sources of research. Its 50th anniversary also provided it with an opportunity to reflect upon achievements and major milestones in the organisation's history. Highlights about its research relevance included ODI staff being consulted informally by the Brandt Commission in 1979, acquiring the editorship of the academic journal *Disasters* in 1990 and building a 1971 partnership with Thames Television on what was at the time a major experiment in public information: twelve hours of programming: *'The Third World War: A Struggle against Poverty'*. These and other milestones were constructed into a timeline of the Institute's history to provide credence to its social, academic and political impacts (ODI, n.d.). Ideational impact is something that needs to be demonstrated and broadcast.

There is little consensus or incontrovertible evidence of when, where and why research has impact. First, there is considerable dispute over the meaning of 'policy' and who is a policy maker. Second, there are many unanswered questions regarding the criteria of 'utilisation'. Some would argue that 'use' means that research affected a decision. Others might suggest that if research is given a serious hearing within policy circles, but not acted upon, then that also constitutes 'use'. Third, the causal nexus is a very complicated one with numerous other contributory factors to the development of policies aside from research. Fourth, what is to be evaluated? Is it a book or a data set that has impact, or an entire body of knowledge? And is it the most excellent research that has impact, or the mediocre? The methodological dilemmas of monitoring and evaluation in this field are well recorded (Struyk and Haddaway, 2011).

As outlined in the previous chapter, contemporary analysis is sceptical of think tanks exerting consistent direct impact on politics. Influence over current political agendas is occasional where capturing the political imagination is problematically dependent on windows of opportunity opening. However, an Institute generally needs to claim successes to demonstrate their social, political or economic relevance. A long-term 'enlightenment' function does not often appeal to donors desiring to deal with immediate issues with practical responses to poverty, economic growth or humanitarian disaster.

At ODI, the metaphor of the 'bridge' is a regular signifier in the Institute's book titles, journal articles, meeting series and pod casts. 'Political explanations' of the social construction of knowledge are also heard in ODI workshops and publications, but they are less amenable to project-related activity. Instead, issues of power and meaning are discussed in workshops, corridor discussions and face-to-face meetings. Or they are found in ODI working papers. Notwithstanding the best efforts by ODI staff to incorporate procedures for deliberative processes with partners or a reflexive awareness of the 'social construction of expert discourse' (Jacobson, 2007: 123), such a priority becomes a time-consuming impulse in the Institute that can become organisationally paralysing.

To be reflexive – consistently (as opposed to sporadically) – places additional demands on executive, administrative and research staff who are already stretched significantly by the day-to-day pressures to fund-raise, write reports, meet deadlines or engage with partners and political audiences. It presents a conundrum for ODI, that is, the paradox of 'knowing' the complexity and contingent character of research communication – especially in the longer term – alongside practical requirements to do something about it immediately by creating communication tools and conducting capacity-building events for policy impact. Such projects are more tangible to Institute stakeholders and development agencies wanting action.

In sum, there are not just varying definitions of (think tank) research influence on policy and different epistemologies for conceptualising the relationship. Unlike academia where there is still an established norm of the creation of knowledge for the sake of knowledge, for a policy institute there is always the question: 'What then, is to be done?' (Court and Maxwell, 2006: 13). At ODI, the step towards action has been recognition of the value of, and investment in, 'policy entrepreneur' skills.

ODI as a policy entrepreneur

A policy entrepreneur is an individual who invests time and resources to advance a position or policy (Kingdon, 1995). One of their most important functions is to change people's beliefs and attitudes about a particular issue. ODI has gone further identifying different policy entrepreneur styles: *story-tellers* whose sense of complex realities is conveyed through simplified scenarios and policy narratives, *networkers* who facilitate coalitions and alliances, *engineers* who are engaged on the ground with street-level bureaucrats in action research rather than isolated in a laboratory and political *fixers* who have a Machiavellian understanding of the policy process and those who hold power in it (Court and Maxwell, 2006: 9).

Not all members of Institute staff could be said to be policy entrepreneurs, or indeed to act as such for much of their time. And as the typology suggests, different personalities and individual traits entail that research communication takes different forms and styles. Yet, policy entrepreneurs are not just individuals. ODI has established itself as an organisational policy entrepreneur by developing advisory ties to governments and international organisations, and institution building of policy communities via networking and partnerships.

For ODI, one of its most important strategic alliances is its long-standing relationship to the UK Department for International Development. Indeed, DfID is the single most important source of funding for the Institute, accounting for well over half its income. But ODI has other national development agencies such as IrishAid and Norad supporting its work, amongst 90-odd funders (ODI, 2006: 44). For instance, in the 2011-12 financial year, the Institute was embedded into the transnational policy community of international development with contracts from 15 donor governments, and ODI was contracted to undertake research for the Gates Foundation, the Commonwealth Secretariat, the European Commission, the OECD in addition to the international financial institutions and 15 UN agencies (ODI, 2012: 1). And there are other kinds of institutional relationships. For instance, ODI is a convenor of APGOOD – the All Parliamentary Group on Overseas Development – for the UK Parliament.

Not only do think tanks seek to act as a bridge between the scholarly and policy worlds, many of them are also interlocutors through their research networks between the regional and the global. Throughout its history, ODI has managed a number of international networks linking researchers, policy makers and practitioners:

- Agricultural Research and Extension Network (AGREN), now dormant due to lack of donor interest;
- Rural Development Forestry Network (RDFN) built around 2900 members but also has faced challenges in maintaining donor support;

- Humanitarian Practice Network (HPN);
- Evidence-Based Policy in Development Network (EBPDN);
- Active Learning Network on Accountability and Performance in Humanitarian Action (ALNAP) for which ODI acts as the Secretariat.

ALNAP is a good example of a network of public–private partnership. ALNAP was instigated by DfID in 1996 when it commissioned ODI to write a concept paper on accountability among humanitarian organisations in the wake of the Rwandan genocide and as humanitarian services increasingly came to be delivered by NGOs. For some time, states had been retreating from delivery and contracting out the delivery of emergency assistance. As donor states increasingly became regulators, the demand for professionalisation and accountability of networks of organisations delivering assistance deepened. Today, ALNAP has consolidated its reputation as a resource hub for evaluation and expertise, best practice and innovation. 'Through its mobilization of UN agencies, national and international donor agencies, humanitarian organisations, and independent consultants ... governance is constructed through the practices of the network and disseminated through its members' (Gross Stein, 2009: 170). As host of the ALNAP Secretariat, ODI is also at the core of the transnational humanitarian assistance policy community.

ODI is also active in the Climate Development Knowledge Network and is a partner in the nascent European Think-Tanks Group. Arising from new proposals to use international financial mechanisms to 'reduce carbon emissions from deforestation and degradation' (REDD+), ODI is also a core partner in REDD-net, a hub for knowledge sharing and resources. These networks provide 'a forum to share and disseminate information, analysis, experience and lessons ...' with the overall aim to contribute to 'individual and institutional learning' (ODI, 2006: 35). For instance, the claim to fame of the forestry network is that it gradually instituted a 'new policy discourse' on sustainability from the mid-1980s onwards. Yet, establishing the causal links of the influence of the network on the thinking of decision makers or the catalytic role of ODI is not subject to definitive demonstration. Instead, it is more a matter of institutional memory among those privy to the forestry policy community.

The networks are 'communities of practice' where inter-personal relationships and social interaction are an important but intangible component of transnational policy communities. Rather than the specific policy analysis papers – or published output – having influence, it is the policy-analytic capacity – or human capital – that has long-term relevance and resonance inside official agencies. ODI is a desirable destination for interns, and is noted for its capacity building and mentorship of budding policy entrepreneurs. These individuals can work on enhancing their experience and personal career prospects through networking, cultivating contacts in the job market. The ODI Fellowship Scheme has been running for 50 years and is one of the Institute's most reputable programmes. In many respects, the Fellowship Scheme is a response to weakened sources of demand for research identified in points 4 and 6 as it mobilises post-graduate economists into employment with 'governments facing capacity problems' (ODI, 2006: 36). These economists enjoy a two-year placement in low-income countries in Africa, the Caribbean and the Pacific.

Like many other think tanks, the Institute is an informal political training ground in development policy where aspiring development practitioners and opinion leaders can practise their hand in policy issues, hone their rhetorical skills and use the Institute as a stepping stone to induct themselves into policy communities. An institute can later trade on the political success of former fellows. As noted in point 8, such movements are not necessarily a loss for the Institute (despite the disruptions that may result and the constant churning of appointment processes). ODI fellows are often 'poached' by the Development Assistance Committee (DAC) of the OECD, or the World Bank. ODI staff moving to positions in DfID, or into the international financial institutions (and sometimes back again), helps embed the Institute in various organisational policy webs as well as build social capital and inter-institutional loyalties in transnational policy communities. The 'revolving-door' of individuals moving between executive appointment and think tanks, law firms or universities is no longer just a US phenomenon. Furthermore, such movements are symptomatic of indirect knowledge utilisation in that ODI researchers bring both their research experience and ODI history with them into the new employer organisation. Likewise, ODI has sought prominent people to sit on its Advisory Council.

Official engagements, fellowships and networks are the formal or institutionalised mechanisms and practices of ODI policy entrepreneurship. There are also the informal connections and ad hoc personal contacts that result from face-to-face engagements at conferences or in meetings with officials. A glance at ODI's meetings programme indicates a continuous rotation of senior officials from UK government ministries, ambassadors and other foreign dignitaries, representatives of the European Commission, the World Bank and other international organisations as well as executive directors of NGOs and sundry professors in development studies. Attracting high-ranking officials and world-renowned scholars contributes to the research reputation of the Institute.

ODI legitimacy in communicating research and analysis is carefully cultivated by building the Institute's epistemic authority (the supply side). ODI also acquires credibility in policy and political circles through both philanthropic and political patronage and funding for its services (demand side). These endowments of research excellence and policy relevance give the Institute some legitimacy in seeking to intervene with knowledge and advice in policy processes. The objective of making knowledge useful is never far from the ODI's public rhetoric:

> We describe ourselves deliberately as a think-tank, because we work at the interface of research and policy. On the one hand, we work hard to help shape the agenda and contribute to debate. That's why so much of our output is short, written in non-technical language and designed to be accessible. On the other hand, our core mandate is research ... to know the theory, apply it to the real world and help develop policy. (Maxwell, 2005b)

ODI also provides consultancy services that include 'monitoring and evaluation', tailored training courses and advice on knowledge management and communications (ODI, 2012: 1). Offering reputable research and analysis, ideas and argumentation or by delivering services such as policy training for civil servants, conference organisations or public platforms for visiting dignitaries, think tanks get used, thereby demonstrating their relevance. In such instances, it is less the case that think tanks have an impact on government and more the reverse case that governments or certain political leaders employ these organisations as partners to provide intellectual legitimacy for policy. The cooption is subtle, incomplete and complicated by strategies of competitive tendering of research contracts (Brinkerhoff, 2002: 25–26).

Media attention also confers expert status on think tanks, but relatively few of these organisations acquire a worldwide profile with the international media. In 2011-12, ODI achieved worldwide coverage *inter alia* on the BBC World Service, Radio France Internationale, *The New York Times*, *The Economist* and *The East African* while its web-site saw 2.3 million downloads (ODI, 2012: 16). Such media attention is a means of indirect re-connection with the public (noted in point 7). Most of the

100+ think tanks in the UK are focused domestically on the UK policy scene whereas for ODI:

> Ouagadougou is every bit as important as Whitehall, Dar es Salaam as Downing Street. ... recognis(ing) the importance of our subject and the global nature of policy problems and solutions. (ODI, 2005)

Due to its development focus, ODI needs multiple voices, and in numerous international forums. This means targeting regional and global decision-making venues such as the international financial institutions and development banks. With the ever changing global context of the Institute's work, 'internationalisation' means that ODI needs to be 'engaged in constant renewal' as well as exploit new venues and tools for research communication (Jay, 2006: 3).

Global knowledge utilisation

Social scientists have long been taxed by questions of how, why and when policy advice and expertise is incorporated into government (see essays in Béland and Cox, 2011). It is a traditional question. A more novel question is to understand *how* policy knowledge is transferred by non-governmental actors between and above countries, that is, to address the trans-nationalisation of research communities – the so-called international 'invisible college' – that has been bank-rolled by international foundations (Roelefs, 2003), universities (Gross Stein et al., 2001) and development agencies. Networks, international meetings and global partnerships are more fluid policy structures than traditional nation-state organisations like government departments. Policy negotiation often moves in an issue-specific and institutionally fragmented manner between (the networks of) bodies as diverse as the G-24, the International Business Leaders Forum, the European Parliament, Transparency International and the International Finance Corporation (just to mention a few of ODI funders 2005–06). For ODI, 'bridging research and policy' means keeping pace with diverse currents of debate within these new and changing venues policy deliberation.

> Some policy issues, of course, are purely local: levels of tax for example, or the precise structure of decentralisation. Even here, however, the typical developing country debate is much influenced by the international zeitgeist, as represented by World Bank or UN reports. Other policy issues are primarily international: UN reform, the future of aid architecture, international trade regimes, and debt relief. In

these cases, bridging research and policy in one country will not do: it is necessary to build 'bridges across boundaries'. (Court and Maxwell, 2006: 7)

The transnational character of policy problems establishes rationales for research collaboration and the international diffusion of policy knowledge. As noted in the previous chapter, think tanks are increasingly interconnected through their own formal networks. As policy agendas internationalise, ODI has interacted with GDN and PASOS in specific projects and many other international NGOs and institutes. Indeed, one of ODI's partners – the Argentine think tank CIPPEC – has produced a handbook for civil society organisations seeking policy influence via global and regional policy networks (Weyrauch, 2007). CIPPEC is also a key instigator behind 'A New ThinkNet', an online community of southern researchers and practitioners studying the link between ideas and politics.

RAPIDity in policy

There is a well-known distinction between 'research on' policy and 'research for' policy. *Research on policy* is more reflective and academic in style, whereas *research for policy* is policy evaluation (Burton, 2006: 187). ODI does both types of research and this is reflected in the RAPID programme. On the first score, RAPID has commissioned literature reviews, contributed to academic books and journals *on* 'bridging' or 'knowledge utilisation' as a scholarly subject. This is the first of RAPID's 'work-streams': understanding the links between policy and practice. On the second score, RAPID projects include workshops, capacity-building activities, case studies, advisory services and toolkits to build individual and institutional competencies *for* bridging activities. This second work-stream is more applied: practical tools to improve skills and capacities.

At the time of RAPID's establishment in late 2001, there was a sizeable literature on knowledge utilisation, but most of it was focused on OECD contexts. RAPID's literature reviews involved synthesis work to make relevant connections to developing-country experiences. A further stage of analytical work was the development of a conceptual framework that could be applied across different policy fields or developing countries (*inter alia* Crewe et al., 2005; Young, 2005). A third step has been to address the particular difficulties associated with transnational dimensions of development policy. RAPID's web-site has become an important resource bank for analysis on knowledge utilisation.

Stepping beyond the analytical work, the first challenge in launching RAPID as a programme of events and activity was finding purchase within the Institute. This has been a gradual process, and not one without disinclination from some ODI staff who considered ODI first and foremost a research body rather than engaged in policy analysis. Even so, RAPID grew quickly. It was consistently promoted by ODI management building on initial pilot research in the late 1990s (Sutton, 1999). RAPID has been able to secure substantial funding and interest from DfID as well as from other donors interested in rectifying what they consider to be a problem of research communication and utilisation.

RAPID objectives have been 'mainstreamed' throughout the Institute and implemented via ODI's standard products – the academic papers, briefings, opinion pieces and meetings. For instance, commencing in 2006, RiPPLE – Research-inspired Policy and Practice Learning in Ethiopia and the Nile Region – was a five-year project of an ODI lead research consortium to advance evidence-based learning on water supply and sanitation focusing specifically on issues of financing, delivery and sustainability.

Diversification on the communication front has also seen ODI create Facebook and Twitter accounts, again as means to ameliorate some of the tensions outlined in point 7. Blogs are one mechanism for ODI to reach to wider audiences on international development issues. These blogs allow ODI 'to respond to events as they unfold – and give you the opportunity to comment and engage' (Maxwell, 2005b). It is a means to break down the 'societal disconnection' (point 7) that think tanks sometime encounter or erect. By making information about international development more current and publicly accessible, one British parliamentarian has suggested that ODI's blog is a mechanism that promotes political accountability (Hudson, 2007).

Within a decade of its establishment, RAPID developed a strong reputation for expertise in research communication. The unit was in a position to offer consultancy services internationally not only to other think tanks but also to international organisations. The RAPID team have undertaken research projects for global networks like GDN (which has its own global research project on Bridging Research and Policy) and numerous other NGOs and development agencies. RAPID staff also help 'clients' with advice, training and programme design on maximising policy impact via research, research communication and operations in organisational development. RAPID also conducts evaluations of the work of research-policy interventions.

One client was DfID's Engineering Knowledge and Research (EngKaR) programme, which provided technical, managerial and policy solutions in the infrastructure and urban development sectors. Over 15 years, EngKaR invested over £100m across some 600 projects. For DfID, the RAPID evaluation provided 'the endorsement of continuing commitment of DfID to research and dissemination activities in the transport, water, and energy sector as supportive to the DfID programmes as a whole and also the contribution to global public good' (DfID, 2008).

The value of external evaluation for the commissioning agency is independent validation of programme activity. Such validation can be crucial in renewal of funding or programme continuation. An evaluation can also be a 'sounding board' and a source of critical feedback to help improve the efficiency of operations. For donors, an evaluation is also a device for transparency and accountability via monitoring and evaluation. This is well known. Less frequently considered is the reward or benefit (other than the fee) for the commissioned evaluator. The government contract provides tangible official affirmation of RAPID expertise and indirect recognition of ODI as a reputable organisation. It is a process of mutual validation. Such 'mutuality' is to be expected among partners but can endanger independent organisational identity 'that comes through processes of compromise and adaptation' to the dominant partner (Brinkerhoff, 2002: 26–27).

In terms of agenda-setting, ODI was very successful in the first decade of the century in tapping growing unrest in the donor community about perception of inadequate knowledge utilisation. The Institute acted as a policy entrepreneur. It quickly took control of the issue in the UK, redirecting the problem stream into its own organisational ambit by initiating research and workshop activity on the topic (in conjunction with others in the think tank, development NGO and policy community). The culmination was to redefine the problem in terms that suited the capacities and growing capabilities of RAPID. The problem and policy streams were joined, providing conducive circumstances for ODI to successfully find funding from the political stream.

Civil society partnership programme

Commencing in 2004, RAPID's flagship Civil Society Partnerships Programme (CSPP) was a seven-year programme funded by DFID with the aim to strengthen civil society use of research-based evidence to promote pro-poor development policy. One key objective is knowledge utilisation 'by establishing a worldwide network for think-tanks, policy research institutes and similar organisations working in international development'. CSPP allows ODI to broach (as in Point 8, above) a wider domain for influence by engaging with a more diverse community via capacity building with civil society organisations and other partner organisations.[1]

As part of the CSSP, the Evidence-Based Policy in Development Network was created aiming to be 'a worldwide community of practice for think tanks, policy research institutes and similar organisations working in international development'. The EBPDN network was characterised by great enthusiasm at its founding meetings, but energy lapsed between meetings as participants returned to their countries, and it was difficult to engineer south–south engagements. As a consequence, the product and activities of the programme was dominated by materials collected by ODI and managed through the EBPDN web-site. The challenges faced were developing mechanisms to create wider ownership among network participants around research themes as well as genuine collaborative projects.

Sustaining reflexivity in an international network is difficult, particularly when the participants are geographically dispersed and face funding dilemmas in their home institutes. Nevertheless, EBPDN annual meetings have confronted issues of elitism, participation, ownership, the 'logic of joint engagement' and governance. Differences of opinion on how to run and fund a network, as well as how research agendas are set, are on-going issues well ventilated in this community.[2] The outcome of this dialogue is that from 2010, RAPID increasingly encouraged its partners to take the lead in many activities. In particular, CIPPEC in Argentina and Grupo FARO in Ecuador are charged with developing RAPID in Latin America to 'provide services that were once supported centrally from London' (ODI, 2012: 11).

Substantive issues of complexity and content – including issues of power and ideology – are also voiced regarding the art and craft of generating knowledge for policy use. For instance, a recent 'practical guide' on *Knowledge, Policy and Power in International Development* (Jones et al., 2012) stresses that policy making is as much about power and politics, if not more so, as it is about rationality and genuine problem solving, that is, the idea that 'power decides what is truth'. Within the organisational culture of the Institute, there is scope to pursue such detailed discussions on the value-based nature of knowledge through the EBPDN and other workshops. But to convey to policy makers equivalence and uncertainty about knowledge claims, and the different social epistemologies of 'utility', is less viable given the instrumental need for policy decisions and programmes that are 'evidence informed'.

Gradually, the orientation of RAPID and its CSSP programme has moved from research on the multi-dimensional nexus of knowledge and power towards using the analysis to plan and execute 'bridging' development projects, that is, creating 'toolkits', drawing practical lessons from case studies (Jones et al., 2012), delivering training workshops and building the EBPDN 'community of practice'. The EBPDN email community and conversations have continued to be active and self-sustaining and, with the support of GDN, responsibility for the network is being devolved to the Centre for Poverty Analysis in Sri Lanka (ODI, 2012: 11). EBPDN is not only indicative of ODI's international entrepreneurship but its capacity to evolve towards more participatory transnational partnerships.

Bridging activities like toolkits and training events appeal to the funding agencies like DfID and GDN, but these agencies focus on practice, products and results. They are rather less concerned to 'understand knowledge and the relationships between knowledge and these [bridging] processes' (Jacobson, 2007: 121, my insertion). Developing practical guides, providing lessons in effective knowledge-policy interfaces and creating 'messages to donors' continue to reflect a belief in the Institute that there will be a rational acceptance within governance circles that one set of interests (think tanks) supposedly provide more credible, reliable and policy relevant knowledge over that of other interests like universities which continue to be stereotyped as theory oriented and out of step with policy realities and political timetables.

Conclusion

Through its networks, its meetings and workshops, the blogs, the publications as well as the more informal behind-the-scenes engagements with officials, personal networks, currying of favour at conferences, the career movements of staff and the invitations to participate in semi-official discussion, ODI embeds itself in a thick web of relationships. As noted by the director of IDRC, ODI's Canadian counterpart organisation, for RAPIDity to occur 'means forming relationships with policy makers that can endure over many years' as well as becoming 'participants in democratic governance, active at every level, from community deliberation and decision making to national and international policymaking' (O'Neil, 2006: 54). At the same time, the Institute needs to maintain a reputation for research that is sound and rigorous *within* its engagements with the policy world. This is secured through a circular process of mutual recognition between ODI as a producer of policy knowledge in conjunction with consumers (often the funder) of the research.

The consequences of brokering research are not neutral. Institutional and individual interests are served through activity that goes beyond the mechanical sharing of information. The communication of development research entails a complex set of reciprocal affirmations: legitimacy for the Institute as a reputable provider of policy research and analysis and legitimacy for the commissioning government department or international agency in having sought an 'evidence base' for decision processes. This circular process of legitimation is buoyed and politically symbolised by the discourse of 'bridging research and policy'. The discourse reinforces the scholarly/scientific/expert credibility of ODI. Official patronage or public funding of 'bridging' projects is then used as 'evidence' of government interaction with the public and incorporating expert 'stakeholder' group in debates on international development even if the critical substance of communicated research might fall by the wayside.

As a point of intersection for the interests of the state, business and intellectual elites, the research and activities of ODI are inflected with the motives of these partners and funders. The Institute is not isolated from broader interests, but interconnected and dependent, requiring support for its ideational work. Importantly, the extensive involvement of ODI in various informal and formal networks and transnational policy communities has a counter effect, in some small degree, by widening the terrain of relevance and audiences. Network approaches are useful in placing think tanks in a web of interdependencies. Yet, such webs also provide scope for independence and manoeuvre that bring some autonomy from sponsors. The network character of the global agora provides scope for not only ODI, but other organisations and KNETS to be present as 'wholly active citizens' in the transnational policy communities of international development.

The focus has been on the Overseas Development Institute because it was one of the first institutes to develop a dedicated programme on 'bridging research and policy'. Nevertheless, the issues faced by ODI are pertinent for similar bodies like the Center for Global Development in Washington DC., ODI's partner institutes like CIPPEC in Argentina, as well as thousands more policy research organisations internationally. It is also relevant to organisations that commission and fund development research, official agencies like DfID in the UK or philanthropic bodies like the Gates Foundation in the USA. The (social) science they fund is not inherently persuasive in debates on international development but contingent on somewhat instrumental partnerships and politicised processes of research communication.

5
Translating Foundation Ideas

Billionaires have become prominent public players in the global agora. Ted Turner made headlines with his initiative donating $1 billion to the UN two decades ago. The Bill and Melinda Gates Foundation was built by the Microsoft entrepreneur Bill Gates in 1994. It has become very active in global health issues and international development. Jim Balsillie, one of the brains behind Blackberry, established the Center for International Governance and Innovation (CIGI) to identify and develop ideas for global change. And George Soros, the billionaire who 'broke the Bank of England' in 1987, is the key figure behind the Open Society Foundations network.

These new foundations and philanthropists complement an older group of foundations like the 'Big 3' – Ford, Rockefeller and MacArthur foundations – that have long been players on the international scene. Old and new alike, philanthropy is cast as voluntary private beneficence. Foundations are generally regarded as civil society organisations operating between both market and state but working towards the public good. In 2010 a US Billionaires Club was established with a 'Giving Pledge' from 40 wealthy families (Clair, 2010). These developments are the 'elite' forms of associational life in civil society. The growth in international giving of philanthropic foundations has been described as 'global civil society making' (Vogel, 2006). This chapter goes a step further to argue that foundations also promote the development of transnational policy making in the global agora through the international spread of funds, people and ideas, as well as through donor partnerships.

National and sub-national venues of policy making are not displaced or disabled, but are inter-connected in increasingly complex fashion as we witness the shift from government to governance. In particular, the spread of norms, knowledge and expertise in which foundations play a more prominent role complements the hard institutional export of policy tools, laws and practices promoted by government agencies and international organisations. Foundations and their grantee organisations are involved in the 'softer' dissemination and translation of prevailing ideas about social and economic organisation.

As suggested in Chapter 1, the porous boundaries of governance in the global agora assists powerful civil society bodies like philanthropic foundations to become an informal part of governance or what some call a new logic of governmentality (Sending and Neumann, 2010). This cascades from top leadership – such as when Balsillie is appointed by the UN Secretary General to join the High-Level Panel on Global Sustainability, a body charged with formulating a new vision for sustainable growth in response to the growing risk of dangerous climate change – through to the micro-level of service delivery with the Gates Foundation in partnership with governments and pharmaceutical companies in Global Alliance for Vaccines and Immunisation (GAVI) by increasing access of poor communities and children in developing countries to immunisation and public health services.

This chapter assesses the policy roles of the Open Society Foundation. It is a private-operating and grant-making foundation based in the US that serves as the hub of the Soros foundations network, a group of autonomous national foundations around the world. Founded in 1993, and known as the Open Society Institute (OSI) until 2010, this collection of national foundations and autonomous organisations operate in more than 60 countries. Originally, the Foundation was designed as a mechanism for the international diffusion of Western expertise and 'best practices' to post-communist countries of Central and Eastern Europe (CEE) and the former Soviet Union (fSU). As the OSF matured, its activities spread to some other democratising nations. Addressing how OSF diffuses knowledge, as well as looking at the content of what is diffused, serves to question commonly held perceptions of foundations as simply being benefactors of social and educational causes, or as civil society bodies independent and separate from government. It is rather more complex than this picture. Instead, OSF's coalitions, partnerships and shared policy initiatives reveal the intermeshing of governance between public and private actors and mutual engagement in policy. More generally, '... philanthropists have taken on the role of the state – essentially setting and implementing policy through their independent funding choices' (Eikenberry, 2006: 588–89).

With their direct engagement with contemporary policy issues of corruption, human rights abuses, civil liberties, rule of law, public health debates, freedom of information and independent media, 'open society' programmes for transition and reform are not only multi-faceted but inherently political. The concern of the Foundation is to give 'voice' to communities at the local level and emerging policy elites in national affairs, through capacity building, the spread of 'best practices' and the translation of liberal norms of the 'open society' into post-communist contexts and democratising nations. Doing so, the OSF becomes a transnational norm broker and reform advocate engaged in what is known as processes of policy transfer (Marsh and Sharman, 2009; Stubbs, 2005).

Not unlike the manner described in the last chapter of how think tanks build their epistemic authority via their relationships with funders and donors, the legitimacy of the Foundation's expertise and the various academics, specialists and consultants engaged by OSF is built through a circular process of credibility construction in the relationship between the knowledge the Foundation sponsors and spreads and the audiences that help legitimise and institutionally consolidate that knowledge. It becomes a mutual validation process, one that assists and gives intellectual credibility to OSF norm advocacy.

The first component of the chapter challenges the idea of philanthropy as a purely private activity undertaken in (global) civil society by examining the policy aspirations of OSF. The discussion introduces another set of policy process theories – the concepts of policy diffusion, transfer and translation – to illuminate the policy practices that the OSF enacts through its network structure. The OSF is constructed as a network, but it is also a participant in various transnational advocacy networks, global public–private networks and knowledge networks of the types introduced in Chapter 2, and thereby implicated in the governance objectives of states and international organisations.

The second section focuses on various OSF programmes and network activities. The third section concentrates on OSF policy research and expertise and how as an evolving organisation it has moved from grassroots mobilisation to a re-envisioning of its organisation focus to take in a 'global turn' and 'policy awakening'. Its current and third reinvention is leadership change and internal professional consolidation. The conclusion returns to the theme of authority construction and blurred public–private boundaries of the global agora.

Policy translations of transnational philanthropy

The Open Societies Foundations network is both a grant giving and an operating foundation with its own initiatives and programmes implemented by OSF staff. The mission of OSF is multi-dimensional, and its policy aspirations are explicit in seeking to promote its norms and agendas on government accountability, rule of law or freedom of information:

- The Open Society Foundations work to build vibrant and tolerant societies whose governments are accountable and open to the participation of all people.
- We seek to strengthen the rule of law; respect for human rights, minorities and a diversity of opinions; democratically elected governments and a civil society that helps keep government power in check.
- We help to shape public policies that assure greater fairness in political, legal and economic systems and safeguard fundamental rights.
- We implement initiatives to advance justice, education, public health and independent media.
- We build alliances across borders and continents on issues such as corruption and freedom of information.
- Working in every part of the world, the Open Society Foundations place a high priority on protecting and improving the lives of people in marginalised communities.[1]

Like the Big 3, and some of the new large philanthropic bodies, the OSF is relatively unusual as a philanthropic body given that it has an international focus. Most foundations are active only on a local and national level.

Participation in international policy dialogues is not automatic. Entrée is determined in large part by the willingness of governments to recognise the validity of the contributions to international governance made by certain non-state actors. The authority and legitimacy for non-state public action in world affairs is not naturally given but cultivated through various management practices, professional networking and intellectual activities. One aspect of the private authority of the Ford Foundation, the Gates Foundation or OSF lies in their establishment as non-profit or charitable organisations. The founders and chief executives can argue on the one hand, they are not compromised by the need to generate profits in proffering their expertise, and on the other hand, that they have independence or autonomy from bureaucracies and political leaders. The annual reports of the Soros Foundations Network are littered with claims about the independence and autonomy of the national foundations (also Carothers, 1999: 273). Such a portrayal coincides with the dominant idea of philanthropic foundations being based in the 'independent sector'.

Rhetorical resort to the professional and scientific norms of scholarly discovery and intellectual investigation also enhances intellectual credibility. Universities have long held this status, and the link of the OSF to its sister institution in Budapest – Central European University – is pertinent to some of the Foundation's activities. This link lapsed a little during the first decade of the millennium, but there are considerable ambitions to revive it via a SPP. The intention is that there would be a two-way flow: OSF expertise and policy experience would feed into the School's activities, helping to ensure its real-world relevance, and the School would help provide the thinking and conceptual underpinnings for Foundation programmes. As George Soros put it:

> I have great hopes for the School of Public Policy. It has the potential to become the leading institution of its kind. It can combine the practical experience of the foundations network and network of networks, which are engaged in practically all the burning issues of our day, with the theoretical knowledge that resides in a university. Currently our practical engagement in these burning issues exceeds our theoretical understanding; in other words, we have more money than ideas. We need to generate more ideas in order to use our money more effectively. If we outsource the process to the school, the school will produce public goods which count as output; if we did it internally, as most foundations do, that would count as overhead. (Soros, 2011: 43–44)

Here, the CEU and the policy studies and intellectual work of the School are portrayed as a 'public good'. Critics are less sanguine: 'Educational philanthropy allows specific social groups, using their economic and social capital, to shape the policy arena not so much by imposing specific policies as by crafting and imposing the tools of policy-making' (Guilhot, 2007: 449). Whilst OSF is recognised as an incubator of progressive social programmes and challenging oppressive social regimes, it is also seen to be a paradox: 'supporting democracy but highly elitist'; non-profit but funded by one of the richest men in the world; independent but pursuing the ideas of the founder; celebrating professionalism and expertise but favouring the appointment of well connected individuals from Soros' clique' (paraphrased from Stubbs and Wedel, 2013).

Other OSF initiatives reinforce this discourse of dispassionate expertise and of the Foundations as repositories of 'specialised subject area knowledge'.[2] OSF sponsors many think tanks such as the European Council on Foreign Relations and the PASOS network (see below). The

Institute of New Economic thinking (INET) was launched in the wake of the global financial crisis and seed-funded by OSF and has now partnered with CIGI and the Martin School at Oxford University to 'nurture a global community of next-generation economic leaders, to provoke new economic thinking, and to inspire the economics profession to engage the challenges of the 21st century'. INET is composed of some of the world's leading mainstream economists 'who have emerged out from the shadows of prevailing economic thought' to address the deficiencies in 'outdated current economic theories'.[3]

Adopting the mantle of protectors of the principles and philosophies underlying democratic societies is another discursive tactic of civil society organisations to claim legitimacy for their policy ambitions. OSF is not unlike many NGOs that lay claim to participation in public debate by 'representing' the interests of minorities or the human rights of oppressed communities and future generations. OSF is well known for its long-standing support for Roma organisations, women's groups and bodies such as Human Rights Watch.

Such discourses of authority and legitimacy are a necessary component in effectively diffusing ideas and propelling them into official domains. Via these three discourses of conduct – first, non-profit, legal and financial independence; second, dispassionate scientific endeavour; and third, democratic representation of oppressed communities – credibility is manufactured for non-state involvement in policy. In creating their credibility to inform policy debates, they also become 'integral to the practices of governing' (Sending and Neumann, 2010: 115), especially when they are treated as 'partners' and 'stakeholders' in international development.

Like most private philanthropic enterprises, the OSF is legally independent and, particularly in the US, is careful to distance itself from any suggestion of lobbying or political advocacy. However, various units of the OSF are to be found in partnership with UNDP, the World Bank, the Council of Europe or parts of the European Commission. With expansion of its 'global agenda, partnerships with other donors are becoming ever more significant' (OSI, 2006: 174). Many more organisations that are recipients of OSF grants are likewise enmeshed in regional policy dialogues, international alliances or multilateral initiatives. Directly and indirectly, the resources of foundations put them in a prime position for promoting norms and ideas to shape policy agendas.

Policy translation

'Policy transfer' or 'policy diffusion' is a transnational policy process. Knowledge about policies, administrative arrangements or institutions in one place is used in the development of policy elsewhere. In other words, transfer can involve specific tools or instruments (such as child-care vouchers) to more general and abstract policy ideas (such as the spread of the 'new public management'). In the case of OSF, it aims to 'open up closed societies' by transmitting Western liberal ideas of markets, civil liberties and freedom of information. Additionally, there are different degrees of transfer from straightforward copying of policy, legislation or techniques as well as various forms of emulation, synthesis and hybridisation. Policy transfer processes can be either voluntary or coercive, involving respectively organisational learning or imposition of policy by external actors. Unsurprisingly, the more placid term of 'diffusion' has been used in World Bank circles (Stiglitz, 2000). By contrast, neo-Gramscians and those of a post-Marxist sensibility (*inter alia*, Bøås and McNeill, 2004; Broad, 2006; Parmar, 2002) regard the diffusion of these ideas as the imposition of a neo-liberal hegemonic project.

It is apparent that policy diffusion occurs between countries as witnessed by the adoption by governments around the world of policy approaches and institutions such as the Ombudsman's Office (Ladi, 2011b) or freedom of information law as well as the spread of tobacco control policies. There is also the 'philanthropic projection of institutional logics abroad' (Heydemann and Hammack, 2009: 7). However, the 'export' or diffusion of ideas is not a single event or unified sequence of exchanges. Instead, it is an on-going *process* of international visitors of experts, collaborations and conferences, funding of publications as well as happenstance meetings and sharing of information, whereby new orthodoxies are both incrementally picked up in public discourse and deliberately propelled to policy circles (Wacquant, 2004: 174).

As noted, one mode of transfer is *coercion*, such as exercised directly or indirectly by powerful nations or international organisations. The Bretton Woods institutions have long been accused of dispensing 'one-size-fits-all' policies coercively imposed through loan conditionality, but these institutions now stress the desire and need of 'putting countries in the driving seat' (Stiglitz, 2000). Coercion is a mechanism out of bounds for a non-state actor like OSF. Instead, developing shared understandings through policy-oriented learning in transnational policy communities is the strategy of non-state actors (Marsh and Sharman, 2009).

This brings us to the idea of translation, that is, not only translation of norms, ideas, institutions and practices within national and local policy communities, but also translation in transnational policy spaces by TANs, GPPNs and the various foundations, think tank, corporate, state and other actors in them (Stone, 2012). The notion of translation reflects a 'move away from thinking of knowledge transfer as a form of technology transfer or dissemination, rejecting if only by implication its mechanistic assumptions and its model of linear messaging from A to B' (Freeman, 2009: 429). It is an idea very much in tune with George Soros' fascination with the notion of 'reflexivity'.

This chapter steps beyond the idea of policy diffusion as a dynamic between governments to argue policy transfer helps create *transnational* policy spaces as well, that is, a locus for percolation, recombination and reinvention of ideas as well as gestation and rejuvenation of 'international policy cultures'. In the dialogues, conferences and negotiations that occur within and among international organisations as well as with partner and client governments, and with foundations and NGOs, further sets of translations take place where policy meanings are distorted, transformed and modified (Lendvai and Stubbs, 2007: 176). There is, for instance, a transnational policy community of 'good governance' (read: anti-corruption) in which bodies like Transparency International are at the centre of public visibility. But there are also other actors like Transparency International Research Institute (TIRI),[4] the Public Integrity Education Network (PIEN) and the Revenue Watch Institute all of which have received OSF support and which play less visible roles in the transnational policy community.

Philanthropic capacity building and grants spread knowledge, transfers practice and transports people. For instance, the OSF is involved in the spread of best practices on transparency and public integrity at a country- and region-wide level. In theory, foundations have the institutional capacity to scan the international environment and undertake detailed evaluations of policy that will help prevent simple or ad hoc copying of policy that feeds inappropriate transfer and policy failure. The strong local ethos of the OSF and the autonomy bestowed on national foundations are designed to promote the most favourable environment for *translation* and 'local ownership' of policy ideas (Carothers, 1996). With 'respect for local decision making', staff of national foundations were trusted to interpret open society values in a manner appropriate to their own countries (Neier, 2011: 336–37).

OSF also supports and diffuses ideas that are in opposition to existing political regime and experts who are critics. OSF-sponsored activists have been accused of a catalytic, behind-the-scenes role in the Rose and Orange Revolutions of Georgia and Ukraine. OSF has been cast as a tool to dismantle socialism, that is, a Western project to 'manufacture democracy' in the former Soviet region (Herd, 2005: 4). Russian President Vladimir Putin accused George Soros of orchestrating the 'colour revolutions'. Such claims suggest that norms and policy activity promoting them can have counter-hegemonic impact. The viral effect of powerful pro-democracy ideas spreading from one neighbouring country to the next is a resource for democracy activists. Yet, OSF was only one among numerous other pro-democracy groups. Any influence it had was a tiny part of the wider movement. 'Open society' principles have had a mixed reception. National foundations have faced real difficulties in Belarus, Uzbekistan and Tajikistan due to the oppressiveness of the incumbent regimes towards most non-state actors. The advocacy of reform ideas or new policy approaches is not uncontested and, for many other reasons related to local context, often do not take root. Undiluted policy transfer is very rare; instead, long-term processes of policy *translation* usually take place.

Without question, the OSF operates as a norm broker for 'open society' values. These norms are embedded in the mission statement outlined earlier. The OSF is a generator and disseminator of ideas and people via network-wide initiatives. National foundations are more involved in implementation and can be seen as both 'norm brokers' within their local policy communities and exercising choice as 'norm takers' when they translate or modify policy ideas or practices from elsewhere (Acharya, 2004: 239–41). The adoption of the notion of translation is also important to contest, or at least qualify, the idea that OSF functions solely as a 'mirror network', that is, a foundation that is 'a mirror network reflecting the values, interests and discourses prevalent in the United States' (Scott-Smith and Baumgärtel, 2011: 280).

Central to its advocacy and norm brokerage has been OSF's structure as a network organisation. Due to the diversity of its operations, sometimes OSF acts like a TAN with its support for human rights bodies like Mental Disability Rights International and the Mental Disability Advocacy Centre (OSI, 2004). At other times, through different initiatives such as INET, the Foundation acts as a KNET. Some OSF projects or initiatives are more normative in character and typified by advocacy and mobilising opinion, such as its work on sex trafficking and human trafficking. In other instances, OSF initiatives are more technical, social scientific and expert driven. Occasionally, certain programme initiatives become bound into GPPNs (such as the Extractive Industries Transparency Initiative (EITI). In each case, these networks represent different kinds of issue-specific governance.

The 'soft' diffusion of ideas and information, people and expertise, has been aided by rapid advances in telecommunications and cheap travel. However, the translation of ideas and best practice into concrete policy programmes and tools is more variable and subject to setback. For all the policy analysis and expertise disseminated between the OSF head offices, the various national foundations and other partner organisations, only a few ideas capture the political imagination to structure official thinking and take shape in reform proposals and new institutions. Many more fall fallow. *Knowledge* transfer and norm advocacy may be more extensive and easier to execute than *policy* transfer and institutional adoption.

Ideas can have the power of persuasion. Even so, ideas need institutions and interests behind them. The non-governmental status of a philanthropic body is a major obstacle to policy transfer and translation. OSF is dependent on governments, international organisations and the local policy communities with which it interacts to see policy ideas accepted and instituted. Increasingly, foundations are often to be found in partnership or coalition with government departments and agencies, international organisations or with other NGOs to achieve their aims.

Foundations of open society

Compared to the 'Big 3', there is as yet little scholarly analysis of the OSF (but see Guilhot, 2007). By contrast, there is a considerable amount of journalistic material that focuses on George Soros as the billionaire hedge fund speculator. The focus is on the individual rather than the organisation. In similar fashion, more attention is devoted to Bill Gates the individual, rather than to the organisational operations of the Bill and Melinda Gates Foundation. The focus on Soros is however compounded by the founder, who regards himself as a public intellectual and is constantly publishing his books, lectures and opinions (Soros, 2011).

Studies that take the source of funding and the motivations of a living donor as the dominant forces guiding and directing the operations of the foundation can overstate the coherence and unity of purpose of an organisation. The reality is more complicated when delving into the organisational 'black box'. Not unlike other large organisations, foundations are subject to internal politicking, deviations from principles, poor implementation records and financial slippages that may or may not occur. Furthermore, other individuals and stakeholders shape OSF mission and operations, and their divergent interests and values further destabilise the idea of the networks functioning as a 'mirror' to US hegemony or 'a channel for extending US power and influence' (Scott-Smith and Baumgärtel, 2011: 280).

Nevertheless, the inspiration for OSF originated with George Soros whose own thinking was informed by the work of Karl Popper, especially *The Open Society and its Enemies* (1945). Popper argued that totalitarian ideologies have a common element: a claim to be in possession of the ultimate truth and which impose their version of truth on society. The 'open society' is an alternative that holds there is no monopoly on truth and that there is a need for institutions to protect human rights, freedom of speech and freedom of choice. In 1979 Soros established the Open Society Fund with the objective of 'opening up closed societies; making open societies more viable; and promoting a more critical mode of thinking' (Soros, 1997). Its initial activities were in the communist societies of CEE, funding scholarly and professional interchange and gradually extending to support the underground democratic movements.

The OSF is a complicated network structure. The OSF overlays and funds a series of *national* foundations created from 1984 onwards. National foundations have been created in over 30 countries. In addition, there are regional foundations, the Open Society Initiative for Southern Africa (OSISA) and the Open Society Initiative for West Africa (OSIWA) and an Open Society Eastern Africa. There is also a growing list of activity in Latin America as well as an Arab Regional Office. Over 30 years, Soros has contributed $8 billion to the network of OSF (Soros, 2011: 2). Annual operating expenditures are now close to $1 billion.

The Open Society Foundations New York office provides the organisation's other offices, affiliates and foundations with administrative, financial and technical support. It is also the main grant-giving centre. The office in Budapest has a large staff and also acts as the administrative and operational headquarters for a number of Open Society initiatives. The London office houses several OSF global initiatives as well as its international advocacy office. The Brussels office addresses European Union policies both inside and outside its borders. OSF-New York also administers many programmes that focus principally on the US.

Due to the strong ethos of localism during the nascence of OSF, as well as a principle of budget autonomy, 'the Soros national foundations are often perceived in their host countries as being organisations *of* those countries' rather than supplicants of OSF-New York or subject to the personal whims of Soros (Carothers, 1999: 273; Stubbs and Wedel, 2013). They operated autonomously with a local board of directors and considerable independence in determining how to translate the ideals of the open society into community initiatives and policy proposals. Since the turn of the century, there have been gradual pressures on the national foundations to become more self-reliant and less dependent on OSF funds. As the chapter is focused primarily on OSF initiatives that are transnational in design, the discussion here overlooks the very great diversity of local and national activities of OSF.

In September 2012, the OSF convened a 'jamboree' to reflect on the past two decades of activity under the leadership of Areyh Neier, a civil rights activist, and mark the changing of the guard with the incoming OSF President, Christopher Stone, a Harvard academic and lawyer. The network had grown large, extending to global reach. In this 'network of networks', as Soros described it, the many different sub-board members and advisors often do not know each other or what other parts of the network are doing. Nor, as he admits, does George Soros (2011). The meeting was a reflection of the need for better communication across the network and preparation for a future where funding would not increase. Instead, a process of de-leveraging some activities was envisioned whilst at the same time maintaining social and policy impact through stream-lined management, internal collaborations and finding other resources. Noted at the first plenary with Soros, a global board member said: 'We change hearts and minds, but results based management asks "how many hearts and which minds?" and that undermines the vibrancy of civil society'. Describing his own management style as 'chaotic' and based on 'trial and error' (Soros, 2011: 44), a recourse to the greater use of indicators and measurement tools signals a change in organisational methods in the network to make an untidy structure manageable (Soros, 2011: 44–46). Some fear these changes will sideline the creativity and local autonomy principles surrounding early practices.

Whilst any organisation develops its own culture, institutional memory and narrative of value and social utility, throughout the OSF network many of its staff and grantees have contributed to policy discourses to help construct the consensual knowledge that defines and establish the boundaries of transnational policy communities. From as early as 1997, the network actively sought to engage in donor partnerships. In the view of Soros, such partnerships are 'a logical interpretation of the idea that no one individual or organisation has a monopoly on the truth (and are) to our benefit to work with others and to learn from one another's perspectives, mistakes, and successes' (Foreword in Bassler and Wisse Smit, 1997). For instance, on the advocacy front, OSF was a donor to the Campaign to Ban Landmines. It has also partnered with 'global public policy networks' such as the Consultative Group to Assist the Poorest and the Global Fund to Fight AIDS, Tuberculosis and Malaria. With the United States Agency for International Development

(USAID), the OSF made in 1998 a ten-year commitment to the Baltic-American Partnership Fund. Among scientific communities, OSF has long supported research in the public health field such as the international knowledge network on extremely drug-resistant tuberculosis (XDR-TB).[5]

The OSF also enables OSF-funded experts to project their ideas into policy thinking across states and within issue-specific global or regional forums. For example, the Global Drug Policy Program, launched in 2008, aims to shift the policy paradigm away from the current punitive approach to international drug policy, to one which is rooted in public health and human rights. The program works with OSF initiatives such as the Central Eurasia Project, the Latin America Program and the International Harm Reduction Development Program as well as with regional, national and local partners. The Global Drug Policy Program also aims to broaden, diversify and consolidate the network of organisations actively challenging the current state of international drug policy to one in favour of 'harm reduction' and the improvement of community health and safety via the incorporation of scientific evidence into illicit drug policies. The program supports, and is part of, a wider international professional community behind the Vienna Declaration: A Global Call to Action for Science-Based Drug Policy.[6] This programme has the character of both a TAN and a knowledge network.

With organisational expertise derived mainly from the transition processes of Central and Eastern Europe and the former Soviet Union, a question arises as to whether the experiences and lessons learned can be transmitted into Central Asia, Latin America or Africa. Organisational dynamics can promote a tendency towards universalisation of standard operating procedures or 'one-size-fits-all'. To assume that a commonality in the Central and Eastern European experience (which already involves a homogenisation of the different country and local experiences) can lead to a policy belief in the replication of the donor experience in other jurisdictions is a considerable leap. Such thinking potentially undermines what was innovative and special in the encouragement of local knowledge and local ability via the national foundations during the 1990s and the light bureaucratic 'touch' of the network in its first two decades.

The bureaucratisation of OSF as a maturing organisation has further prompted a universalising dynamic that is in tension with the reflexive spirit favoured by George Soros. It presents a challenge for OSF management given their limited resources and where staff expertise is founded on post-communist transition experiences. The growing geographical spread of the foundations could prompt a default to second world lessons for third world contexts.

The encouragement of the national foundations to be more autonomous and independent brought a gradual transformation within the network. The sources of diversity and difference were increasingly filtered by the growing centralisation of power. OSF shifted from a 'bottom-up' capacity-building approach in local and national communities and headed in the direction of a 'top down' professionalised mode of policy interaction with decision makers and other elites. With consolidation of decision-making in New York among growing cohort of career officers, OSF matured more into the mode of a traditional foundation. This is a step change away from public action that is focused on capacity building at local and national levels (built in the historical context of post-communist transitions) to activity aimed on the one hand at transnational levels and on the other at higher-level policy processes. The centrifugal dynamic to New York has created a more hierarchical set of relationships among OSF constituent parts and with its grantee organisations.

It is quite a transformation from the original intentions of the founder. OSF was never meant to be a permanent project. As George Soros (2011: 41) states:

> When I established the Open Society Foundations, I did not want them to survive me. The fate of other institutions has taught me that they tend to stray very far from the founders' intentions. But as the Open Society Foundations took on a more substantial form, I changed my mind. I came to realize that terminating the foundations' network at the time of my death would be an act of excessive selfishness. A number of very capable people are devoting their lives to the work of the Open Society Foundations; I have no right to pull the rug out from under them.

Not only foundation staff but also grantees and partner organisations find additional reasons, and constituencies, in favour of OSF survival and expansion.

Importantly, the power of private philanthropy is substantially mediated by the strong institutions and the healthy and usually competitive political cultures of stable liberal or social democracies. Multiple actors and processes of translation also modulate impact. However, philanthropic interventions into transitional or fragile states can be more decisive, for good or for ill. Local interests may also have political reasons for exaggerating their influence by demonising foundations, NGOs and other, often 'western' agents as alien imports or foreign forces that are undermining national policy processes and traditions.

Likewise, in the weakly institutionalised global agora, where authority structures are still emerging, the initiatives of private philanthropy can have more forceful longer-term implications than would be the case in a national context where state institutions exercise stronger command and control. In the absence of strong and effective institutional architectures of global and regional policy making, the capacities and policy concerns of well-resourced philanthropies strongly motivated to create partnerships with other powerful actors are amplified and accredited in the governance voids.

Open society expertise

Throughout its existence, the OSF has been 'promoting policy research, evaluating policy options, initiating and disseminating best practices, and monitoring policies ...' (Krizsán and Zentai, 2005: 169–70). It does so via the individual expertise cultivated within initiatives as well as through a range of scholarships, fellowships and other grant giving. The OSF web-site was reconfigured in 2012 to provide a link to 'experts' available for the media and public commentary. The following discussion will focus on only two initiatives to promote expert analysis and advice: the Open Society Fellowship and the Think Tank Fund.

Established in 2008, the Open Society Fellowship in New York supports individuals pursuing innovative and unconventional approaches to open society challenges. Its launch saw the demise of an older International Policy Fellowship scheme managed from Budapest. The new scheme seeks 'idea entrepreneurs' who not only challenge conventional wisdom but who push the boundaries of current thinking and carry lessons that can be applied to a variety of settings.[7]

The transfer of 'lessons' about transnational policy issues were dominant among projects undertaken by the 2012 Fellows. An American think tanker, Thomas Feffer, interviewed leading thinkers, activists and writers in Eastern Europe to gauge lessons that may be applicable to other societies experiencing similar transformations. From the Brookings Institution, Vanda Felbab–Brown addressed the human security management issues associated with the drug trade, maritime piracy, the smuggling of gems, illicit logging and the illegal trade in wildlife. A journalist, Mark Gervisser, examined the reach and effect of the growing global campaign for the rights of gay, lesbian, bisexual, transgendered and intersexed people with a particular interest in mapping the global 'culture wars' that have emerged between those who argue for 'human rights' on the one hand and those who claim to defend 'traditional values' and 'cultural sovereignty' on the other. Gregg Gonsalves sought lessons how the HIV/AIDS scale-up can be applied to other global health challenges, such as mobilisations to fight drug-resistant tuberculosis and to protect maternal and child health. Ian Johnson, a Pulitzer Prize-winning journalist, studied the intersection of religion and civil society in contemporary revival among many faith-based groups. Another investigative journalist, Ken Silverstein, looked at hidden forms of corruption in the international energy business. Sarah Spencer investigated the provision of essential services to irregular migrants across Europe. Martina Vandenberg established The Human Trafficking Legal Resource Center, bringing together pro bono attorneys with human-trafficking survivors seeking legal assistance.

While all these projects were comparative or transnational in orientation, their impact on policy practice has been, to date, negligible. However, the objective of the fellowship programme is to 'enrich public understanding', which is not readily amenable to measure. The outputs of projects are broadcast both locally and internationally in the hope that the ideas may receive good· reception and publicity, and perhaps some policy traction. But this is done in a relatively undirected manner. The capacity of Fellows to 'stimulate far-reaching and probing conversations *within* the Open Society Foundations and in the world' is more open to assessment. For the OSF the value of the programme is that it is a means to bring in new talent and new ideas into the organisation, to inform OSF practices and programmes.

Established in 2007, the Think Tank Fund supports independent policy centres that strengthen democratic processes in their countries by identifying and analysing policy options, monitoring policy processes, consulting with the government and advocating their recommendations. Such policy centres also involve stakeholders outside of government circles in policy debates and make their findings widely available to the public. The Think Tank Fund (TTF) fosters institutions that carry out non-partisan policy-relevant research and promote inclusive policy change. TTF was founded on the view that a healthy policy process is one that is informed by evidence and open to wide participation. Consequently, a diverse think tank community is regarded as one safeguard against societal or political attempts to stifle dissent and assistance to them a mechanism to implement open society principles.

Establishing the TTF was the culmination of a variety of disparate initiatives brought under one envelope. Previously, the Local Government and Public Sector Initiative provided assistance to think tanks. Now disbanded, one of the programmes it funded was PASOS, a network of 40+ policy institutes from CEE and fSU. In large degree, PASOS was designed to promote policy transfer given its aim 'to ensure the lessons of transition are understood, shared, and applied'[8]. But the TTF has moved beyond these original OSF initiatives to fund a wider universe of think tanks, or aspirant think tank bodies that might be based in NGOs or certain universities in Europe and the South Caucasus. The secretariat have occasional informal liaison with the IDRC Think Tank Initiative.

The TTF has targeted both managerial capacity of the centres and their capacity to prepare better policy documents and advocacy (through training workshops and mentorship). The transfer undertaken is of Western standards of policy professionalism contextualised to local conditions with time spent coaching on matters such as grant writing or how to construct viable policy research projects as well as workshops on research communications and policy advocacy. More generally, the Fund has sought to integrate the activities of some grantee organisations with OSF anti-discrimination programmes and Roma initiatives.

The TTF is managed from Budapest and housed in the CEU complex. Its current director is a graduate of the Department of Public Policy. The Chair of the TTF, Thomas Carothers from the Carnegie Endowment, is adjunct faculty with new SPP at CEU. Another board member, the author, was the foundation professor establishing the public policy teaching programmes at CEU. Notwithstanding historical and individual ties between OSF and various parts of the CEU, in general the relationship between the two organisations has been marked by different trajectories. As is the case in many universities, disciplinary boundaries are firm: faculty stick to their departments and disciplinary interests and often disdain participation in OSF advocacy. However, the SPP may draw part of the university back into the constellation of OSF activity via adjunct teaching, internships and joint research projects.

The Foundation's image as a knowledge actor helps sustain its authority. Many of OSF board members have social status as leading experts, and many of OSF staff and consultants are regarded as reputable policy analysts. Attributed as public-spirited and with a steadfast commitment to independence, objectivity and scholarly enterprise bestows authority on OSF in a dynamic that also boosts the reputations of the individuals associated with it. These groups (and sometimes the media in its quest for expert commentary) legitimate OSF staff as 'serious' and 'expert' persons. To maintain their organisational reputation and repudiate accusations of politicisation, advocacy and lobbying, or ideological polemic, OSF has encouraged engagement with academic communities. In general, the links to various higher education institutions, think tanks and other expert bodies give the OSF some credence as a 'knowledge network'.

OSF in the global agora

At the end of last century, internal debates on globalisation heralded a change to OSF programmes. OSF leadership began to consider the social and political challenges faced by emerging democracies not only in a post-socialist but also in a global context (Palley, 2003; Krizsán and Zentai, 2005). This debate coincided with OSF concerns about the crisis of sustainability for many civil society organisations in CEE as donor attention shifted to Afghanistan and the Middle East (Koncz, 2006). Another reason George Soros was less inclined to close down OSF developed along with his personal interest in globalisation. In his view: 'Our global open society lacks the institutions and mechanisms necessary for its preservation, but there is no political will to bring them into existence' (Soros, 1997: 7). With the havoc wrought by the global financial crisis, this has become more rather than less of a concern.

Grant giving to transnational advocacy programmes is especially apparent in the fields of human rights and anti-corruption. In 2003, funding went to bodies such as Global Witness, the Data Foundation (for educating the US public about debt relief, aid and trade), the Altus Global Alliance, TIRI and long-standing partners such as Human Rights Watch and the International Crisis Group (OSI, 2004: 190). A decade later, funding continues to many of these bodies.

A further symptom of the 'global turn' is the degree of interaction and partnership between OSF and international organisations. These include the World Bank, the European Union and the Council of Europe as well as a range of other non-state international actors (OSI, 2006: 174). OSF had a memorandum of understanding with UNDP for a number of years. One important example of the Foundation's incorporation in transnational governance has been the long-standing record of work regarding Roma communities, support for the establishment of the European Roma Rights Centre and the regional Roma Participation Program. On the one hand, much work revolves around civil society monitoring, that surveys and data gathering simply to understand the dimensions of the situation faced by Roma and prevailing social attitudes on xenophobia and racism. On the other hand, there is direct engagement with policy institutions: In 2003, the World Bank initiated the 'Decade of Roma Inclusion: 2005–2015' in partnership with OSF. The two institutions subsequently brought to the partnership most regional governments as well as that of Finland and Sweden, the European Commission, UNDP and the Council of Europe (Krizsán and Zentai, 2005: 175–80). Even so, whilst there exists a transnational policy community concerned with the deterioration of literacy, employment and health levels among Roma communities, a change in social attitudes and policy practice within local communities and inside national administrations has been considerably slower.

The 'global turn' has many dimensions. It involves the internationalisation of civil society at national and sub-national levels through capacity building initiatives to educate local communities and policy actors into the impact of globalisation and regionalisation. OSF partners with international organisations and governments in arrangements that it has also identified as 'global public policy networks' (OSI, 2006: 174). The global turn is also apparent in the re-articulation of the network's driving principles for a 'global open society' where it regards itself exhibiting 'global leadership' in the OSF's promotion of freedom of information, advocacy of budget transparency and the effectiveness of international institutions 'all of which contribute to global governance on critical issues that must be addressed transnationally' (Aryeh Neier in OSI, 2009: 3). It takes specific shape in the support given to programmes like INET, amongst others.

Nevertheless, the global turn does not penetrate all OSF activity. Few of the national foundations work on regional issues, or on international organisations, or even on other countries. Instead they are focused on domestic policy issues. Although George Soros likes to speak of the global character of OSF as a 'network of networks', the 'global turn' is more pronounced in OSF initiatives directed from New York or Budapest and increasingly London and Brussels. Only the tip of the iceberg is global.

Related to the 'global turn' is its 'policy awakening'. As the Foundation network matured, it has advanced from a focus on capacity building to using built capacity to inform policy. The early work of national foundations and the initiatives was disposed towards human rights and civil liberties issues at local levels with grassroots associations and community groups. But the need for state engagement was recognised and increasingly incorporated into the design and implementation of some OSF programmes. Institution building and open society advocacy have not been supplanted. Civil society strengthening remains a core component of OSF. But as 'the collapse of a repressive regime does not automatically lead to the establishment of an open society' (Soros, 1997: 10–11), the absence of a blooming of a tolerant and diverse civil society, a stronger policy orientation took root in OSF. As stated about its anti-corruption work:

> After an initial period of largely focusing on awareness raising, recipient governments and donors must now concentrate on the crucial implementation stage. The commitment to fight corruption must go beyond the pledges on paper. It must be worked into the day-to-day practices of the state, in its interactions with citizens and business. (OSI, 2004: 139)

Also indicative of the policy awakening is not only the support given to TTF and the Open Society Fellowships but also the establishment of the Brussels Office in order to engage with the EU.

The policy orientation is succeeding the early strong base in civil society initiatives and capacity building. The shift imposes new or additional demands on programme staff as well as grantees. The shift also reflects the different skills and talents of new generations of Western trained policy entrepreneurs and opinion leaders making their mark in CEE, fSU and other parts of the world.

The OSF's structure as a network of national foundations overlaid with different programmes and initiatives creates an 'octopus' organisation with each tentacle representing different styles of advocacy, analysis, information-sharing and norm promotion. Taken as a unified whole, the OSF messily mixes activities with normative aspirations and advocacy alongside scientific pursuits and policy analysis. To this extent, more by accident than by design, the network is 'a mechanism of bridging knowledge production and policy ...' (Krizsán and Zentai, 2005: 169). In reality, the different programmes act quite independently. One consequence of the global spread of OSF offices is that staff or board members in one tentacle are unconnected to the other limbs.

While norm advocacy and knowledge generation does create some tension, there are also positive outcomes that consolidate the mission of the OSF. The network structure potentially facilitates the incorporation of local expertise into more traditional and elite research approaches. Different entities within the network can be engaged in different stages of the policy process from conceptualisation (such as is hoped with the link to SPP) through to policy advocacy, concrete action and programme monitoring (Krizsán and Zentai, 2005: 174, 182).

The OSF operates differently to the ODI discussed as a policy entrepreneur in the previous chapter. But by re-inventing itself from an open society norm broker in opposition to communism to become a body with stronger policy-analytic capabilities, OSF has also sought to bridge social science and praxis. OSF seeks to provide the normative principles, the governance approaches and the empirical lessons that become the prevailing views of those making policy in transition or developing countries, and in policies for communities at risk. OSF does not act alone in such intellectual action but in coalition with like-minded thinkers and activists in journalism, the professions and universities. For instance, through its funding of Caspian Revenue Watch, Global Witness and the Publish What You Pay coalition, the Foundation was an early player in starting development debates about the 'resource curse' and the role of resource wealth on state revenues in authoritarian, developing or corrupt states. Advocating mandatory disclosure of payments by resource extraction companies to governments, OSF and its NGO allies were central in getting the resource curse issue onto the international agenda, into public consciousness and providing a civil society momentum behind EITI. Even though EITI (one example of a GPPN) only promotes voluntary disclosure, it nevertheless represents a form of soft regulation.

Finally, its partnership activities and policy aspirations undermine popular understanding of philanthropic foundations located in a separate domain of civil society. Although OSF is a non-governmental public actor it is nonetheless part of a dynamic where 'philanthropists and philanthropic groups can become "mini-governments"' (Eikenberry, 2006: 589). Firstly, OSF is symptomatic of a 'governmental rationality where political power operates *through* rather than *on* civil society' (Sending and Neumann, 2010:131). In tandem with the financing and delivery of community services, education programmes and scholarships along with training and induction into Western policy norms and protocols, amongst many other programmes, OSF becomes the medium of governance. Secondly, OSF 'ends up "governing" other NGOs' (Stubbs, 2005: 81) through its grant mechanisms and auditing requirements. As the OSF consolidates as a traditional foundation rather than a grassroots capacity-building donor, combined with its 'global turn' in its 'policy awakening', OSF-New York, London and Budapest become more distant from local associations and closer to traditional governance institutions and transnational policy communities. The international processes of policy transfers help create transnational policy spaces even if ideas, tools and practices subsequently go through phases of translation and localisation. While OSF has origins as a grassroots civil society actor in the post-communist countries, it is maturing as an elite global policy organisation.

Conclusion

The source of OSF influence does not lie in numbers; it cannot seek electoral support, and it is not a social movement. Nor does it have the power and authority of public office. It is legally located in civil society. In terms of material power, OSF is puny compared to that of corporations and the economic clout of business, notwithstanding the billions dispensed by its founder. Instead, the sources of its power in policy lie in the appeal of its ideas, expertise and partners, that is, norms of the open society and human rights that are bolstered by knowledge creation via think tanks, university scholarships and grants, alongside policy fellowships.

While OSF operates from global civil society, the promotion of Western and 'open society' values and practices in international policy transfers dissolves the notion that it is in a hermetically sealed 'independent sector' separate from state or market. Rather than a simple blurring of boundaries between public and private, the OSF – and numerous other transnational actors – carve out new transnational spaces for public action. Instead of a simple co-option into governance, OSF also helps create transnational policy *spaces* via its own international network infrastructure, the policy transfers and translations it sponsors as well as through a kaleidoscope of international policy partnerships.

Within the global agora, OSF has been consolidating its own credibility and authority in part by creating its own audiences and reference points. Funding intellectuals, NGOs, the CEU and other academic centres helps build clientele relationships between these grantees and the Foundation, as well as with other foreign donors. This is not exceptional to OSF (Roelofs, 2003: 188). However, the extensive nature of OSF's more or less permanent as well as occasional partnerships undermines criticism that the network operates as a 'mirror' to US interests. OSF subsidises various experts and intellectuals to persuade professional or bureaucratic audiences of the superiority of OSF values and principles, and how to transform them into policy. Instead of the linear transmission of knowledge that puts OSF as a one-way conveyer belt of policy ideas, a recursive process is in operation. Just as is the case with ODI, the clients and constituencies of OSF are sources of its legitimacy. Another way in which the organisation normalises its legitimacy is also by transferring, and translating to the global agora, its own institutional logic in conjunction with the partnership principle. That is, the role of private philanthropic organisations – whether it be the OSF, the Aga Khan Foundation or CIGI – in global affairs is naturalised and promoted such as via the pronouncements from the Giving Pledge of billionaires and laudatory comments from world leaders. Likewise, the logic of global public policy networks and multi-stakeholder initiatives becomes embedded and accepted as an appropriate and effective mode of governance and regulation in the global agora.

6
Informal Diplomacy
of the ASEAN-ISIS Network

For several decades a number of Asian think tanks have had research programmes concerning economic affairs of the Asia Pacific and, later, security cooperation. Their role has been at the earlier stages of regional cooperative efforts, that is, agenda-setting. Rather than focusing on political and economic interests involved in the tangible features of building political institutions of regional cooperation, the focus of this chapter is on these earlier efforts of agenda-setting undertaken through research, advocacy and networking of the ASEAN-Institutes of Strategic and International Studies (ASEAN-ISIS) with political elites in the region. ASEAN-ISIS has played a proactive and sometimes influential role in regional debates on Asian economic integration and, more prominently, security cooperation.

'Informal diplomacy' is a mode of private networking and policy influence in the global agora. Such networking entails unofficial activities involving academics and intellectuals, journalists, business elites and others as well as government officials and political leaders 'acting in their private capacity' (Jones, 2008: 2). Think tanks and university institutes have often provided the 'neutral territory' outside the architecture of the state for the conduct of informal diplomacy. These processes are discussed in detail in the first section.

The second section outlines the formation of ASEAN-ISIS. The association is a mix of university research institutes, state-sponsored think tanks and (later in the genesis of the network) research units of foreign affairs ministries. These think tanks and their directors sought to promote social learning and help create a sense of regional identity at an elite level amongst nascent regional policy communities. This contribution to regional cooperation was through a 'repeated cycle of interaction, interpretation and internalisation' (Johnstone, 2005: 189) conducted via intensive networking and informal diplomacy.

The third section assesses the agenda-setting activities in the 'habit of dialogue' among the ASEAN-ISIS 'interpretative community' (Johnstone, 2005). Through long-standing interaction at conferences or workshops, the shared experiences among individuals have forged strong links between institutes. The decade of policy-related research conducted by think tanks for ASEAN and home governments, combined with their policy entrepreneurship, contributed to political understanding about the possible benefits of cooperation. Ideas and interpretations of 'region' and their debates on policy practices of economic and security cooperation both preceded and accompanied political attempts by governments to create regional institutions. ASEAN-ISIS deliberations contributed to what has come to be known as the 'ASEAN Way' of soft regionalism discussed in the fourth section.

As has been the case with previous chapters, the concern here is to address the *mechanisms and agents* through which the diffusion and adoption of ideas, in this instance about regional cooperation, occurs. Similar to previous chapters, it introduces an additional policy concept, that of informal diplomacy to embed the discussion. Through the policy process of 'informal diplomacy', ideational policy entrepreneurs had access to government, business and other political elites and their decision-making forums (Rouhana, 1995). As an interpretative community, ASEAN-ISIS was an innovation in the Southeast Asian region as a network, but also spurred new institutions of regional governance. Collectively, the Southeast Asian think tanks created a transnational network to sustain a space for governance discussions on regional cooperation. Thus, the network and its component organisations created, synthesised, legitimated and disseminated expert knowledge on 'region' and played a significant role in the emerging regional governance system.

In its role as a venue for informal diplomacy, the picture of ASEAN-ISIS as a non-state actor becomes complicated. Informal diplomacy is undertaken for public purposes, and is usually sanctioned by foreign policy elites, some of whom take part in these off-the-record discussions. Even though ASEAN-ISIS was created as an NGO, its practice of informal diplomacy rests on unclear distinctions between 'public' and 'private' as well as a false division between knowledge and power. The research and analysis emanating from the interpretative community was not 'independent' or 'autonomous' or created in a domain separate from policy and politics that is only utilised when contracted or called upon by government actors. Instead, the ASEAN-ISIS network became deeply deposited in policy making as an important cog in the nascence of regional governance. Rather than a mere resource for other interests, knowledge actors and knowledge discourses are a form of power essential to the construction of region. These processes of region-building are not in contest with the idea of a global agora. Instead, regional discussions driven by informal diplomacy, or by other processes, can be considered to be one space of Assembly in the agora. The participating institutes and individuals can be viewed as 'wholly active citizens' taking initiative to generate frameworks and legitimating discourses for regional coopera-tion on specific policy concerns.

Informal diplomacy

Informal diplomacy is not state-centric and incorporates a more diverse range of actors than bureaucrats and politicians in international nego-tiations. Track One (T1) diplomacy are diplomatic efforts of bureaucrats to resolve conflicts through official channels of government (Kaye, 2007: 5). However, official diplomats in Track One increasingly share the world stage with and make use of the growing cast of non-state actors; what has become known as Track Two (T2) is an arena for non-governmental public action. T2 is symptomatic of the breakdown of traditional distinctions between foreign policy making and domestic policies (mirrored in the academic fields of international relations and public policy, respectively). Track Three (T3) diplomacy occurs among civil society groups.

To complicate matters, the notion of Track One-and-a-Half (T1½) is also used to describe something between an autonomous T2 and official diplomacy (see Nan, Druckman and El Hor, 2009). The ideas of T1, T1½, T2 and T3 may be thought of as points on spectrum from state-exclusive and often secret processes at one end to non-state public processes at the other. Hence the preference in this paper for the term 'informal diplomacy' given that T2 can morph into T1½ over time (Capie and Taylor, 2010: 365–67) and terminological nuances in different political cultures (Job, 2003: 250; Rouhana, 1995). T1½, and on occasion, T2 can also be thought of as transnational executive networking.

T2 diplomacy entails 'unofficial dialogues often facilitated by an impartial Third Party and involving individuals with some connections to their respective official communities, focused on co-operative efforts to explore new ways to resolve differences over, or discuss new approaches to, policy-relevant issues' (Jones, 2008: 4). It is conducted through closed dialogues 'either because of government uncertainty on how to proceed with sensitive discussions, or because of a lack of professional expertise'

(Kim, 2001: 38). It can include academics and intellectuals, journalists, business elites and others as well as government officials 'acting in their private capacity' (Ball, Milner and Taylor, 2006: 175). This diplomacy usually takes place in an 'off-the-record' setting. That bureaucrats and politicians are acting in their private capacity is to be treated as a 'polite fiction'. Official and non-governmental participation in seminars, conferences and organisations is 'mixed' or 'blended', suggesting that the demarcation between official and unofficial involvement is unclear (Kraft, 2002). Some processes can be secretive such as the Oslo Process in the Israeli-Palestinian conflict (Chataway, 1998; Fisher, 2006). In the ASEAN-ISIS case discussed here, T2 was a more public albeit quite an exclusive process.

Whilst Track Two incorporates figures from civil society, it is distinct given the direct ties to, and sometimes long-term involvement of, government officials and politicians in network building and their patronage of institutes and or input into developing research agendas. T2 diplomacy is semi-official, a hybrid form of diplomacy that uses interlocutors to mediate between state actors. This occurs in situations where governments wish to express intentions or to suggest methods of resolving a diplomatic situation, but do not wish to express a formal position. In reverse, informal diplomacy also provides windows of opportunity for non-state actors or policy entrepreneurs from the interpretive community to independently influence government by providing analysis or evaluations (Chataway, 1998: 275; Lee, 2009).

Publically regarded as independent organisations, think tanks can create neutral territory in the form of private dialogues where all parties to a common concern or conflict can meet to discuss possibilities for resolution. In a facilitating role, they act as the 'honest broker', inviting all interested parties to sit down behind closed doors to address a particular problem or proposal. They provide 'a middle ground' where new forms of cooperation or controversial approaches to regional conflicts can be explored without fear of public exposure. Such an activity is useful to governments if the think tank is a prominent organisation of which foreigners leaders have heard, and more importantly, if it can draw together a network of distinguished states-people, business leaders, diplomats, military officers, experts and scholars.

Informal dialogues are also valuable at times when for whatever reason, official dialogues are stalled or official relations strained (Chataway, 1998: 273). On the negative side, governments can use the Track Two process and think tanks for the purposes of public symbolism. Non-officials are given the impression that their advice and analysis is useful although this could be illusory. As noted by a senior participant in T2 dialogues:

> ... Track 2 specialists, unencumbered by governance responsibilities, can gaze into the future, anticipating issues that could become international problems and thus devise coping strategies. However, outside experts may also be co-opted by governments to justify policy positions taken by states prior to Track 2 investigations. In such cases, Track 2 activities may be used to lend prestige to official decisions reached independently of outside expert inputs. (Simon, 2010: 78)

At issue is whether T2 experts are simply used as puppets by governments or if they became part of agenda-setting and decision-making processes.

In mainstream IR, sceptical assessments prevail among policy practitioners who see few if any concrete results from such unofficial endeavours (Jones, 2008: 2; Kaye, 2007: 3). Realists in international relations scholarship have a tendency to see dialogues and multilateral discussions as little more than 'talking shops'. That is, the various policy dialogues may offer little more than an amenable social and intellectual exercise for participants. However, other realists would argue that their key concerns about 'balance of power' continue to permeate T2 dialogues (Rüland, 2002: 93; Lee, 2009).

> The 'realist' school tends to favour explanations of international affairs which stress interest based bargaining, the competition for power between states and zero-sum games. Social-psychological and constructivist theories tend to stress interpersonal relations, community building and the development of norms. While neither realism nor constructivism is so definitive as presented here, most Track Two is more comfortable in the latter tradition. (Jones, 2008: 11)

The interpretive community framework adopted here goes one step further than constructivism to argue that policy is dependent on, and framed by, knowledge and ideational forces. In this perspective '... it is a mistake to believe that T2 diplomacy is merely dialogue for dialogue's sake ... (for) it creates a positive atmosphere that is conducive to the formation of regional identity' (Kim, 2001: 4). With the emphasis on consensus building, the filtering and re-assemblage of ideas and the socialisation of elites, the focus is more on discourse and interpretation by the institutes of ideas about regional cooperation. That is, the routes and processes through which vague and general concepts are transformed into policy practices and political objectives (Schmidt, 2008). Notwithstanding theoretical debates about the impact (or not) of T2 processes in general, or the ASEAN-ISIS network in particular, the pace of informal dialogues accelerated and diversified in Southeast Asia from the 1990s, and continue to attract both official sponsorship and unofficial patronage from governments in the region and beyond.

The formal network structure of ASEAN-ISIS and the informal diplomacy processes it cultivated were the mechanisms by which new ideas were created, moulded, elaborated, disseminated, expounded and adjusted to practical realities. The ideas were picked up due to changing geo-political realities in the region in the post-Cold War era. The interpretive community gestated within ASEAN-ISIS built trust and understanding among Southeast Asia's policy communities. The network was a vehicle for policy learning. It was not sufficient for 'vague' ideas or policy research on security cooperation to be 'diffused' through traditional processes of academic publication or public speaking for such ideas to find their way into policy discussion by serendipity. There is no automatic process that new policy ideas will seep into the consciousness of political and policy elites. Instead, it is necessary to focus on the discursive constructions and agency of policy entrepreneurs, their research institutes and their networks in the shaping of policy agendas.

Southeast Asian policy institutes

Most prominent Southeast Asian think tanks are different to their 'nongovernmental' and 'intellectually autonomous' Western counterparts. The institutes discussed in this chapter have both formal and informal ties to national political elites and the state apparatus (Nesadurai, 2011). 'State and non-state actors in ASEAN have proceeded in a very complex environment that displays authoritarian and democratic features simultaneously, a high degree of power monopoly on the part of a small circle of elites consolidated by the infrastructure of an interventionist state' (Manea, 2009: 37). In some instances, the ASEAN institutes may be better described as GONGOs – governmentally organised NGOs – or even labelled as MANGOs – manipulated NGOs. Even so, long-term dynamics towards democratisation in Southeast Asia, the maturing of higher education systems alongside 'knowledge for development' capacity building can alter over time whether or not institutes are classed as MANGOs.

When ASEAN-ISIS was rising to prominence in the 1990s, Asian think tanks were considered by many Western observers to have an unhealthily close relationship with government. Some critics claimed that these bodies were 'state-directed' (Jayasuriya, 1994). Their importance to the state was in their capacity to amplify messages that come from the top down to the rest of society. Consequently, Asian think tanks tended to be 'regime enhancing' rather than 'regime critical' (Yamamoto and Hubbard, 1995: 45). This also applied to regional institutional initiatives as think tanks began to engage in policy dialogues across borders. Thus while depicting their dialogues as T2, in reality the close political connections of think tank directors of that time suggested their activities were rather more T1½.

The launch of ASEAN in 1967 and its slow institutional consolidation over the 1970s and 1980s gradually generated a regional source of demand for policy analysis. The ASEAN secretariat had lacked sufficient strength and staff to conduct policy research and sophisticated advisory functions. There had been a policy analysis vacuum in the formal structures of regional governance. This lacuna provided a window of opportunity for think tanks and university institutes in Southeast Asia to provide research and analysis on security and economic cooperation via ASEAN-ISIS. This does not mean that T2 displaces T1. However, ASEAN was reliant on the Institutes (and other actors) to provide the convening, the conference organisation, the dialogue vehicles and other activities that allowed a 'habit of dialogue' to become a reality and on-going practice in the growth of the regional policy community.

The ASEAN-ISIS was launched as a formal association in 1988 (although there were informal meetings in years earlier). It was founded by think tanks in four of the core ASEAN countries:

• Centre for Strategic and International Studies – CSIS Indonesia
• Institute for Strategic and International Studies – ISIS Malaysia
• Singapore Institute for International Affairs – SIIA
• Institute for Security and International Studies – ISIS Thailand
• Plus an individual, Professor Carolina Hernandez, and subsequently, Institute for Strategic and Development Studies – ISDS in the Philippines from 1991

The ASEAN-ISIS network is legally designated as an NGO. At the domestic level, however, most institutes are linked to the state via funding relationships or legal location within the bureaucratic apparatus. For instance, ISIS Malaysia directors often acted as speech writers for their Prime Minister. Such formal and informal links have made informal diplomacy a very effective mode of policy influence. Nevertheless, these institutes are both policy institutes and scholarly bodies, although the balance differs from one nation to the next. ISIS Thailand was originally founded in 1981 as part of Chulalongkorn University before it acquired independent status. Likewise ISDS was founded by scholars from the University of the Philippines.

The objectives of ASEAN-ISIS are research oriented, as would be expected from think tanks and university institutes. ASEAN-ISIS seeks to:

- strengthen and increase regional cooperation in the development of research,
- increase the effectiveness and efficiency of research by intensified communication and coordination,
- contribute to ASEAN cooperation by promoting public knowledge and understanding of problems and issues faced by the ASEAN communities.

At face value, these three concerns do not signal an explicit policy orientation.

Complementing these objectives, ASEAN-ISIS has three flagship activities of which the first has been most significant in policy impact:

1. Asia Pacific Roundtable (APR) for Confidence Building and Conflict Resolution from 1987;
2. ASEAN-ISIS Colloquium on Human Rights since 1994;
3. ASEAN People's Assembly in 2000.

The APR is its oldest activity and most closely associated with T2 diplomacy (Soesastro, Joewono and Hernandez, 2006: 2). Indeed, it has been described as the 'grand-daddy' of all T2 in the region (Butcher, 2009). Hosted by ISIS Malaysia, APR has 'the consistent and unwavering patronage of successive Prime Ministers, Deputy Prime Ministers and Foreign Ministers of Malaysia ... (who) have delivered the bulk of the keynote addresses at the APR since its inception'.[1] The other two activities emerged later, but these activities engage with civil society to a greater degree. Unlike APR, the People's Assembly as a T3 venture did not gain traction with official ASEAN.

With the widening of ASEAN to the new member countries of Vietnam, Cambodia and Brunei, newly created government institutes were brought into the fold:

- Institute for International Relations in Hanoi
- Cambodian Institute for Cooperation and Peace

- Brunei Darussalam Institute of Policy and Strategic Studies
- Institute of Foreign Affairs, Laos

Growing recognition of ASEAN-ISIS as a space and place for policy dialogue had the effect of prompting institutional development at the national level in those countries where think tank development was not known. There was a 'boomerang effect' of regional dialogue and networking, which spurred national-level institutional development. The new national institutions could then participate in the regional debates on economic integration and security cooperation. That is, a replication process took place that not only helped to consolidate the network structure but which was also paralleling the composition of the formal inter-governmental ASEAN organisation.

A 'relentless conversation' about region

A shared idea of regional identity is a necessary but not sufficient condition for the states of the region to establish a framework for political and economic cooperation or harmonisation of policies. States also depend on each other, in part, for the creation of these interpretations, and furthermore, the strategic interaction of states further contributes to shared understandings (Wendt, 1994). Political leaders of Asian countries have often talked of 'Asian values' in their regional security community or economic dialogues. In constructivist thinking, 'states are engaging in discursive practices designed to express and/or to change ideas about who "the self" of self-interested collective action is' (Wendt, 1994: 391).

Engaging in cooperative acts can become a self-reinforcing dynamic that allows actors to reassess core beliefs and come to new understandings. By teaching themselves and others to cooperate, they effectively create new identities. Part of the learning and interactive process occurs through the strategic narrative practices designed to persuade others to change conceptions of their interests. The greater the degree of conflict in the international system, the more likely states will fear each other and defend their 'egoistic identities' (Wendt, 1994). By contrast, where there are positive shared understandings and mutual recognition of sovereignty among states, there is potential for collective identity formation. States are also more likely to identify their interests with others, when they share a common fate and cannot act unilaterally to undo that fate. Aspects of egoistic identities increasingly become redundant provided states do not respond defensively to their vulnerability. The discourses of cooperation can aid collective action by helping create a sense of solidarity. The discourse of ASEAN-ISIS became an elite system of meaning for the policy community that ordered the production of interpretations of the social world in the context of the post-Cold War security vacuum in the region. A major concern 'was the need to prepare ASEAN to anticipate impending changes in the regional and global order' (Sukma, 2006: 91). ASEAN-ISIS ideas and interests transcended the nation-state.

'Interpretive communities' are not neatly defined. Instead, there are overlapping communities; those involved in the economic cooperation movement in East Asia (Nesadurai, 2011) also sometimes feature in ASEAN-ISIS debates on security or human rights. In the words of one Japanese think tank director, these communities develop regional networks, 'thus providing encouraging opportunities of establishing regional institutional linkages and facilitating individual networks and collaborative relationships, a prerequisite ... of community building in Asia Pacific' (Yamamoto and Hubbard, 1995: 3). At issue is whether the actors within the ASEAN-ISIS network were acting solely in the interests of their states with their research and advocacy of Asian cooperation, or whether the ASEAN-ISIS affiliates developed their own *raison d'etre* as an interpretive community.

An interpretive community rests upon 'professional interpreters' who, as outlined in Chapter 2, create 'texts'. In the case here, think tank directors, research fellows, university scholars and others operating in ASEAN-ISIS formed an interpretive community (or what might also be called a 'discourse coalition'). Many strategic studies scholars have frequently referred to Southeast Asia's T2 dialogue groups as 'epistemic communities' (Acharya, 2004; Kim, 2001; Rüland, 2002; Simon, 2010). While the experts associated with ASEAN-ISIS often shared normative or principled understandings concerning the benefits of regional cooperation, they were not bound together by common notions of validity based on inter-subjective, internally defined criteria for validating knowledge, and they lacked shared causal beliefs. The experts from the ISIS institutes are better thought of as an interpretative community.

The texts of ASEAN-ISIS are the web-sites, meetings, publications and policy commentary (briefs, speech writing, etc.) produced by the interpreters. The situations and 'field of practice' are constituted through T1, T1½ and T2 networks where think tanks articulated new meanings of region in a situation of state preferences for sovereign decision-making.

Asian think tanks in general (not only ASEAN-ISIS) played a catalytic role in region building because they represented an intersection for the movement of opinion formers and decision makers, that is, a cross-road for policy entrepreneurs. This network and others provided forums where new social realities were constructed, debated and interpreted as individuals came into contact and interacted. Over time and through multiple discourses and venues, the concepts of region become an organising logic or coordinative paradigm. Expert discourses, such as the 'ASEAN Way', become a structuring force.

Rather than seeking legalistic and formal institutions (such as characterised in the development of EU), Asian economic and security cooperation is of a more informal, unstructured and consensual character. It 'has been called the "ASEAN Way" (and) was presented by some Asian leaders as a culturally-rooted notion, focusing on organisational minimalism, avoidance of legalism, and an emphasis on consultations and consensus decision-making' (Acharya and Johnstone, 2007: 34). The non-governmental T2 dialogue activities of think tanks are not simply a manifestation of the style of Asian cooperation. From a discourse institutionalism perspective they are constitutive of regional cooperation, that is, 'a *relentless conversation* of ASEAN that may have been the essential ingredient in creating ... meaningful entities ...' (Milner, 2007: 579, my italics). The 'relentless conversation' was essential to interpreting and normalising new ideas about cooperation.

By no means is this a smooth linear process. Official reception of new ideas is not automatic and 'government officials are often sceptical or even disdainful of Track 2, which they often see as full of "wannabes" or "hasbeens" seeking to play intergovernmental roles themselves and dispensing unsolicited advice' (Morrison, 2004: 550). The identity-building dialogues, Roundtables and regional workshops were easily unsettled. The 1997-98 Asian financial crisis saw funds dry up for regional activities when states reverted to their focus on national interests of economic recovery (Ball, Milner and Taylor, 2006: 176). Egoistic identities re-asserted. Weathering the current global financial crisis better, and propelled over the past decade by a range of non-traditional security threats, ASEAN-ISIS adopted new research agendas for regional cooperation and coordination. Research programmes were initiated in areas such as piracy and the maritime commons, contagious disease (especially in the context of SARS and Avian flu) and environmental crime.

As 'wholly active citizens', ASEAN-ISIS institutes performed three important tasks. Firstly, they acted as *innovators* by providing new policy ideas about economic or security cooperation at the regional level. Secondly, they *broadcast* these ideas and their policy recommendations and started the ball rolling for a 'habit of dialogue' (Sukma, 2006: 89). Thirdly, through their *networking*, joint research and other collaborative ventures intra-regionally, and for some through their involvement in the political processes of their home states, the institutes helped shape the political choices made by state elites.

To date, most analysis on Asian regionalism has concentrated on the more tangible institution-building exercises and disputes of business and government actors concerning Asia Pacific Economic Cooperation (APEC) with the research community tending to be portrayed as playing a subsidiary analytical service role. This is not unusual. As think tanks are considered to be independent NGOs (erroneously in this case) operating at the margins of politics with only the powers of persuasion at their disposal, they have not been accorded significant influence in policy making (but see Acharya, 2011; Nesadurai, 2011). Another reason why non-state public action is lost from sight is that it operates primarily at a discursive level. This is labelled by regional players as the 'habit of dialogue'. The phrase pertains to the meetings and dialogues, the workshop reports and conference proceedings as well as the countless informal discussions and web-site postings that are all part of the 'relentless conversation', that is, modalities of Assembly in the agora. This long-term 'conversation' is process-related activity. As such, it is relatively ephemeral and less concrete than tangible new institutions created by governments such as the ASEAN Regional Forum (ARF).

Generally, multilateral security institutions have been slow to emerge in the Asia Pacific. The Cold War in Asia was conducted through a set of bilateral relationships with a resulting absence of European-style alliances. The end of the Cold War and the rapid decay of the former communist regimes provided a window of opportunity for new thinking in security cooperation. The formation of the ARF,[2] the Asia Pacific region's first attempt at multilateral security cooperation, illustrates this clearly, with scholars explaining its formation as the outcome of both strategic power shifts and leadership provided by middle powers, in this case by ASEAN (Acharya, 2004).

The ARF operates on the basis of cooperative security rather than common security. Unlike common security approaches, cooperative security is less fixated on the rapid development of formal multilateral institutions, preferring the establishment of habits of dialogue. The ARF replaced the Cold War security structure (which was based primarily on bipolar power-balancing and bilateral alliances) with a multilateral diplomatic approach that emphasises consultation, inclusiveness and engaging 'adversaries'. The latter has been termed 'soft regionalism' or 'soft dialogue' as opposed to the 'hard dialogue' associated with formal institutions (Acharya, 2004).

While these dialogues have been strongly influenced by European ideas, the evolving discourse necessarily has a distinctly Asian flavour and regionally specific institutional 'field of practice'. For instance, the main elements of a cooperative security discourse include emphasising political dialogue at both the governmental and non-governmental levels, a non-confrontational approach to dispute settlement, establishing comfort levels, frequent consultations and consensual decision-making. In short, ideas about common and cooperative security have been translated or interpreted and then adjusted, modified and adapted in unique ways (Kjaer and Pedersen, 2001: 221) to the particular regional and historical context of East Asia. That is, 'the ASEAN Way' and a home-grown Asian strategic culture.

T2 processes, especially through ASEAN-ISIS, have been crucial to the leadership role played by ASEAN in establishing the ARF. This was significant as ASEAN had generally been averse to multilateral security cooperation in the past. Discursive institutionalism offers insights into *why* political institutions change by zooming in not only on sentient agents' cognitive and normative ideas about what they were doing and why at different levels of generality – policy (in this case, security cooperation), programme (the ARF) and philosophy (ASEAN Way) – but also on their discursive interactions regarding who spoke to whom, where, when and why in the process of generating those ideas in a 'coordinative discourse' of policy construction (Schmidt, 2008). ASEAN-ISIS also generated a venue for 'communicative' discourse of public deliberation and their conferences, analysis and publications provided one source of legitimisation for subsequent policy positions. However, this communicative discourse was pertinent only to the 'wholly active' and 'standing members' of regional and international policy forums. The citizenry of most Asian countries have been mostly passive or disinterested in regional initiatives and unaware of the activities of the institutes of ASEAN-ISIS.

This process of opinion formation and consensus building over decades is another reason why the impact of unofficial actors can be underestimated. Many of the initiatives and policy proposals of the ASEAN-ISIS for security cooperation have touched on areas where ASEAN governments were known to have serious reservations; for example, ideas to convene a multilateral security dialogue go to the core of sovereign insecurities. According to one Singaporean insider to ASEAN-ISIS: 'It is an on-going process ... rather than episodic undertaking ... a process that shadows the official inter-governmental, state processes' (Tay, 2006: 129). This 'shadow' process is masked from public scrutiny where its relevance and influence is caught in the multiplicity of conversations, briefings and professional relationships built through successive meetings.

Indeed, T1 to T2 dialogues and research activities throughout Asia have proliferated so extensively that the Japan Centre for International Exchange (another government-supported think tank) maintained the *Dialogue and Research Monitor* to map the web of meetings and dialogues. The web-site provided an inventory of trends in research dialogues concerning East Asia, and it lists major multilateral governmental and non-governmental meetings and significant studies. In 2007, marking the 40th anniversary of ASEAN, the adoption of the ASEAN Charter, and the 10th anniversary of the Asian financial crisis, there were 278 Track One and 284 Track Two dialogues.[3]

The interpretive community has many institutional bases, and it evolves over time. Yet, in terms of setting the agenda towards economic and security cooperation in the 1990s, this community consolidated in regional non-governmental organisations. This is not to suggest an uncontested or consensual pattern of research or debate within interpretive communities. Significant divisions among scholars, institutions and nations exist. These differences are readily found in the literature, and further undermine notions of epistemic coherence among researchers. Even so, the close personal ties and friendships between the directors and senior fellows of the ASEAN-ISIS institutes, particularly in its earlier days, was quite remarkable. The social capital that they built has been recounted by a number of 'insiders' in a book on *Twenty Two Years of ASEAN ISIS* (Soesastro, Joewono and Hernandez, 2006) with retrospectives from self-dubbed 'ASEAN thinkers' and 'true believers in ASEAN'. They saw each other regularly at the annual APR and in between at issue-specific meetings and workshops. It was a tight and very sociable community. Today, they are concerned about generational renewal and the need to bring younger scholars into ASEAN-ISIS leadership positions (Butcher, 2009; Sukma, 2006: 95).

Notwithstanding on-going scholarly debates and intellectual divisions, the body of policy-related research built by the institutes, combined with their policy entrepreneurship via the ASEAN-ISIS network, contributed to wider political understanding about the possible benefits of regional cooperation. Their discursive practices have helped create new regional modes of governance via informal diplomacy as well as opening transnational spaces for policy making by making discursive and social sense of that space.

The 'ASEAN Way' of the intellectuals

ASEAN-ISIS is registered with the ASEAN Secretariat as an ASEAN NGO. Its Charter mandates that only research institutes based in ASEAN member countries may join ASEAN-ISIS. However, ASEAN-ISIS also maintains extensive regional and international networks of institutional linkages with leading think tanks outside ASEAN. Although ASEAN-ISIS is non-governmental, as noted above its non-governmental status is questionable. But is it a MANGO? As indicated in this quote from Paul Evans, a long standing Canadian participant-observer in ASEAS-ISIS events and expert on Asian security, the distinctions between official and unofficial are very cloudy.

> In structural terms, while it has been an avowed leader of non-governmental or unofficial initiatives, the dividing line between non-governmental and governmental is thin to non-existent in several of the participating institutes. Some institutes are based within governmental ministries and led by government officials. For example, the Institute of International Relations in Hanoi is part of the Vietnamese Ministry of Foreign Affairs. The same is the case in Laos. The management and staff at ISIS Malaysia are government employees and the government provides the lion's share of the Institute's funding. At the other end of the spectrum, ISDS in the Philippines has a loose connection to the University of the Philippines but is independent from government and the university in funding, personnel and operations. The Singapore Institute of International Affairs is a self-standing and self-financing organisation, though does receive government funding. CSIS in Jakarta has evolved from having a close relationship to government to being an autonomous institution in the past decade. (Evans, 2006 99–100)

The demarcating line between unofficial T2 and official T1 diplomacy is blurred to such an extent that it often becomes indistinguishable (Ball, Milner and Taylor, 2006: 184). The grey areas in the status of ASEAN-ISIS as part public, part private is very convenient for all parties to informal diplomacy. The distinctions between T1, T2 and increasingly T3 are more than simply symbolic and have functional value in agenda-setting processes. 'This "disclaimer" erects a mythical separation of private and public diplomacy and allows sensitive issues to be discussed without the burden of official accountability' (Kim, 2001: 2).

Within the tense security environs of the early 1990s, ASEAN-ISIS was able to emphasise its non-governmental status – neutral territory at the regional level – in promoting sensitive ideas and policy recommendations on security cooperation. At the same time, the (semi-)official status of key members attending T2 activities and dialogues meant that state interests were protected and pursued in a safe setting. In reality, the public and the private were very blurred, deliberately so. Through the symbolic distinctions of T1 and T2, the 'mythical separation' of official and informal diplomacy has practical advantages in creating forums for discussion of threat perceptions and other delicate issues in low-risk settings.

Influence has been a gradual process. And it has not been a constant one. The first steps towards substantive engagement with ASEAN came in 1991. The ASEAN Institutes meeting of that year in Jakarta produced a memorandum – *A Time for Initiative*. It was not only timely in its recommendations but captured the imagination of not only ASEAN Governments but also ASEAN Dialogue partners like Japan, Australia and Canada that were also interested in establishing an arrangement for the Asia-Pacific like the Commission on Security and Cooperation in Europe. As a sources of inspiration, however, it was a CSCE-like 'tool kit minus the normative substance' concerning democracy and human rights as it would have directly confronted the ASEAN principle of non-interference in domestic affairs (Rüland, 2002: 89; Manea, 2009).

ASEAN-ISIS ideas were submitted to the Fourth ASEAN Summit in Singapore in 1992 as well as in a series of constructive proposals to ASEAN governments to initiate an official dialogue process at the end of each ASEAN-PMC (Post Ministerial Conference). The official ASEAN response was cautious but not dismissive since ASEAN Foreign Ministers agreed to study the idea further. ASEAN-ISIS was attempting to establish a new regional agenda and 'was somewhat ahead of the official position' (Kerr, 1994: 403). It was not until two years later after the ASEAN Ministerial Meeting that the ASEAN Regional Forum was formally established.

The ARF's creation in September 1993 was greatly influenced by a climate of opinion generated through T2 activities. Indeed, the ASEAN Foreign Ministers acknowledged the role played by non-governmental bodies in the genesis of ARF and, in particular, commended ASEAN-ISIS for exploring and promoting the ideas that enhanced security cooperation (Kerr, 1994: 397). The ASEAN Secretariat states on its web-site: 'Efforts of the Governments to foster an enduring regional order, stability and prosperity are supplemented by various non governmental institutions on the non-official track. (...) ASEAN has found useful several studies and proposals put forward by the various institutions represented in the ASEAN- ISIS'[4].

ASEAN-ISIS built a set of multilateral processes through which new thinking in security cooperation could be informally and openly discussed before these ideas were taken up at the official level. While these new ideas have been strongly influenced by European ideas of 'common security', 'cooperative' and 'comprehensive security', 'confidence building measures' and 'transparency', the evolving discourse has a distinct regional or Asian character. This enabled these new ideas to be accepted at the official level by ASEAN states.

As ASEAN political leaders usually only meet where there is an official summit, such informal dialogues are all the more important. The ASEAN Regional Forum meets only once every summer for a day. National leaders do not have time to become acquainted with the intricacies of issues or have the luxury to appreciate the reasons for different perceptions. Consequently, the T2 community becomes an important vehicle for building constructive relationships at a lower bureaucratic level. As ASEAN-ISIS evolved, it also moved in different directions. T2 widened beyond the Southeast Asian nations to embrace a broader concept of region than that composed of the ASEAN states.

A wider T2 process

The Council for Security Cooperation in the Asia Pacific (CSCAP) is another T2 initiative. Established in 1993, it also complements the governmental (T1) mechanisms for developing security cooperation. It is a more diverse grouping than ASEAN-ISIS on two fronts: first, it is of wider national reach and, second, CSCAP convenors are university, think tank and governmental organisations[5] (and other relevant individuals such as consultants, senior journalists or leading corporate executives). By contrast, ASEAN-ISIS is constituted by government research bureau, university institutes or independent think tanks.

CSCAP was established with the purpose of serving as the ARFs Track Two mechanism. This has involved delivering 'the necessary support activities for the ARF agenda, and make recommendations which are relevant for policy implementation' (Kerr, 1994: 404), improved communication among like-minded states as well as more ambitious objectives of instituting cooperative security approaches that transcend ideological divisions and existing alliance structures. It provides a more structured process for regional confidence building. CSCAP does not aspire to become the region's sole Track Two channel but to help coordinate efforts and avoid redundancy.

The idea for CSCAP was first aired in 1992 at a conference on 'Security Cooperation in the Asia Pacific' in Seoul. This meeting was jointly arranged by Pacific Forum, the Japan Institute of International Affairs, the Seoul Forum for International Affairs and ASEAN-ISIS. Thus, ASEAN-ISIS played a key role in creating CSCAP. However, participation in CSCAP was extended to all countries and territories of the Asia Pacific. The establishment of CSCAP has not been without difficulty or some scepticism. There were the usual teething problems as it sought funding and members and as founding partners tinkered with structures and administration. Concerns that CSCAP represented an overly optimistic attempt to promote cooperation that does not sufficiently appreciate the tensions and hostilities that continue to abound in the region have been borne out. These include unresolved sovereignty and territorial conflicts, uncertainty about the extent of US commitment to the region, anxiety over the arms build-up in China and arms proliferation in general. Furthermore, whilst there is an apparent 'habit of dialogue' in Southeast Asia, such a habit is weak in Northeast Asia. More fundamental collective action difficulties arise from the differing perceptions of the enterprise held by a larger number of participants (that also includes Russia, the US and India) than is the case in the more homogenous ASEAN-ISIS.

ASEAN-ISIS also broadened but in terms of its research agenda to include a wider array of human security and development issues. This has included partnering with parallel T2 processes like the Asia Economic Forum. With T3 ambitions, ASEAN-ISIS also engaged with civil society bodies through ASEAN People's Assembly to promote 'regionalism from below'. However, the T2 to T3 process has had a short and chequered history leading 'some civil society organisations to accuse ASEAN-ISIS of restricting rather than opening channels for dialogue with ASEAN' (Collins, 2008). Participatory regionalism also requires ASEAN governments and officials to create space for these groups in ASEAN deliberations. In reality, 'ASEAN has not always been supportive of APA'. When ASEAN officials attended APA Annual Forums 'in their private capacity', so as to allow for a frank exchange of views, this happened rarely 'because many officials could not step out of their official roles' (Nesadurai, 2011).

The establishment of a 'habit of dialogue' is an important but intangible outcome of the ASEAN-ISIS. It has built a history among participants encouraging loyalty and learning. In other words, the Association has helped build an *esprit de corps* and a sense of ASEAN solidarity among members. Information is shared and views on sensitive matters are aired helping to clear doubts and uncertainties if not to resolve tensions. Its activities promote information exchange and transparency in the region. Admittedly, this sense of identity is a fragile one that has encountered many setbacks and challenges. Yet, there is enough going on for a former Singaporean parliamentarian to speak of ASEAN identity construction:

> ASEAN ISIS and the individuals involved in their work have in some ways been fore runners in creating a sense of the region. ... Moreover, they are often less closely wedded to a national interest perspective, and can try to see the common interest of the region as a whole. Through the media, and in their various conferences and symposia, the ASEAN ISIS think tanks promote the understanding of ASEAN. (Tay, 2006: 126)

The notion of ASEAN identity and community raises the question of the identity of whom? From its inception, the ASEAN project has been very much an elite affair or an 'exclusive club'. Not until after the Asian financial crisis of the late 1990s did civil society engagements become recognised and routinised. Indeed, it was not until the Bali Concord in 2003 – some 30+ years after ASEAN's establishment – that an ASEAN Community was proclaimed and recognised that ASEAN was founded on three pillars: the ASEAN Economic Community; the ASEAN Security Community and the ASEAN Socio-Cultural Community. This third pillar is testimony to a perceived political need to engage the wider ASEAN community beyond its business and political elites (Caballero-Anthony, 2006: 55). Through its flagship ASEAN People's Assembly, ASEAN-ISIS wanted to help build the third pillar, but APA was one contested by other stronger regional gatherings of civil society associations (Collins, 2008: 322). ASEAN-ISIS suspended APA in 2009. Moreover, the idea of an ASEAN Community remains an elite civil society project. The ASEAN Community idea is very weakly embedded and barely recognised in the national societies of the region.

The success of ASEAN-ISIS in the 1990s prompted imitation as well as replication (such as CSCAP or the Asia Pacific Water Forum Regional Consultation Meetings). Other venues of T2 have become equally important in regional debates on community building if the *Dialogue and Research Monitor* inventory is taken as a guide to the multiple institutional bases of the interpretive community. The innovative agenda-setting influence of ASEAN-ISIS region construction may also be time-contingent. Today it operates in a different environment from the early 1990s: At a domestic level, national bureaucracies have matured, professionalised and increasingly function with in-house research and analytic capacity. At the regional levels of ASEAN and the Asia Pacific, ASEAN-ISIS is now but one venue for T2 activity.

New T2 dialogues have entered the field of which NEAT – the Network of East Asian Think Tanks – is one example, albeit a low-key one, and the Sentosa Round Table is another. Additionally, the Shangri-La Dialogue convened by the London-based International Institute for Strategic Studies touts itself as 'the most important regular gathering of defence professionals in the region and has become a vital annual fixture in the diaries of Asia Pacific defence ministers and their civilian and military chiefs of staff'.[6] and is seen by some as having overtaken ASEAN-ISIS (Butcher, 2009; Capie and Taylor, 2010). It certainly receives greater 'airplay' in the media and on the internet than other T2 processes. As an established T2 venue, CSCAP is also experiencing competition from the Shangri-La Dialogue and the Boao Forum hosted in Hainan (Desker, 2010: 231). Finally, regional institution building is subject not only to the persuasiveness of interpretative communities, but also to the dynamics of material interests and power plays of political and economic interests where 'official responses to T2 suggestions are usually influenced by the neo-realist mentality of state governments' (Lee, 2009: 209).

Conclusion: Interpretative networking

As a KNET, the achievements of ASEAN-ISIS were to create and help sustain a regional interpretive community. Signs of ASEAN-ISIS impact are numerous: (i) It was an early entrepreneur, and initiated new T2 processes in Southeast Asia; (ii) it built a regional network that continues to prosper as a regional research community despite its declining policy influence; (iii) it prompted the launch of new think tanks in Laos and Cambodia in order for those countries to have representation in the network as well as other T2 initiatives; (iv) it attracted official patronage from national governments; (v) it has institutionalised meetings with the ASEAN Senior Official Meeting (SOM), has acknowledgement of the role of ASEAN-ISIS in the Joint Communiqués of the ASEAN Ministerial Meetings, and the solicitation by ASEAN SOM of ASEAN-ISIS views on issues that ASEAN senior officials would like to have studied and (vi) it has developed collaborative research projects and dialogues that have attracted scholarly interest. Had it failed, the ASEAN-ISIS would have slowly retreated into the academic domain or disintegrated. Instead, it expanded with new activities that continue to attract public funding and official patronage. Imitators, who also operate with a certainty in the power of ideas, have copied ASEAN-ISIS via additional T2 networks. All this suggests that ideational work is essential to institutional innovation at a regional level, and by analogy at the global level.

The cross-cutting theme in previous chapters concerning the ontological separation between the scholar-researcher and the policy practitioner is exemplified in this chapter by the very terms T1 and T2. However, a focus on the networking, the relentless conversations and habit of dialogue via ASEAN Way informal processes of diplomacy destabilises and undermines a strict separation between public and private as well as between the research and policy-making worlds. Instead, knowledge and power are seen as intertwined and inseparable. 'Region' and institutions of regional cooperation first needed to be 'thought' – researched, critiqued and debated – before they could be created. In this framework, the research/interpretive community that is drawn from universities and think tanks becomes central to governance. This is in contra-distinction to traditional Realist and Liberal perspectives that would regard think tanks and T2 networks simply as 'interlocutors' or 'ideas brokers' in between the research world and the state, that is, operating solely as 'reinforcement for T1 processes' (Morrison, 2004: 551).

The research/interpretative community is not based in a separate or independent domain distinct from policy and politics feeding ideas in a one-way transmission to decision makers. Nor are intellectuals, institutes and their networks merely hinged or fused onto political processes to legitimate inter-governmental cooperation. Instead, they are inextricably bound with such processes. This is not just blurred lines between public and private. Rather, knowledge is mutually constituted with governance. Nevertheless, the 'mythical separation' of official state-directed T1 diplomatic processes vis-à-vis private NGO-led T2 initiatives is maintained because it is useful for ASEAN governments to sponsor so-called independent 'thinking outfits' to act as non-state sources of information gathering, elite mobilisation and intellectual validation. Not dissimilar to the manner in which ODI interacts with DfID and other sponsors as an evidence provider, these finely honed distinctions become a method of legitimation.

Informal diplomacy is well recognised as being a means to manage either sensitive or highly technical policy concerns between states. In this case, informal diplomacy was means for policy innovation and regional construction. Over a period of two decades a field of practice was created, and continues to be sustained, by the ASEAN-ISIS and many other T2 initiatives in the interpretive community. This is not to say that regional identity acquisition is learned automatically through processes of T2 communication and social engagement. Identity creation is a much more variable process. It is fragile, prone to setbacks, and at this point in time, is mostly limited to regional policy elites in the business and political worlds rather than having roots in wider society. These regional spaces are weakly institutionalised and 'soft' in the sense that they are based often on a 'habit of dialogue', consensus building and informal processes of diplomacy rather than formal multilateral organisation. Yet, these informal processes remain a necessary if not a sufficient condition for the development of formal inter-governmental structures such as the ARF. Where institutions are weak or under-developed, discourse can be a strong and determining force. This is reflected in continuing proliferation of T2 and T3 activity witnessed in the region and which is bank-rolled by governments, business and philanthropy alike. While ASEAN-ISIS may now be of less policy significance in the more crowded and competitive realm of informal diplomacy, its experience shows how 'interpretive communities' composed of like-minded think tanks, independent experts and university scholars can be central to the articulation, formation and legitimation of new regional governance arrangements.

In its past as well as in its future, ASEAN-ISIS is primarily regarded as a knowledge network. It only achieved occasional and partial status as a transnational executive network when political power was operating through informal diplomacy to achieve discourse institutionalisation with the ARF. The height of ASEAN-ISIS influence as a regional policy network was in the late 1980s and 1990s. But its influence was of an agenda-setting nature, providing coordinative and communicative discourses on region, rather than becoming part of either decision-making or implementation as is the case with TENs and GPPNs. Nevertheless, the ASEAN institutes represent a valuable regional example of the overlapping networks of private and public initiative in the global agora.

7
Bankrolling Knowledge Networks

There are many research networks in existence but few so grand in ambition as the GDN created by the World Bank. Why has the World Bank devoted so much effort and so many resources to this network? Some of the answers lie in broader objectives of the World Bank to be the 'knowledge bank' and to provide access to research, data and analysis as a global public good. Outlined in the first section, the World Bank's policy discourses of both 'knowledge for development' and 'global public goods' form the back drop to the discussion of its expanding activities sponsoring networks in the global agora.

The GDN represents one programme to operationalise these policy discourses, and its formation by the World Bank and its subsequent growth are laid out in the second section. As a driver of development, the Network is designed to allow greater scope for 'home-grown' policy, information-sharing and enhanced research capacity in and between developing countries for the co-production of local, regional and global knowledge. An important theme in this section is the manner in which the public and private status of the GDN has changed over time and how these shifts in its organisational or network identity contributed to GDNs' authority and status in the global agora.

The World Bank and other sponsors of the Network are promoting the creation and distribution of a global public good – knowledge. Stimulating the supply of both the quantity and quality of policy-relevant research aids the transmission of international 'best practices' which is argued to improve the scope for social and economic development. The role of the GDN as a provider of global public knowledge goods is addressed in the third section along with some of the criticisms the Network faced. Such great expectations behind the design of the GDN were broadly welcomed within the development studies community despite concerns among some donors about the uncritical view of knowledge and the assumptions about how that knowledge is utilised. There is a rationalist tendency within the GDN that portrays (scientific) research as independent from its social context. Knowledge is utilised as an intellectual tool that allows rational policy actors to reduce and control uncertainty in decision-making and advance social progress.

Frequently, the GDN has been criticised as a mechanism for the spread of the (post-)Washington consensus and neo-liberal ideology. It is evident that GDN research is broadly supportive of open economies and free market research. This does not mean that the GDN is in the hegemonic grasp of neo-liberal economics. Knowledge is contested and debated within the Network and the ideology is diluted by other narratives. Accordingly, the fourth section considers whether the GDN is a particular 'species' of network such as an epistemic community or an ideologically oriented 'embedded knowledge network'.

Creating knowledge and sharing research to promote development has best served the interests of the institutions advocating the knowledge agenda and the researchers in their orbit. 'Knowledge for Development' serves a particular kind of interest. The fifth section considers this 'cognitive interest' of researchers in their professional regeneration and advancement into new institutional arrangements such as global policy networks. In conclusion, the Network represents an example of the many partnerships and global programmes that the Banks sponsor in conjunction with other donors and decision-making groups.

Knowledge banking

There is considerable substance to the notion of the World Bank, predominantly a lending institution, being a knowledge bank. This aspiration has been translated into policies and practices to improve dissemination of knowledge. The Global Development Gateway was the most ambitious initiative for dissemination, aimed at harnessing information and communication technologies to the development process. Other initiatives included the Knowledge Networks for Sustainable Energy in Africa complementing older knowledge-based programmes hosted by the World Bank such as the CGIAR.

Today, the 'core priorities' in the World Bank's evolving 'Knowledge Agenda' are 'global practices, partnerships and knowledge governance' (Wheeler, 2009: 1). At an individual level the academic credentials of many staff, the adjunct teaching that some staff do in universities and their orientations to research contribute to the culture of the knowledge bank. Indeed, a former vice president describes the Bank as 'comparable to an American or Anglo-Saxon university in its organisational culture' (Ritzen, 2005: 110). Critics, however, point to a mono-disciplinary hegemony of economic thinking (Broad, 2006). Inside the Bank, global research on development is equated usually with 'development economics' (Ravallion et al., 2010: 32). For critics from both within and without the organisation, the concentration on economic thinking, methods and approaches has promoted a 'crony intellectualism' (Kapur, 2006) that has 'elided any discussion of the political economy of development' (Bebbington et al., 2004; also Broad, 2006).

That the World Bank is associated with a particular economistic perspective to development issues is neither surprising nor unusual. International bureaucracies, in general, impose particular constraints on research agendas to bring such agendas in tune with management objectives and operational necessities (Toye and Toye, 2005; Broad, 2006). The Bank has policies that need to be defended, and as is the case with most public institutions, it employs staff to do so (Ravallion et al., 2010). This does not mean that staff officers are mere cyphers of Bank policy: Many staff are internal critics; others are reformist in motivation while yet others move into different organisations sometimes with the explicit aim to develop alternative policies and perspectives to those of the Bank. Nevertheless, the research agendas and priorities of the Bank are in line with its institutional interests with the objective to 'generate knowledge to guide the Bank's corporate strategies, policy advice, lending operations, and technical assistance' (World Bank, 2012: 2).

The frequent rationale for maintaining extensive in-house research capacity is to inform and help maintain high-quality standards in the Bank's operational work (Ravallion et al., 2010: 31). Sources of in-house research include the World Bank Institute (WBI), which was noted for its work on governance, especially corruption and transparency. WBI is now much less engaged in research and more a 'global connector' of practitioners and institutions with the knowledge they need to 'scale up' innovations and their applications to development problems. While the Independent Evaluation Group does not regard itself as a research unit, nevertheless, its evaluation reports are often used as a research resource. Some of the Bank's global programmes in the Development Grant Facility (DGF) also finance research.

The Development Economics Research Group (DECRG) is the 'theoretical core' of the institution and often associated with the 'more orthodox and institutionally sanctioned positions on development, albeit with notable exceptions' (Bebbington et al., 2004: 45, 41; Kapur , 2006).

The Research Group is complemented by the Data Group (DECDG) and the Prospects Group (DECPG) which provides analysis on global trends in the world economy, especially on trade, financial flows, commodity prices and remittance flows, and the impact of these trends on developing countries. DEC is the main centre for development research in the Bank and is responsible for collecting, studying and sharing information relating to development. In the words of a former Director of Research in DEC, and subsequently GDN Director, the Bank 'has a clear comparative advantage' in 'applied, policy oriented research often with a strong cross-country dimension' (Squire, 2000: 110). A strong in-house research capacity is believed to ensure that research of relevance to developing countries is undertaken and disseminated to policy makers (Dethier, 2007). Through its research capacity, products such as the annual *World Development Report*, its two in-house journals and as a major provider of statistical data, the Bank has been able to shape the analytical terms of debate within the transnational development policy community. In an external evaluation of World Bank research the high quality of Bank research was recognised and lauded, despite some criticisms as to how it was sometimes used (Bannerjee et al., 2006). The Bank's internal report *Research at Work* (2012: 3) continued to laud its researchers as 'both prolific and prominent in the field of development'.

Through 'knowledge sharing' (as well as knowledge creation), the Bank also casts itself as a 'global public good' provider. For students and their teachers interested in development, a number of public services are available from the Bank, including scholarships but also extensive online resources. For practitioners there are the e-learning tools, professional development courses, knowledge exchange partnerships and web-based libraries built by WBI. For scholars, there are data bases, working papers, journals and other research resources. In the public eye, the Annual Bank Conference on Development Economics (ABCDE) and its regional events are platforms for knowledge exchange for contributing ideas to the international development agenda.

Sponsoring various research activities and knowledge networking allowed the World Bank to pursue its objective of becoming a 'knowledge bank'. Knowledge production inside the Bank as well as knowledge sharing (such as the Open Data initiative) and capacity building has given considerable substance to the policy discourse of the Bank as a 'global public good' provider. Sponsorship of GDN and many other networks has helped legitimise the Banks claims of building partnerships not only with civil society organisations such as research institutes but also with other development donors and NGOs. As a result, development economists in the World Bank, in 'client' countries and the regional networks, were given new opportunities to extend their professional interests into these global knowledge networks. But as has been noted of 'knowledge management for development' generally, there is a dichotomy between:

> ... goals, which are geared toward more participatory knowledge networks, and its active knowledge management practices, which reflect rationalist tendencies. Knowledge management on these premises risks becoming counterproductive to development efforts by perpetuating transfer of representational knowledge of development elites. (Ferguson et al., 2010: 1807)

It is important to understand how units within the Bank conceive of development, the manner in which capacity building is operationalised and how and with whom they do knowledge networking in order to understand the short but eventful history of the GDN.

Networking development research

The GDN – an association of research institutes and think tanks – was launched in 1999 by the World Bank in cooperation with the UN, the Governments of Japan, Germany and Switzerland, seven regional research networks and other private and public international development institutions. The three broad objectives of the GDN were to 'create, share and apply knowledge'. The Network was intended to incorporate the 'research community' of developing and transition countries more efficiently into development policy. Today it is composed primarily of university research centres and think tanks. The assumption was that 'the generation of local knowledge which when shared with local policy makers will ultimately lead to the solution of local problems' (GDN, 2001).

Central to GDNs design was that it be a co-ordinating mechanism – a 'network of networks'. The building blocks on which the Network was created were seven regional research networks. These regional consortia were established over the decade prior to the launch of the GDN.

- Africa Economic Research Consortium
- Centre for Economic Research and Graduate Education – CERGE
- East Asian Development Network – EADN
- Economic Education and Research Consortium

- Economic Research Forum (Middle East and North Africa)
- Latin American and Caribbean Economic Association – LACEA
- South Asian Network of Economic Institutes

Aside from the pre-existing LACEA and the Eastern European network, these regional bodies were established with support from DEC. In later years, the GDN expanded to include other networks to give it more global coverage:

- European Development Network – EUDN
- Bureau for Research and Analysis of Development in North America – BREAD
- GDN Japan
- Oceania Development Network

With the inclusion of these networks, the core constituency developing countries and transition states has been diluted. This has been compounded as the Network moved from a membership base of individuals, to focus on its 'network of networks' identity.

GDN consolidated rapidly from its launch in late 1999 in Bonn. Five core activities emerged to define the GDNs roles:

1. Global research projects;
2. Awards and medals;
3. Annual conferences;
4. Regional research competitions and
5. GDNet – the web-site to disseminate research and connect the GDN community.

The goal of the GDN is to enhance the quality and availability of policy-oriented research and strengthen the institutions that undertake this work, that is, 'to generate, share and apply knowledge about development'. Pursuing its own 'global public goods' orientation, the GDN seeks to provide better information about and access to resources such as research funds and professional development programmes. For example, access to high-quality data was viewed as a major constraint for researchers in developing countries. Accordingly, DECDG offered access for GDN-affiliated institutes to the Statistical Information Management and Analysis database. Additionally, the GDN also helps to coordinate and to disseminate multi-disciplinary research efforts and build research capability for institutes and individuals in developing countries.

Global research projects conduct collaborative studies in many countries simultaneously. Likewise, the regional research competitions are based on open, competitive allocation of research funds. However, the disciplinary focus and dominance of the regional networks in this process has meant research agendas are structured around economic questions, analysis and solutions. Yet, this 'mobilisation of bias' in favour of economic research varies significantly between the regional networks. Compared to CERGE in Eastern Europe, the more recently established EADN in Asia was not as dominated by economics. Moreover, the GDN Governing Body has regularly requested the regional networks to open themselves to 'other' social science perspectives. This call to multidisciplinarity was also done as a gesture to secure additional funding support from a more diverse group of donors.

Criticisms of the GDN as a World Bank 'spawn and pawn' was a driving consideration in GDNs exit from the Bank. At the 1999 launch conference in Bonn, a few large donors sponsoring other established programmes with research institutes and think tanks were concerned that GDN would squeeze out existing initiatives or duplicate effort. Some criticism was that the Bank was diverting resources to its favoured group of policy institutes, excluding more radical views or simply alternative political economy approaches. Other issues raised by donor groups revolved around lack of multi-disciplinarity, the lack of transparency in the Network decision-making procedures and insufficient representation of user groups – donors and policy makers. These issues, compounded by perceptions of the GDN–World Bank relationship being 'too close', created sufficient pressure on the World Bank for the Network to separate, amicably, from its parent organisation.

The GDN was incorporated as non-profit organisation and moved outside World Bank offices in mid-2001. Whilst this was a significant re-drawing of its legal boundaries, the Network retained close cultural affiliation with its parent organisation. The GDN Board of Directors includes a Bank representative and a number of other board members also have experience of Bank service. The first GDN Director (Lyn Squire) was a research manager in DECRG; the next Director (Gobind Nankani) was World Bank's Vice President for the Africa Region before coming to the GDN in mid-2007. The third Director (Gerardo della Paolera) is a former university president and economist. The Director appointed in 2012, Pierre Jacquet, was previously Chief Economist of the French Development Agency. The head of GDN's administrative staff previously worked in the World Bank as did the first appointed senior economist in the Network. They brought with them many of the styles and procedures of organisational operations found in the Bank. Each year, the GDN conference brings in a number of Bank staff as keynote speakers or 'resource persons'. In the first five years of its existence, the GDN was heavily dependent on Bank financial support through the DGF.[1]

Nevertheless, donors such as the Japan Bank for International Cooperation and the UK DfID soon supported the awards and the web-site, respectively. These and many other subsequent partners have additional interests in supporting multilateral knowledge partnerships. Funding support has diversified considerably to twenty-plus major donors over the last decade, including during 2011: AusAID; the Bill and Melinda Gates Foundation; Inter-American Development Bank (IDB); Ministère des Finances, Government of Luxembourg and the OSF, amongst others. Rather than squeezing out existing knowledge networks and partnerships, there has been a rash of additional 'knowledge for development' initiatives over the past decade such as the IDRC-Hewlett initiative and AusAid's 'Revitalising Indonesia's Knowledge Sector for Development Policy' programme.[2] The rapid institutional development of GDN, in partnership with the World Bank and other like-minded donors, put knowledge as a 'global public good' firmly on the development agenda helping to prompt other initiatives.

There is one further and important step in GDNs' organisational development that has improved its international standing and status. From 2001, GDN became an NGO under the laws of the State of Delaware, USA, and legally, if not yet financially, independent from the World Bank. In effect, GDN became a private body based in civil society. Over the next few years, there were further moves that diluted the relationship with the Bank. Although an office was maintained in Washington DC, GDNs headquarters were established in New Delhi in late 2004, and new sets of relationships emerged with new partners and stakeholders. The online community managed via GDNet was administered by a team in Cairo almost from the beginning. This departure and distancing worked for both the GDN and the World Bank. The GDN could legitimately claim to be an independent body. By the same token, the World Bank could claim that it was partnering with a civil society organisation. However, 2005 marks the transformation of GDN into an international organisation when Egypt, Italy and Senegal signed the GDN charter. India, Sri Lanka and Spain were later signatories. The GDN became a public entity with formal inter-governmental status. This new legal identity as an international organisation strengthened GDNs' claim to scholarly independence and organisational autonomy in creating and disseminating global public knowledge. As an international organisation, the Network operates with enhanced public authority in the global agora.

Created inside the World Bank in the late 1990s, the Network was 'spun-off', in effect privatised by the Bank as a new NGO. Even so, the status of the GDN as an NGO simply represented an extension of the World Bank's public action via alternative means. It was the first step in the blurring of domains between civil society and international organisation. A second step in the reconfiguration of the GDN as a public entity resulted with initiatives from the GDN Secretariat and Governing Body to shed its private, non-governmental identity in pursuit of state-based recognition as an international organisation.

Global public knowledge

An important platform of thinking behind the GDN is that it provides a 'global public good'. GPG delivery is central to the public discourse of the World Bank and has been one important source of inspiration for the GDNs' adoption of the discourse. But there were also other sources of scholarly sustenance. One of the first appointed members to the GDN Governing Body was Inge Kaul, then Director of the Office of Development Studies at UNDP (Kaul, 2001). She is credited with the conceptual development of the idea of GPGs and convincing UNDP to engage in public advocacy of the framework. The GPG discourse was subsequently picked up, at a rhetorical level at least, by many other international agencies given the 'positive connotations' inherent to the concept (Long and Woolley, 2009: 117). It has become a coordinative discourse. Likewise, current GDN Board member, Ravi Kanbur, has conducted research and publication on what he refers to as 'international public goods'. Another founding GDN Governing Body member Richard Cooper (2001) also has created a body of research in this field. World Bank Chief Economist, Joseph Stiglitz, was another who advocated research on the notion of knowledge as a global public good (Stiglitz, 1999, 2000).

A 'pure' public good is one that is 'non-excludable' – no one can be barred from its consumption. Further, if the good can be consumed without it being depleted, then the public good is 'non-rivalrous' in consumption. By contrast, private goods are those that are excludable. In other words, such goods can be produced and distributed according to their demand; their ownership can be transferred against a price and property rights are attached to them. These goods can be consumed privately. Public goods are those that have benefits as well as costs that are not confined to a 'buyer' (or set of buyers). Once provided, such goods are enjoyed freely by others. As a consequence, public goods suffer from market failure. A profit cannot be gained by the private sector if it produces non-excludable goods. Non-market interventions are required to ensure that certain public goods are produced.

In reality, public goods do not exist in pure form. They can be made more or less 'public' as a result of subsidy or regulation. Codified knowledge – education, libraries, Internet-based information – is often portrayed as a public good but usually it is a local authority or government financing open access to the resource that often has the effect of making it a public good. Likewise, advances in technology can make certain goods more public, such as the ability to download in a non-rivalrous fashion, books and articles via the Internet. Thus, there are extremely few instances of 'pure' public goods (Long and Woolley, 2009).

Examples of global public goods include a world free from malaria, sustainable fisheries or a clean environment. Public goods are 'global' if they are 'quasi-universal': covering more than one group of countries, covering all population groups and meeting the needs of current generations without foreclosing opportunity for later generations. We are more likely to encounter global public bads: pollution, water crisis and pandemics. For instance, the public is not excluded from the ill-effects of climate change and must consume the costs of environmental damage. Similarly, inaccurate research or poor policy analysis incorporated into decision-making can contribute to perverse policy outcomes. These global public goods and bads can be localised in their impact but are also a feature of the global agora. Global networks have emerged mostly in response to counter the effects of public bads but also as mechanisms to facilitate the delivery of public goods. The GDN is such a global network to create research and spread knowledge about successful (and failed) policy experiments and innovations of one country that may be of benefit to other countries and communities.

'Knowledge gaps' or an inadequate supply of policy-relevant research entails that policy in developing countries is often formulated without access to the best research and analysis. It is beyond the self-interest of any one country to engage in a systematic global analysis of policy to overcome 'knowledge gaps' as the costs are carried by one, whereas the benefits are likely to be enjoyed by many. Policy research is consumed by 'free-riding' actors such as journalists, the educated lay public, the intelligentsia of other countries, colleges and students, civil society organisations and companies who do not usually contribute (directly) to the costs of knowledge production. It leads to under-investment and under-supply in policy research and analysis. Accordingly, the GDN was conceived as an intervention to facilitate both the increased and improved supply of a global public good, development research about 'best practice' (Squire, 2000: 113–14).

Whilst the global public goods concept has become an important rallying concept mobilising numerous international organisations, countries and non-state actors into joint action or joint financing, there are also practical limitations to the concept as a coordinative discourse. Overcoming the public goods problem of the lack of locally generated policy research does not ensure its effective application or utilisation. Research does not by necessity 'trickle through' into policy, particularly when policy-relevant research is ignored or even repressed by governments. This dilemma was well recognised by the GDN Governing Body and Secretariat, which cooperated closely in its early days with the ODI in London to develop its own programme on 'Bridging Research and Policy'.

The public goods framework is also apolitical. It treats knowledge as homogenous, technical and neutral. As discussed in Chapter 2, policy-making deference to 'evidence' does not signify a single body of knowledge that is commonly recognised. To the contrary, a 'battle of ideas' between different worldviews and 'regimes of truth' prevails. For many critics of GDN, the real issue was not the creation and dissemination of knowledge but the kind of knowledge that was produced and the kind of knowledge that dominated policy debate. Little is provided in public goods accounts about the socio-political functions of knowledge or issues of power and hegemony.

Nor has the 'global' 'public' 'good' terminology been unpacked. It is unclear who constitutes the 'global public' or what constitutes the 'global good'. Instead, these are abstractions in the same way that the public good of a healthy or educated society is intangible. 'In the abstract, knowledge benefits everyone; yet patents exclude, as do educational institutions' (Long and Woolley, 2009: 111). Furthermore, the preferences of individuals, communities and nations are not homogenous: Some will have a greater preference for public goods of a clean environment and sustainable fisheries, whereas others may favour financial stability or national defence and security. Nevertheless, the involvement of civil society and other stakeholders in GPG delivery can have an important effect of making international negotiations less statist (multi-actor) and less territorial (multi-level governance) (Kaul, 2001).

The notion of knowledge as a 'club good' goes much further towards accommodating the idea that the benefits of knowledge sharing are limited to particular groups. That is, the benefits of the club, or network, are non-rivalrous for members but excludable. Those selected to participate in GDN conferences or in Global Research Projects become part of the GDN club. Those who have Internet access are able to freely access GDN (or other network) resources. And it is those who have recognised professional qualifications and social science expertise who participate in the Network.

Finally, the public goods approach tends to focus on outcomes – production of public goods. However, a focus on process – addressing decision-making procedures or resource allocations – draws attention to the kind of knowledge that is reproduced and then circulated in the global agora. Within GDN, development economics has dominated. GDN Governing Body members were announced at the second Annual Conference in Tokyo in 2000. The dominant composition of (male) economists drew sharp rebuke from the assembled audience. One representative of the European Association of Development Research and Training Institutes (EADI) complained about the 'exclusive economistic ways of looking at development phenomena'.[3] Over a decade later, EADI had long departed on a separate trajectory from both GDN and EUDN, and the renamed GDN Board of Directors was still composed primarily of economists.

The dominance of the economics discipline was reflected in other activities. From the outset, the Network's 'Global Development Awards' attracted international attention and were an effective mechanism to advertise the aspirations of the nascent network. The first were awarded in Tokyo in 2001. The 'Outstanding Researcher' committee comprised economists, four of whom were former Bank employees, including Nancy Birdsall from the Carnegie Endowment (a former Director of Research at the World Bank and now the Director of the Centre for Global Development in Washington DC.); Francois Bouguignon (subsequently Chief Economist of the World Bank), Takatoshi Ito from the Japanese Ministry of Finance and Nobel Prize winners Amartya Sen and (former Chief Economist) Joseph Stiglitz. Overall, nine of the twelve research awardees in that year were economists. In subsequent years, a high proportion of awardees in the research competitions continued to be economists (albeit much less so the case of winners of the Japanese Award for Most Innovative Development Project).

Within the GDN, the dominant conceptualisation of knowledge is research undertaken by suitably qualified experts in recognised institutional contexts, that is, research institutes. The GDN promotes *techne* or technical knowledge which requires expert mastery of the communication codes referred to in Chapter 2. It is a 'codified' under-standing of knowledge that allows meaningful 'sharing' between the highly educated and technically qualified. Knowledge is framed predominantly by the methods and models, professional norms and standards of economists even though it depicts itself as a social science network. This orthodoxy is not accidental but symptomatic of the pur-suit of 'cognitive interest' by professional researchers.

Placing 'knowledge' (and more specifically research) central to the development process was a profound re-conceptualisation of develop-ment not only in the World Bank but also in other development agen-cies that adopt similar language concerning the benefits of knowledge and research for development and the advantages of 'evidence-based policy'. One implication is that the creation, management and diffu-sion of knowledge becomes one of the primary pivots for cooperation on development. Capacity building on development research and then 'knowledge sharing' via the GDN, or other knowledge networks, also has an effect on governance: 'Capacity building in the field of develop-ment, for example, can be viewed as an apparatus of rule that establishes a diverse range of rationalities for building institutional frameworks, enhancing the skills of people and mobilising knowledge through the formation of new partnerships' (Ilcan and Phillips, 2008: 715). This is captured in GDN's 'theory of change' that places 'science' central to resolving complex problems of social and economic development:

> Most of the problems that developing and transition societies face are complex. Yet they are increasingly addressable through scientific pursuit. Many, if not all, necessitate new ways of producing, structur-ing and mobilizing knowledge through open, collaborative, multi-disciplinary, and global research collaboration(s).[4]

In this formulation, the challenges of development do not rest in power differentials, intractable problems of poverty or unequal social condi-tions, but in the lack of public knowledge goods.

Sharing what knowledge

Knowledge networks are venues equally for the construction as well as the delivery or dissemination of knowledge public goods. Originally, the GDN was conceived as a network where individual researchers as well as organisations were members. Today, individuals register with GDNet (rather than the Network). This mode of (virtual) membership entails dispersion of GDN information and expertise outwards and downwards to relatively isolated individuals. Close to twelve and half thousand researchers are registered, and they enjoy access to many knowledge products and online resources. As a group, however, they are not organised in any meaningful sense. As noted of think tanks in Chapter 3, the relationship is a top-down one from the global and regional networks. Instead, it is the senior players within the regional networks that are structured into the decision-making dynamics of the GDN and who are better positioned to develop themes for the Global Research Projects or the Awards. Each of the regional networks nominates a representative to the GDN Board.

Capacity building involves sharing 'best practices' in research methodologies, data analysis and research communication. The spread of research standards is achieved subtly and indirectly via the award criteria and benchmarks set in Global Development Awards, the now-ended IMF fellowship scheme, or through selection for participation in the Global Research Projects and for presentation of papers at the annual conference. Exposure to some of the world's most noted development thinkers, or research collaborations, can have a demonstration effect helping to lift standards or, at least, to communicate international standards of research practice. Network interactions such as these help form common patterns of understanding – an elite consensus – regarding the appropriate developmental questions and research methods that can help devise policies to stimulate economic growth.

The GDN was also designed to share knowledge of researchers with decision makers for policy formulation. World Bank Chief Economist Joseph Stiglitz advised the GDN partner institutes at the time of its launch that if developing countries were to be 'in the drivers' seat', steering social and economic reform, greater capacity for independent economic analysis was needed:

> Local researchers, combining the knowledge of local conditions – including knowledge of local political and social structures – with the learning derived from global experiences, provides the best prospects for deriving policies which are both effective and engender broad-based support. (Stiglitz, 2000: 27)

This process of adaption moves away from the apolitical language of knowledge 'diffusion' from development agencies – notwithstanding notions of institutes 'scanning globally' to download 'best practice' – to prepare against developing and transition countries being 'cognitively dependent recipients of the main messages ... of bureaucratic "reason" in the development agencies' (Stiglitz, 2000: 37). Local research institutions and think tanks are necessary institutions to cultivate in order for effective 'transplanting' of development knowledge to local conditions as well as to avoid 'intellectual colonialism' (Stiglitz, 2000: 33, 37). In this regard, it is worthwhile to ask whether, or if, the GDN functions as an epistemic community or an 'embedded knowledge network' or a transnational discourse community. This questioning provides an opportunity to assess not simply how GDN research and policy ideas might be shared, but what kind of knowledge is disseminated.

Chapter 2 argued that the 'epistemic community' approach highlights the role of scientific opinion and the weight of consensual knowledge of expert groups in shaping policy agendas, especially in circumstances of uncertainty. The dynamics of policy uncertainty, the scope for interpretation over global problems and the low level of institutionalisation at the international level drive policy makers towards the use of expert analysts and epistemic communities. Policy actors puzzle over the intractability of poverty and other development problems, which gives rise to demands for information in an attempt to understand and decode a complex reality. Epistemic communities that can offer information and interpretation for policy makers, that is, a scientific coordinative discourse, are in a pivotal agenda-setting position. Two types of epistemic community operate. An 'ad hoc coalition' aims to solve a particular policy problem, whereby the problem shapes the community. The 'life' of such communities 'is limited to the time and space defined by the problem and its solutions' (Adler and Haas, 1992: 371). The other kind is more constant and is aimed at the establishment and perpetuation of beliefs and visions as 'dominant social discourses'. An example would be the neo-liberal orthodoxy described as the (post) Washington Consensus which is refracted from the GDN.

The GDN has epistemic qualities given the disciplinary character of its partners. However, the Network is not an institutional embodiment of one epistemic community. At best, it is a forum where 'techne' is valued and a number of epistemic communities can interact. The Network as a whole could be described as 'epistemic-like' where it is simply one node in a wider community of applied development economists rather than an organisational embodiment of a community. Nevertheless, the label 'epistemic community' has considerable caché given that the concept concords with the dominant idea of knowledge within GDN as being based on facts and empirically discernible realities, a basis from which 'truth speaks to power'. For many, the Network is about *episteme* and 'the pursuit of knowledge – global knowledge about general principles, local knowledge about how those principles play out in the multitude of global contexts over our vast globe – knowledge based on well constructed theories and meticulous analysis of the empirical evidence' (Stiglitz, 2000: 40). This aspiration was crystallised in GDNs' mission and first strap-line: 'Better Research, Better Policy, Better "Developing" World'.[5]

In contrast to the idea of the GDN operating as a network vehicle for epistemic communities in the development field, the 'embedded knowledge networks' framework captures the ideological functions of technical knowledge or (social) scientific expertise and how the Network is linked normatively and cognitively to material interests in the international financial institutions. One critic argues that the 'World Bank can rely safely on the GDN network of think tanks to secure information in this process ... of large-scale transformation of global development politics ... and to develop new layers of transnational knowledge circuits' (Plehwe, 2007: 526). By providing capacity building for research on development or poverty alleviation, the GDN also seeks to embed itself the regional networks and other developing-country research institutes not only as authoritative actors in development debates but also as ideational infrastructure.

Notwithstanding the public good attributes of knowledge, in sponsoring increased capacity for 'independent' research and analysis, the interests of the World Bank and other development institutions are served as their policy prescriptions are broadly in favour of pro-capitalist growth approaches to reduce poverty. There is considerable space for scholarly difference and debate within GDN; there are a diversity of methodological approaches and distinct sets of research questions arising from different disciplinary foci. Nevertheless, a prevailing set of social relations favour a development discourse that is in tune with prerequisites of major partners and supporters. Knowledge networks represent the 'micro-politics of contemporary hegemony', whereby think tanks and research institutes are enrolled as part of a strategic element within globalising capitalism. In other words, GDN knowledge – research results, data, information about 'best practice' – is flavoured by the values and policy preference of the post-Washington Consensus – privatisation, deregulation, financial liberalisation and macro-economic stability (Kaul, 2001: 591).

The GDN and its constituent elements – research institutes, university centres, the regional networks and individual researchers – are enlisted in 'partnerships' with its major donor to act as an amplifier of World Bank perspectives and priorities. Specific policy approaches are reinforced by partner organisations in their national context and through building regional networks to share information and spread policy lessons. The GDN represents one mechanism for the intellectual sustenance of the neo-liberal capitalist order through the reproduction of ideas supportive of it. The 'embedded knowledge network' framework is more useful in highlighting how a private network ascribes authority through collective action. Through patronage from, and partnerships with, multilateral agencies and governments, GDN institutes are recognised and legitimised as expert sources of policy research in the transnational development policy community and who reinforce a dominant ideology.

However, there are voices of critique and dissent within the GDN. Furthermore, not all who are part of it would regard their research work as subsidiary to interests. While the disciplinary discourse of economics may have achieved the structuration of policy debate to become 'coordinative', it is not necessarily stable and set, or uncontested discourse. Implicit in debates over multi-disciplinarity in the Network are differences about what constitutes quality research. GDN is composed of many contradictory research narratives and 'coded ways' of representing development problems that are played out in the annual conferences, GDNet and the research projects. However, the discourse communities represented in the GDN are not on an equal footing. A discourse coalition of development economists has been able to set most, but certainly not all, research agendas.

Moreover, the structure of the Network allows it to absorb diverse sources of development research and diffuse it without necessarily undermining network coherence at the core revolving around the Secretariat, the leadership of the regional networks and key GDN partners. Network hegemony is incomplete and partial. GDN sponsors have changed over time with a waxing and waning of enthusiasm, or as specific collaborative projects came to their natural end. A grid-like complex of ideas shaping consciousness and dominating the global order gives little credence to the many alternative worldviews and sites of intellectual resistance within and beyond the GDN. This is not to dismiss studies of the ideological character or disciplinary preferences of the Knowledge Bank and its partners (Broad, 2006; Kapur, 2006; Bebbington et al., 2004), but suggests it is much less strategic and often without direction.

The GDN rhetoric of promoting applied social science, 'best practices' in research capacity and in knowledge sharing, and its portrayal as a global partnership to produce public goods de-emphasises the ideological character of the Network. GDN emphasis is on *knowledge management* and devices such as training materials on research communications, building the GDNet community and improving opportunities for researchers from the South through funding news alerts, a document delivery service or toolkits on proposal writing. In pursuit of GDN aspiration to achieve a critical mass of researchers who are globally interconnected and produce good research to impact public policy leaves less questioning on the content of knowledge. What is 'shared' indeed, disseminated and broadcast globally via the GDN are broadly similar sets of policy paradigms or development discourse. While access to the GDN is open, full participation is in reality restricted to those individuals and institutes that display competence of *techne* and dominant discourses.

Despite substantive differences regarding how 'episteme', 'ideology' and 'discourse' relate to policy philosophies and programmes, these concepts help take an understanding of global policy partnerships, like the GDN, beyond public goods analysis, which tends to presume a progressive and benign public benefit. It allows a focus on processes of exclusion and unequal (but shifting) positions of power in privatised domains of policy formulation. Instead of discarding two of these concepts in favour of a preferred approach, they each provide different lenses of interpretation. Outsiders to the Network have criticised it as one ideological weapon in the hegemonic arsenal of the neo-liberal project of the post-Washington consensus. The GDN Secretariat and Board draw attention to the diversity of analytical and policy discourses fed by multi-disciplinary debates. For those who steer and fund the GDN, the official discourse is about *episteme*: 'to generate and share applied social science research to advance social and economic development'.[6] Yet the GDN is not an epistemic community of development economists. Development economists share many common professional standards, but often disagree on the causes and components of economic growth and poverty alleviation. And what is missing among the GDN community that would make it 'epistemic' is a common policy project and reform agenda. Nevertheless, building research capacity to international standards of quality among social science communities of developing countries, as the basis of 'evidence-based policy', represents logic of governance rationality spread by the international institutions and development donors.

Embedding knowledge

In the first two years of its existence, the GDN was on a path of development that structurally favoured certain groups of researchers – development economists. This was evident in conference participation, awards procedures and allocation of funds to early research pro-grammes. The constriction of research agendas had implications not only for the kinds of researchers attracted to the Network but also for the manner in which development issues have been framed, problems defined and solutions proposed. This was noted by the GDN Governing Body, which introduced measures to rectify perceived imbalances in the early days of network consolidation (GDN, 2001).

The dominance of economic frameworks and thinking has resulted to great extent because of the apparent relevance of the discipline to development questions. But it is also a consequence of the 'cognitive interest' of embedded knowledge actors (development economists but also other consultants and experts) in professional regeneration and institutional entrenchment. Given the resources and patronage of official and private development agencies and international organisations were devoting to the network, it is unsurprising that professional communities mobilised to secure control over resources, prestige and position within the Network. As a result, the GDN became more supply led by researchers than a demand-driven initiative.

If researchers are to be 'suppliers of solutions' through policy research, they need to define development problems in such a way as to encourage recourse to their expertise. Not doing so would mean that researchers define themselves out of consideration as possible providers of solutions. As noted earlier within the frame of the public goods policy narrative, a lack of knowledge is defined as part of the (development) problem. As a result, experts and researchers have a professional stake in the 'knowledge agenda' of the 'knowledge bank' and of other international organisations. The 'cognitive interests' of development researchers are served, in some small degree, through the GDN with its capacity-building support for research institutes (grants and scholarship information, training and data initiatives) and the dissemination of knowledge (Knutsen and Sending, 2000).

This general tendency within the GDN coincides with the more specific professional dominance of economic thinking and prescription within the World Bank. If 'theory is always for someone and for some purpose', then the 'public goods concept works for some economists as an economic rationale for government' (Long and Woolley, 2009: 117, paraphrasing Robert Cox). Or in this case, the global public goods framework helps to legitimate the global policy programmes and international development assistance roles of various international organisations. Traditionally, economics has been the most important discipline for Bank staff recruitment. Not only are development economists 'embedded', they also have a cognitive interest in the selective use of their mode of problem definition, methodological approaches and policy solutions. Consequently, cognitive interests not only compete in scientific terms but also compete to gain access to resources and recognition.

In addition, there are difficulties for researchers outside to breach the edifice of Bank professional consensus. As put by two DEC insiders:

> Over the years, generations of economists who have been recruited by the Bank have created an argot within the Bank that is closely aligned with the argot of economics, which in turn creates high entry costs for other disciplines. Competing perspectives cannot enter without translation which dilutes their clarity and effectiveness; this, in turn, only reinforces the (often disdainful) views of economists regarding the rigor and relevance of other social science disciplines, thereby creating a vicious circle. (Rao and Woolcock, 2007: 480)

This institutional tendency towards disciplinary monopoly permeates into knowledge networking where further sets of negotiations, contests and alliances in between disciplines as well as with the development policy community are enacted.

Development economists in the World Bank and their partner organisations attempt to extend their professional interests into the GDN. This is no surprise: Individual researchers and organisations will seek to take advantage of opportunities that promote their careers, provide access to resources or represent potential for mutually beneficial partnerships. Yet, their preferred pursuit of technical knowledge becomes a self-reinforcing dynamic that encourages resistance to other disciplinary approaches as well as to practical, grassroots or indigenous knowledge.

Notwithstanding these tendencies, it is not the case that the World Bank is a monolithic entity with a united and coherent position on all questions of development to which staff happily subscribe. To portray the Bank in this fashion misses the complexity of perspectives in the organisation. There are constant bureaucratic battles that modify and dilute hegemonic uniformity and consistency of purpose in Bank operations. This does not mean that there is not a broad policy consensus amongst many Bank personnel as well as among many of their counterparts in 'client countries'. However, epistemic neo-liberal unity exists only amongst some and it is in constant contest with other perspectives. In other words, the discourse of poverty reduction is shared, but there are divergent positions on how to achieve this aspiration.

Similarly, the GDN is a research community driven by scientific competition among the social sciences as much as other, more altruistic motives to produce GPGs. The tendency towards disciplinary monopoly is not uncontested. Nor is it unchangeable. Once outside the Bank, and based in India, the GDN was increasingly subject to pressures from a more diverse range of stakeholders. However, cultural change comes about slowly in large, federal global networks. The GDN research agendas, services and publications continue to be in broad conformity with the precepts of development economics perpetuated in many of the world's leading development agencies. The GDN is one vehicle not only for intellectual renewal and induction of new generations of development researchers but also for advancement of the development economics as an applied, policy-relevant discipline *sine qua non*. Other disciplinary insights on development are not excluded but incorporated more towards the margins of the Network life to bolster the legitimacy of the GDN as a social science entity. This is to be expected given that Network sustainability is in part dependent on cognitive connection and research resonance with its funders and supporters – that is, development economists institutionally embedded in the IMF, World Bank, UN agencies or other development agencies.

The tussles over which disciplinary concepts and methods are adopted and privileged are central to the GDNs' more mundane activities of network management and partnership activities. It brings into focus as the micro-infrastructure of governance and the routine practices through which power and authority are enacted. That is, '... routine practices can give rise to an innovative reading of neoliberalism that is not understood as an ideology or current expression of a capitalist agenda, but rather as an 'assemblage of rationalities, strategies, technologies, and techniques that allow "government at a distance"' (Ilcan and Phillips, 2008: 715, quoting Aihwa Ong). GDN is just one small mechanism in the messy 'assemblage' of global policy making and symptomatic of how global organisations govern conduct through the use of knowledge networks or civil society partners. The mobilisation of knowledge for development gives credence to participatory relations and partnership building via 'diverse forms of knowledge generation, global bench marking and training programmes to shape the conduct of individuals and groups around the world' (Ilcan and Phillips, 2008: 718). GDN built capacity for research among developing-country scholars and early career scholars around two pillars: one of scholarly standards of excellence and the other oscillating around bureaucratic requirements for policy relevance and operational technologies. Its engagements as an independent body with international organisations and other powerful donors in development have the effect of governing the field of development by defining what constitutes knowledge for development and determines those who are the credible actors to create and disseminate this knowledge.

The form of knowledge that is mobilised by the World Bank is primarily focussed on economic liberalisation and market globalisation. Unsurprisingly, the World Bank partners with organisations that exhibit common values and norms. Furthermore, the structural power of World Bank in shaping not only the supply but also demand for development knowledge is significant. Political themes and policy approaches are reinforced by Bank capacity-building programmes for research institutes at a domestic level and through building regional and global policy networks to share information, spread policy lessons and promote technical knowledge on the causes of, and solutions to, poverty and stalled economic development. Alternative perspectives on development and grassroots knowledge are not excluded in either the Bank or the GDN but can face a more difficult passage into the lime light.

Conclusion

Through its sponsorship of the GDN, the Bank was able to demonstrate that it is implementing its policy on 'knowledge', point to civil society partnerships and co-financing arrangements, diffuse 'best practice' (or what others call neo-liberalism in apolitical, technical guise – Broad, 2006) and use the Network to extend its policy discourse and worldview. In reciprocity, the World Bank as a partner empowers the salient agendas of the GDN. This is not an undiluted bilateral relationship: Other partners – individuals and institutions – also bring their latent agendas where their priorities are usually formed independently of the Bank. Likewise, the degree to which individual researchers become 'embedded' varies according to their regularity of engagement and depth of commitment to Network projects.

The World Bank has not acted alone in its nurturing of the GDN – it is a multilateral initiative. The IMF, the UN and the OECD amongst others are highly professionalised organisations with core research staff, which can also be thought of as 'knowledge organisations'. Similarly, the world's major foundations like the Ford or Gates Foundations and the civil servants based in national development agencies like DfID, AusAID or the Japan International Cooperation Agency have strong 'cognitive' interest in the research they fund informing policy. Research organisations and individual experts adapt to the 'knowledge for development' discourse coming from donors. They also meet the challenges and opportunities afforded by new multilateral partnerships to pursue their cognitive interests in global policy networks, in general, including the GDN. A coordinative discourse has been the global public goods framework which provides a basis in economic theory for the public intervention of governments, international organisations and their non-state partners to jointly deliver or finance public goods. In the process, new quasi-public entities emerge. As a global knowledge network, the evolution of GDN from a small 'knowledge for development' project inside the World Bank to become an NGO and then develop into a fully fledged international organisation in less than a decade is a remarkable trajectory in reconfiguring private into formal public authority.

Conclusion

The Rise of Knowledge Networks and the 'Turn' of Think Tanks

Ideas matter, but ideas also need to be made to matter. The new social technology of networks is one important mode of making ideas matter. While ideas matter in the formulation of policy, so do interests. Likewise, ideas matter in shaping institutional innovation or reform, but so too institutions exert their own historical and organisational dynamics on patterns of policy. Ideas matter alongside institutions and interests, but increasingly so, information technology has also become an important social and economic force and which entwines all three elements in complex interplays – intertwingularity – in politics and policy making.

This concluding chapter is organised into two parts. The latter half returns to the theme of the global agora and the intermingling of private and public spheres. The first part, however, addresses the contemporary role of knowledge organisations, especially think tanks, and their possible future trajectories in the Internet age. This part returns to issues that were raised in the Introduction to argue that researchers and their organisations have become transnational actors, aided by the Internet and digital communications, largely in response to cross-border regional and global policy quandaries increasingly apparent in the twenty-first century. Research organisations respond to international organisations, governments and global policy programmes requiring data, evidence and analysis that is reputable, sound and rigorous to help map, monitor and interpret pressing policy problems.

The expert status of both private and publicly funded policy-analytic organisations has been constructed by the 'two worlds' metaphor of bridging research and policy. The policy roles of think tanks, research NGOs and philanthropic foundations have been legitimated when and if they are incorporated into a transnational policy community and contracted by governments and international organisations. Knowledge networks and organisations are not mere dispensers of evidence, on the academic sidelines, to be used by others in making policy. Many have become co-constitutive of global and regional policy processes. A central theme across all chapters has been to dispute the notion of a smooth linear transfer of scientific truths or socio-economic evidence from (knowledgeable) researchers to (uninformed) decision makers in policy formulation as a one-way process.

Knowledge organisations and transnational policy

Over the past century, the think tank organisational form has spread around the world and boomed in numbers. The think tank has become ubiquitous. As societies and economies have developed and diversified, the demand for policy analysis and advice has grown in parallel. Think tanks represented custom-designed organisations for brokering academic research to an educated lay public, for synthesising or translating dense theoretical work or statistical data into manageable artifacts for use in policy making and for then 'spinning' or communicating these policy-relevant items to political parties, bureaucrats and other decision makers or regulators. The effectiveness, and legitimacy, of think tanks as knowledge organisation within the public sphere informing policy rests in the analytical service they (claim to) render in connecting 'research and the real world', 'knowledge and power', 'science and politics'.

Ideas matter but so do interests. While policy research and analysis may be under-girded by sophisticated and rigorous methodologies in order to produce an evidence base for decision-making, nevertheless, such analysis enters a political domain where it can be distorted or put towards uses other than intended. For governments and international organisations, it is politically useful to sponsor so-called independent 'thinking outfits', especially if they are civil society based as it provides a democratic patina of consultation. It is also convenient for policy communities and decision makers to buy into the myth of the separate world of science and social inquiry and the popular representation of think tanks and other knowledge-brokering institutions as 'bridges'.

This volume has advanced two seemingly contradictory arguments: knowledge organisations and networks, as well as their funders and patrons, have a vested interest in the public myth of knowledge and power as separate domains, and then notwithstanding this 'myth', the two worlds need to be brought together via research brokerage, 'bridging' strategies and networking. On the first score, the various policy narratives that reflect a deeper ontological separation of knowledge and power have captured the social and political imagination. The discourse of separate worlds of science and policy has had an effect of structuring collective thinking. It is seen in diverse domains and is certainly not limited to think tanks:

- UNESCO Chairs are hailed as 'think tanks' and 'bridge builders' between the academic world, civil society, local communities, research and policy making.[1]
- AusAid funds a leadership programme, organised annually three times at the Australian National University for potential research leaders in the Asia Pacific region on 'Bridging the Research-Policy Divide'.[2]
- The African Development Bank has been cast as a 'knowledge broker' with a role 'linking research to policy'. (Jones, 2011)

Countless other examples could be provided and some were elaborated in earlier chapters. Internationally, the RAPID programme at ODI has been central in advertising and applying this organisational practice, marketing it to other institutions and sometimes adopted without critical reflection (for example, Jones, 2011). Similarly, the informal diplomacy role of ASEAN-ISIS functioned as a 'bridge' between policy makers and the research community of the Southeast Asian region.

'Bridging' is a simple idea. It is easily explained and resonates well with electorates and the educated public. There is power in its simplicity and the assumption that an unmediated transfer of scientific results between experts and decision makers is possible. Not only linking the scholarly and the political, the think tank bridge also connects state and society as well as the national and local with the regional and global. More importantly, it is a policy narrative that helps justify government, philanthropic and international organisation resourcing of knowledge brokers. As a communicative discourse it also demonstrates that funding agencies want value for their research buck spent on universities, NGOs or consultants as much as think tanks, in a reverse cycle of research communication back to electorates or tax payers.

Instead of well-preserved social, legal and professional boundaries between politics and evidence making, knowledge networks and policy networks present a more messy reality of research engagements. The networking, joint policy dialogues, commissioned studies and collaborative ventures between researchers and research organisations with officials and policy-making organisations entangle and entwine both ecologies undermining the 'myth' of two separate worlds. This recognition allows analysis to go beyond a dualism of science on one side of the bridge, and the state or governance on the other, to address the more complex relations between expertise and public policy. Viewed in this way, ideas are neither 'pure' nor in opposition to 'interests'.

At dispute is the enlightenment notion that with time, and with the correct institutional mechanisms between scientists and policy makers, rational opinions will come to dominance in policy making and 'truth' will prevail. Instead, a more chaotic perspective has been presented: research will be interpreted and reconstructed – alongside other forms of knowledge – in the process of its use. Policy makers are not empty vessels into whom to pour knowledge. As the first three chapters discussed, problems do not have predetermined solutions to be discovered (notwithstanding the interests of some researchers or research organisation to chase problems with their solutions). Moreover research and scientific endeavour do not exist only to solve problems. Research also aids critical reflection and helps problematise social and economic phenomena in a dialogue between the researchers and the users of knowledge: critique and interpretation takes place in both realms.

The knowledge brokerage field

The massive advances in telecommunications as well as social networking have fundamentally altered the landscape for think tanks. They are not alone: universities face significant challenges in operations with the onset of MOOCs – massive online open courses – accessible to anyone with an Internet connection. Where universities were once equated as the sole providers of higher education training, now other providers have also entered the industry. A similar predicament arises with think tanks as other policy analysis providers enter their traditional terrain.

The last century witnessed the rise of the think tank as an organisational form. This century may well presage their decline. The think tank increasingly faces competition from new types of research and analysis organisations as well as new platforms and media for communication. Today, there is more 'interchangeability between the think tank public intellectual and the academic public intellectual' (Misztal, 2012: 128). Universities have established their own policy research centres rivalling the independent or 'stand-alone' institute. As discussed in Chapter 3, many of the world's leading NGOs have developed a strong in-house capacity for policy research. Business associations, multi-national corporations, professional bodies and trade unions are better able to proselytise their policy perspectives with in-house research units. Global task forces are convened from time to time to address pressing cross-border issues. For instance, the Global Commission on Drugs is a private initiative, which is part financed by the OSF, but also supported by other foundations, think tanks, institutes and advocacy groups to deliver an alternative evidence and policy perspectives on 'harm reduction' and drug control. As discussed below in more detail, the Group of Twenty (G20) now attracts a range of 'free advice' providers.

Not only is there a greater range of knowledge-brokering organisations, the individual researcher or 'policy wonk' also functions in a changed landscape. No longer are they as reliant on intermediary organisations to promote or publicise their work in policy-making circles. Today, the university researcher can circumvent the think tank and go direct to the blogosphere. New vehicles such as *The Conversation* have emerged. Launched first in Australia in 2011, rolled out later in Europe and India, *The Conversation* (2012) is 'an independent source of analysis, commentary and news from the university and research sector – written by acknowledged experts and delivered directly to the public'. It is complemented by other new media outlets like the *Huffington Post* and the *Open Democracy* portal amongst many, many others.

YouTube and Ted-Ex have launched many 'talking heads' as minor celebrities, albeit often short-lived ones. Massive experimentation with information technology and the Internet in pedagogy is already well underway. Research communication can be unmediated in a direct connection with parliamentary interns, World Bank staffers, naval officers, politicians, electoral research officers, personal assistants to CEOs, departmental heads – all of whom can trawl the Internet for information if they have the time and inclination. Interlocutors and research brokers will continue to be important. Equally important is the need for talented editors and skilled curators, organisations as much as individuals, to help those within policy processes to quickly discern the credibility and quality of knowledge(s) from disparate scientific and advocacy groups. The Future World Foundation (2013), for instance, claims it does so through its new 'information portal of the Global Agora'. Information technology also makes knowledge sharing a fast and cheap process compared to the situation three decades ago when newspapers and books were published only in hard copy.

> In the past, conversations could only be intertwingled across paper memos, faxes, written reports and email. Until the advent of the Web it wasn't possible to intertwingle conversations, networks, analysis and work in near-real time and global scale. Now that's trivial and essentially free with basic Web access. (Lloyd, 2010)

The rapid dispersion and at the same time the massive proliferation of knowledge complicate the absorption of information by policy-making communities. A problem of governance, as much at local as it is at transnational levels, becomes one of 'editing' the over-supply of evidence and analysis from research NGOs, universities and advocacy groups for the most reliable expertise and scientific advice. This potentially represents a space for the reinvention of think tanks both to protect their brand name and to provide new services.

As Chapter 2 argued, demand can be distorted by the politicisation of research and scientific findings via selective use, de-contextualisation or misquotation. However, it can also be the case that knowledge providers and the relationships they develop with consumers and funders of their services can also skew or inflate perspectives of what constitutes timely or worthwhile analysis. Growing scepticism about think tanks is exemplified by the weary comment of a *Financial Times* columnist about their self-serving behaviour:

> The story was given further padding by a study from an ambulance-chasing Washington think-tank, which warned that it would continue to convene media conference calls until its quixotic and politically suicidal plan to ameliorate whatever crisis was gathering had been given respectful though substantially undeserved attention. (Rachman, 2008)

Another factor challenging think tanks may well result from their own initiatives to collaborate. Their research partnerships and networks indirectly build the research communication skills and policy capacity of their partners, in some small degree diluting the organisational impact of individual think tanks. Policy analysis capacity and reputation becomes vested in the network of a wider constituency of experts, advisors and knowledge providers. This was the fate of the think tanks in ASEAN-ISIS outlined in Chapter 6. In the 1980s and 1990s, these elite-level institutes almost had a monopoly on the policy analysis function in their respective nation-states. They formed a tight interpretive community fortunate to see their discourse on regional security structure policy debates and inform political agendas. Today, there are many competing sources of analysis from within their countries as the media, university sector and NGOs strengthen.

Demand for policy analysis and expert commentary, and the character of its utilisation, has also altered with 'the changing boundaries between public, private and voluntary sectors; to the changing role of the state' where 'the informal authority of networks supplements the formal authority of government' (Rhodes, 2012: 32). The venues of governance have widened alongside the growing array of international commissions, global public–policy networks and transnational decision-making domains and which act as magnets for advisors and analysts.

This book has outlined the manner in which knowledge agents are intertwined in a double devolution of governance: first, a sideways partial delegation of governance responsibilities to non-state or quasi-state actors, and second, there is an upward decentralisation of governance among transnational policy forums. In these two dynamics, experts exercise power by virtue of their possession of, or access to, evidence and high-quality information. Accordingly, a third devolutionary dynamic of governance comes from the ability to constitute, control and legitimise the very issues that are the subjects of political deliberation and public debate. Renditions of John Maynard Keynes' famous dictum are often recounted to convey the impact of intellectual influences:

> The ideas of economists and political philosophers ... are more powerful than is commonly understood. Indeed the world is ruled by little else. Practical men who believe themselves to be quite exempt from any intellectual influences, are usually the slaves of some defunct economist. Madmen in authority who hear voices in the air are distilling their frenzy from some academic scribbler of a few years back. (Keynes, 1936: 383)

Yet, this quote also maintains the distinction of two separate worlds of ideas and practice. Those in positions of authority are gradually 'enlightened'. Knowledge is assumed to have a 'trickle down' effect. However, as has been argued: 'Rather than understanding power and discourse to be properties of particular actors, which assumes that knowledge and interests are distinct, expert ideas and discourses can themselves be powerful entities' (Fischer, 2003: 45). To illustrate, one principle that underpins the recently launched Future World Foundation (2013) 'is that contemplating the future allows us to create it'.

Ironically, Keynes was one who traversed both the scholarly and policy worlds. But Keynes was reflecting on an era where the individual could often be seen to make an impact. Scholarly communities were much smaller. There was a greater degree of social interaction between political and intellectual elites usually drawn from a common elite milieu. It was a time when scholars and intellectuals built their reputations on independent research often as a lone scholar. Today, of the seven million scientists and researchers that The Royal Society (2012: 5) estimates to be working worldwide, relatively few have direct engagement with bureaucracy or policy making. Instead, they are identified as much by their employing organisation, professional association or academy as they are for their individual research and analysis skills. Increasingly, science and technological innovation advances on the basis of teams in laboratories or research consortia. The major grant programmes and national science academies exhort such collaborative endeavours.

As suggested in the case study chapters, rather than influence resting in the scientific work of significant individual scholars, it rests in the collective contributions of the research community that develops consensual knowledge or an evidence base over time. In short, in a more complex social and economic world facing many intractable problems of governance, the organisational base and affiliation of an 'expert' – and the necessary but costly resources the organisation provides such as computing facilities, libraries, access to databases and publication outlets, etc. – becomes an essential component of knowledge agency and brokerage. Instead of an analytic focus on individual 'thinkers' or 'public intellectuals', this study has focused predominantly on one type of knowledge organisation – the think tank. Even so, other types of knowledge organisation like philanthropic foundations, NGOs, consultancy firms and commissions of inquiry also populate the *ecology* of policy research and analysis.

The most recent evolution brought about by both communications technology and a growing preponderance of networks and consortia among knowledge organisations, and with other more diverse actors in the knowledge ecology, suggests that traditional think tank functions are being unravelled from the think tank organisational form. Global forums and national policy dialogues continue to draw upon the expertise concentrated in think tanks. But they are not dependent on these organisations to hone and tailor practitioner knowledge, professional expertise and scholarly insights into digestible policy formats. The types of knowledge-brokering organisations have widened. Both DAWN and Oxfam are advocacy organisations but have also developed a credible policy research profile. As noted, the Internet often provides a short cut to independent policy research. Competition and e-communication are eroding, gradually, the unique client base of think tanks.

Second, the upward decentralisation of governance among an array of new global and regional decision-making forums of mixed public–private composition also disaggregates and disperses knowledge functions. As Chapter 2 outlined, civil society-based transnational advocacy networks have proliferated. Gatherings of experts and policy practitioners such as the World Economic Forum in Davos on general matters of global governance, and others on specific matters such as the Evian Group on trade policy, also engineer elite policy dialogue between corporate leaders, public sector officials and specialist social scientists. These are non-state actors feeding advice and analysis to policy makers and the media in the hope of changing policy agendas. But it is the global public policy networks, like GDN, and a host others such as Global Forum for Health Research or the Global Road Safety Facility that represent new domains of the public sector. They are symptomatic of a governmental rationality where policy objectives are pursued *in partnership with* non-state actors in the private sector or civil society.

The network modality itself has also been diffused as a tool of governance to be adopted by governments around the world. In Canada, 'knowledge-based networks' are promoted by the government as its 'approach to development' (Gross Stein et al., 2001, viii). The burgeoning of global programmes and public–private partnerships has a 'network effect' of interoperability. That is, the more frequently this governance modality is deployed, the more effective it becomes, and the more likely it will be deployed yet again.

But knowledge networks are also a mode of governance. This is a third involution rather than an outward devolution of governance from public agencies. As the global agora features a lower degree of institutionalisation of *de jure* legal and political processes than at the national level, then the governance impact of knowledge organisations and networks may be more pervasive in terms of problem formulation, agenda-setting as well as monitoring and evaluation. The policy discourses of networks do not just describe reality but also help constitute it. For example, Chapter 2 mentioned that the European Commission through its Frameworks Programmes sponsors research consortia across the sciences, humanities and social sciences. In the social science ecology, for instance, both EU-GRASP (a programme on Changing Multilateralism: The EU As a Global-Regional Actor in Security and Peace) and GR:EEN (short for Global Re-ordering: Evolution through European Networks) address the role of the EU as a global and regional actor.[3] They do not simply do research but, in the minds of their funders, are 'large scale integrating projects' for the EU to enhance and embed the European project. Collaborative research on European regionalism and the diffusion of 'Europeanisation beyond Europe' has the effect of repeating and replicating the discourse, establishing the discourse as dominant, notwithstanding the sceptical and critical tributaries running through these research endeavours (Börzel and Risse, 2012; Beeson and Stone, 2013).

Similarly, CGIAR undertakes international agricultural research but is also constituted as a global policy partnership with developing and industrialised country governments, foundations, and international and regional organisations. Established for well over 30 years, it was the first model with which the World Bank had within its arsenal to offer as a broad template, or inspiration, for subsequent global programmes. With official patronage, ASEAN-ISIS constructed the scholarly concepts and elaborated policy narratives of security cooperation, that is, a policy discourse on which governments could then proceed to build new institutions of regional governance and a mode distinct and different to that diffused from the EU (Beeson and Stone, 2013). These networks become part of the ecology of governance but, simultaneously, the network logic is reinforced.

In sum, knowledge brokering and research communication of policy analysis is no longer hinged to the custom-designed organisation, or social technology, of last century – the think tank. Nor for that matter is print media as important as it once was in this role. Governance at local, national and transnational levels still requires input of expertise, evidence and evaluation. Yet, information technology and the multi-actor character of policy networks level the playing field in many forum of governance debate.

The title of this Conclusion implies a bold thesis, but it is one that is better cast as a question. Think tanks will not die out. These organisations will continue to play a vital role in policy debates. Numbers may well continue to grow for some time yet. Moreover, many of these organisations have adapted rapidly to the opportunities afforded by new information technology. The leading think tanks have highly sophisticated web-sites and communications programmes. The solid reputation of the elite institutes for rigorous analysis may also shed a favourable light across the entire industry. The 'social prominence' of the think tank in public debate is high. However, maintaining quality and reputation with competence in the communication codes and disciplinary specialism associated with universities and the professions entails equally high costs. Not all think tanks can sustain such costs, nor desire to do so when the dynamics of digitised (new) media generates demand for celebrity 'policy wonks' who are noted more for their contribution to 'info-tainment' than for their scientific pedigree (Misztal, 2012: 128).

Policy processes in the global agora

The idea of the agora being transnational or a digitised domain has growing recognition (*inter alia*, Laine, 2012; McNutt and Pal, 2011). The metaphor of global agora has been developed further here to convey a fast changing, multi-level domain where new policy responsibilities are taking shape but where what is 'public' and what is 'private' becomes unclear. Politics, markets and societal forces do not simply intersect; instead, elements of each intermesh in numerous configurations. The global agora is also disordered: institutions are underdeveloped and political authority is dispersed through networks. At a more extreme level, the Internet further 'intertwingles' and interconnects all in a deeper and more complex manner.

Intertwingularity is a portmanteau phrase from 'entwined' and 'intermingled' developed to capture the complexity of interrelations in human knowledge. 'Intertwingularity is not generally acknowledged – people keep pretending they can make things hierarchical, categorizable and sequential' (Nelson, 1987: DM37). From this perspective, the rationalist project is artificial in that it fails to comprehend and accept the cross-connected nonlinear informational state of multiple contexts. Applied to the global agora, intertwingled policy making is a condition that defies simplistic categorisation as a consequence of the diversity, decay and constant renewal of networks, transnational programmes and 'experimentalist governance' (Sabel and Zeitlin, 2012).

While acknowledging intertwinglularity as a useful idea in conveying heightened complexity, this volume takes some steps backwards from the notion of 'everything being deeply intertwingled' all at once. Indeed, the emergence of initiatives like Future World Foundation (which has also adopted the term 'global agora') or *The Conversation* or other portals suggests that the current state of intertwingling is indiscriminate, and rather random, without editors and resource banks. Furthermore, the preceding chapters have introduced networks as coordinating structures in the agora as well as venues of policy processes, that whilst not linear and sequential, are at least guided more or less by frameworks that seek to steer decision-making in line with norms and principles.

Policy change is also geared around powerful interests and institutional forces that exert some control and regulatory pattern over social and economic development. For example, the centralising management dynamic to New York in the OSF 'network of networks' is also seen in the gravitational pull to Washington DC., with the CGIAR (The Royal Society, 2012: 85). Concentrations of power will continue to create strong nodal points in the global agora imposing some order and coordination. While Chapter 3 suggested that the welter of information creates 'white noise' or 'static' in governance processes, nevertheless, at the same time new niches emerge for knowledge 'editors' to weed out and validate the reputable analysis and quality research in order to distinguish it from that which is of low quality or sub-standard. Patterns of power re-assert themselves amidst the complexity.

However, rather than being simply editors of content, there is also a growing recognition of there being both space and demand for 'curators of dialogue'. As social networking and the blogosphere expands to become more of a digital and visual sphere, new social norms develop and experimentation with ideas about 'Internet civics' emerge. Twitter has become a 'forum' for civic conversation. Mobile phone technology allows for 'civic crowd funding'. That is, a twitter campaign is mounted to seek funds for a rejuvenation of a local park or a city-based social service project. It is an alternative funding route for the provision of a local public good rather than the more traditional sources found in local government or a local charitable organisation. The Internet and mobile phone communications become the infrastructure of a digital public sphere in the global agora (Castells, 2008).

As yet, there is poor understanding of the dynamics within this public sphere. 'Clicktivism', or the flooding of requests for funds, friends or social foment, is one of the negative consequences that saps time and attention. Even so, the notion of 'digital citizenship' also contains the idea that it is incumbent upon individuals and communities to maintain their literacy level in order to function effectively in global agora. This kind of literacy might increase awareness of the governance roles and powers of the growing number of transnational executive networks and global or regional public–private networks. The transnational policy communities and networks that help create the transnational public sector could be a force for democratisation by creating new spaces for 'stakeholder' interests and participation. However, as Chapters 1 and 2 argued, the arcane interests, the professional communication codes and issue-specific technocratic character of many GPPNs and TENs can be exclusionary. Networks may be 'gateways', but they can also function as 'gatekeepers' in the global agora, restricting access to closed circles of professional elites. GPPNs and TENs use technologies and techniques that facilitate 'government at a distance' but which also creates technocratic distance from national publics.

Creating a discourse of a global agora – of global policy, global programmes, a transnational public sphere – places discussion in tension with the traditional discourse of state power and sovereignty. The state is not in demise. As noted by UNESCO MOST, yet another programme promoting links between research, policy and practice:

> International fora are useful for advancing the establishment of shared languages and common terms of reference. However, change towards social development remains a distinctive national affair and this despite the profound influence and work done by international governmental organizations or NGOs. (Papanagnou, 2010: 36)

Likewise, The Royal Society (2011: 36) notes that the 'global science land-scape is underpinned by national infrastructures, which reflect the research priorities, capacity and strengths of individual countries'. Sovereignty as a principle and the practice of sovereign policy making remains well entrenched even though state capacity in asserting sovereignty differs substantially between an advanced industrial economy of the OECD in contrast to, say, a failed state in sub-Saharan Africa. Although inter-state cooperation is necessary and will persevere, the negotiation difficulties, slow progress and setbacks associated with traditional international responses to global problems inevitably entails experimentation with networks and other kinds of governance coalitions.

Political strategies and visions are always challenged. Indeed the very idea of a global agora would be rejected by those of a realist persuasion and resisted more generally by those who see enduring power vested in sovereign states. Networks and global programmes not only unite some interests but also divide them from others in the debates over defining and managing the global agora and the dialogues over who should have the responsibility for transnational administration. For example, the G20 is one venue where such deliberations take place. To illustrate, the G20 has become a magnet for attracting expert advice: it shows first, how the knowledge–policy nexus fuels the constitution of the agora; second, the centrality of networks as the social technology in support of global summitry; and third, the truncated technocratic character of the public sphere in the G20 orbit.

Think20

The G20 is the premier forum for international economic cooperation with members from 19 countries and the EU. G20 leaders, finance ministers and central bank governors meet regularly to address global economic and financial challenges. In December 1999, the finance ministers and central bank governors of advanced and emerging countries of systemic importance met in Berlin, Germany, for an informal dialogue on key issues affecting global economic stability. Since then, finance ministers and central bank governors have met annually. In 2008, US President George W. Bush convened a meeting of G20 leaders in Washington DC as the magnitude of the global financial crisis threatened to engulf the entire global economy. The G20 was viewed as the most suitable forum for achieving a high-level coordinated response, given that it represents both advanced and emerging economies from all corners of the world. In addition, its relatively small membership allows the group to reach agreements. Since then, the G20 has held numerous Leaders' Summits to seek agreements on global economic matters.

The G20 is an important international meeting and summit. However it is not an international organisation like the IMF or UN. It lacks inter-governmental treaty status. It operates without a charter, votes or legally binding decisions. The G20 is an informal forum for debate among systemically important countries. It is, in effect, a self-appointed club of nations, where members interact as equals and emphasis is given on reaching consensus.

The G20 has a 'deputies' process' that prepares the ground for meetings of finance ministers and central bank governors (the 'ministerial'). G20 deputies meet at least twice a year before the annual meeting of ministers and governors, which is typically held in the late autumn. The 'ministerial' is the capstone meeting of the year. It is hosted by the chair country. Workshops and seminars for deputies are also organised through the year in support of the year's agenda (and may be hosted by other countries). The number of workshops and seminars has varied, but three has become customary.

Importantly, the G20 lacks a permanent secretariat. Instead, G20 deputies establish a management Troika consisting of the previous, current, and immediately upcoming chairs. This innovation was to serve the continuity of the Group but otherwise the host country provides secretariat services. Among its duties, the Troika proposes agenda issues for the G20, selects speakers in consultation with members, and deals with the logistics of meetings. It also gives the current and upcoming chairs ready access to the experience of the previous year's chair.

In 2006, study groups were introduced on an *ad hoc* basis. Their purpose is to 'maintain momentum of analytic work in the G20 that may not be carried by the main agenda' (G20, 2008: 24–25). Each chairing country establishes a G20 web-site for that year. In addition to background information available to the public, a confidential members-only site is maintained to circulate background papers and other material for meetings and to archive documents. Work of study groups is also posted for discussion. The interactions among the Sherpas, the study groups and the deputies are characteristic of a 'transnational executive network'.

The G20 has formally recognised that its activities are enriched by the contributions of academia and think tanks, or specialised research centres. The Mexican Presidency of the G20 in 2012 organised a meeting of think tanks in Mexico. It was the first time researchers were invited to take part directly in the discussions of a G20 Presidency. The rationale behind the incorporation of think tanks and research institutes was that 'think tanks significantly contribute to the transparency, analysis and evaluation of public policy', including the G20 process.[4] That is, invited think tanks would play a role in following up previous results and commitments. Moreover, they would deliver a collective Think20 report with specific recommendations to the next G20 Sherpa Meeting the following month.[5] Whether such report writing and analytical support is taken on board is a moot point. Indeed, as one participant noted somewhat tongue-in-cheek: 'It will come as no surprise that, in a gathering of think tankers, the area of greatest consensus was on the role of think tanks themselves' (Thirlwell, 2012).

Although touted by some as being initiated by the Mexican Government and organised by COMEXI – the Mexican Council on Foreign Relations – Think20 has a history going back nearly three years prior to a meeting at Langdon Hall in Canada convened by CIGI. Three of the most important rationales proffered by the think tankers of the utility of Think20 initiative were as follows:

- Serving as an ideas bank, and providing new ideas and policies for G20 governments.
- Providing a potential source of accountability through monitoring how well G20 governments delivered on their commitments.
- Working to deliver buy-in to the G20 process, through helping to explain the importance of the G20 and of (at least some of) the policies it is trying to promote. (Thirlwell, 2012)

In short, Think20 was designed to provide ideational support and research services for G20 processes – coordinative discourses. In addition, in its public outreach it would help provide a communicative discourse for the educated lay public. Knowledge and policy become intermeshed in global summitry.

Although a young international grouping, the G20 has evolved quickly. Debate has intensified as to whether 'the G20 can move from being a crisis committee to being a steering committee' (Cooper, 2012: 1). Institutionally, it remains weak without a permanent secretariat and dependent on host country capacity for preparations and continuity. Indeed one of the recommendations of the first Think20 Report was to state that the Troika Process was not working and that serious consideration be given to creating a 'Bureau'. The Report also went on to recommend that the G20 'institutionalize the Think-20 to serve as idea "banks", monitoring and accountability mechanisms, and help deliver feedback and buy-in from sceptical publics to accept correct, but painful, policies. The Think-20 can also be asked to craft assessments of potential agenda items' (Think-20 Mexico, 2012). Other recommendations on process were deeper institutionalisation and embedding of the G20 in the global agora.

The creation of Think20 also raises issues about participation and representation in the global agora via knowledge organisations and networks. The following remarks are not exclusive to Think20. This initiative is illustrative. It is feasible to raise similar matters vis-a-vis the World Economic Forum or the Global Drug Commission or Future World Foundation.

First, the process for the group's composition was not a transparent one. This might reflect on the credibility of G20's intent to make itself more democratic. One assumption could be that think tanks invited to Think20 were selected on the basis of G20 membership. Most members in Think20 are represented by a country-specific research organisation. Yet the February 2012 meeting of Think20 included a Singaporean body (which is not a G20 member). Some G20 members such as Saudi Arabia or Argentina were not included. However, the institutes behind Think20 argue they are neither an advocate nor mirror of the G20, hence no need to copy its composition when useful or relevant research from elsewhere can be drawn in.

A second critique suggests the roles and responsibilities distributed among Think20 institutes are in tension with aims of the G20 to give a voice to emerging and developing economies. One criticism is that the organisation and management of Think20 resides in a club of institutions from the G20's advanced economies, thereby perpetuating traditional North–South relations and under-representation of developing economies' interests. For example, 'A flagrant example of misrepresentation is that the African continent is represented in Think20 by only one regional forum, while the EU is represented by four research institutes' (de Ridder and Sánchez Díaz, 2012). Another critic suggests that it is not simply a limited range of think tanks involved, but that academics have been left out of the G20 altogether (Kirton, 2012: 1).

New initiatives are easy to criticise as their architects scramble to raise funds and mobilise interests. As yet, it is too early to say whether Think20 will have some determining force on G20 processes. Its role is advisory and informal, notwithstanding the formal invitation extended by the Mexican Chair followed by Russia and Australia. Unless its expert services are more systematically incorporated into G20 processes recommendations, Think20 could become intellectual ornamentation to the G20's democratisation process. Indeed, this new think tank summit operates in tandem with a proliferation of forums surrounding the G20, including the B20 (for business), L20 (for labour unions), Y20 (for young people) and the CS20 (for civil society organisations). All will be clamouring for attention and for adoption of their recommendations. It may mean that Think20, like the others, may become no more than the 'side event' they are credited with on the official G20 Mexican Presidency web-site.

This is not so much scientific competition as competition among knowledge brokers and policy entrepreneurs. For example, the Council of Councils includes 'leading institutions from nineteen countries, roughly tracking the composition of the G20' and represents an alternative to Think20. Another G20 Foreign Policy Think Tank Summit was called mid-2012 by the University of Philadelphia and co-sponsored by Fundação Getulio Vargas (Brazil). The Future World Foundation also claims to build 'on a request from the G20 to create a community of think-tanks' (2013).

Along with the clutter of competing networks and knowledge brokers, there are also never-ending struggles between different 'discourses', 'worldviews' and 'regimes of truth' (Jacobsen, 2007). Rather than 'truth speaking to power', as the myth of separate worlds of knowledge and power would have us believe, any policy-making consensus is a communal construction. Expert organisations or knowledge networks do not stand apart from the agora in order to impose solutions upon it. Instead their role is to intervene in a way that facilitates awareness and dialogue so that the stakeholders understand jointly the collective problems of relevance to them to pose corresponding questions and explore possible solutions. It is in this sense that knowledge is co-produced. Authorship of knowledge does not reside solely with the experts, but also with the whole gamut of stakeholders who participate in these deliberations.

The G20 is symptomatic of contemporary reconfiguring of the agora and reflective of how knowledge organisations and networks in its orbit are remade as entrepreneurial agents of governance. This is evident in the 'global public policy network' literature and equally apparent in many of the 'global programmes' sponsored by the World Bank and UN. Global and regional networks and their subjects (stakeholders, donors, international organisation staff, support professionals and government and corporate sponsors) are better integrated into new processes and experimental procedures of global management and transnational regulation. Rather than the neo-liberal world order being understood as an ideology or conscious expression of coherent capitalist agendas, it is better comprehended as garbage can of rationalities, network strategies, coordinative discourses and expert techniques that allow devolved governance and collaborative policy making. Policy solutions become 'temporary truces in a constant struggle over ideals; they are the passing discursive constructions of a reality always in motion' (Papanagnou, 2010: 26).

Within the global agora, network knowledge practices continually feed into and inform political discourses by interrogating sovereignty and conceptualising new modes of governance above the state (Djelic and Sahlin, 2012). Networks – whether they act like TANs as the OSF sometimes does, or as GPPNs like the GDN – can be regarded as technologies of governance that regulate, normalise and discipline. They help to introduce and to deepen the administrative rationalities associated with network governance. The knowledge and expert meanings produced by Think20 or the Council of Councils are representative of policy thinking and debates within the parameters of the dominant but sometimes disrupted neo-liberal discourse on the predominance of market mechanisms and limited powers of state.

The sphere of public debate is widened by the activities of knowledge networks and policy networks in the global agora, but in a contained fashion. Not dissimilar to the manner in which 17th century salon became an extension of European court society, the multi-actor policy network/knowledge network is an extension of governance in the global agora. Contrary to accounts of the salon as an oppositional public sphere (Habermas, 1989), salons were populated by members of high society who either disdained public opinion or lacked popular engagement with it. The transnational policy communities that serve the G20 or circulate around international organisations and global public policy networks are partially privatised domains of public deliberation with participation limited to stakeholders, office holders and designated experts. For instance, interest in the procedures of the Global Gas Flaring Reduction initiative, unsurprisingly for most readers, appeals primarily to a narrow specialist audience of engineers, mining companies and development specialists.[6] Similarly, ASEAN-ISIS was a gathering of regional policy experts in the agora. Networks such as these are elite groupings restricted, in the main, to those who have professional mastery of the communications codes or to those who have either material power or political control over a given policy problem that is very often defined by these codes.

The co-construction of knowledge and analytical frames for the purpose of ordering the global agora does not imply that either policy analysis is participatory or that decision-making is democratically deliberative. Participatory policy deliberation in transnational spheres is not feasible in the sense that a local community can convene a town hall meeting, public hearings or a local referendum. The local community is a geographically concentrated interest. Notwithstanding the benefits of the Internet, the transaction costs of transnational hearings would be extremely high. And 'there can be no *global* public sphere because of the impoverished state of the existing global media, which address merely an aggregate (and culturally nonspecific) public chiefly as a passive spectator' (Eckersley, 2007: 333). The default is to the quasi-public knowledge networks–policy networks, of limited representation, that help weave together the joint initiatives of states, international organisation and non-state actors. These transnational policy communities that implement network agendas are the 'wholly active citizens' of the global agora.

To date, these networks are notable more for their coordinative discourses for efficiency and effectiveness in delivery of global public goods, than for their communicative discourses with publics. Transnational public sectors are evolving through the network interactions and the partnership programmes of governments and international organisations. Yet, these issue-specific sectors of policy activity are not tied to any one sovereign authority. By contrast, 'public sphere theory has always been implicitly Westphalian and/or nationalist; it has always tacitly assumed a Westphalian and/or national frame' (Fraser, 2005). This disconnect has implications for the re-creation of the public in the global agora: It takes shape within partnerships of public and private where publicness is diluted or transformed. Public cognition among national citizenries of a transnational public sector and of specific network initiatives is stunted. As a consequence public participation is dissipated and, for the most part, citizenries are 'passive' publics facing a plethora of quite technical, issue-specific transnational policy programmes, commissions and consultative groups.

Constituted as networks, public action in the global agora often has a private face or a chameleon-like character as both public and private. The case studies of this book were chosen for their shifting public–private identities: ODI as private NGO in civil society but enmeshed in a range of networks and funding relationships with public sector entities; OSF as a private philanthropy but which partners with governments and international organisations to introduce and establish neo-liberal logics of governance and organisation; ASEAN-ISIS as a regional NGO network composed of a mix of independent and state-supported policy institutes engaged in a semi-official processes of informal diplomacy and GDN with World Bank parentage, spun off as an independent NGO, then re-inventing itself as an inter-governmental organisation. The case studies were also chosen as they are not glamorous or topical subject matter in either policy studies or IR scholarship. Instead, the case studies are indicative of the lower order, every-day mechanisms and processes of transnational policy making. They are a few examples of pinions or gears in the machinery of transnational governance. Many more yet need investigation and analysis. And as noted elsewhere: 'Who can enter the agora and participate in the political discussions?' (Laine, 2012: 17). At one level, the public events, products and web-sites of ODI, GDN and OSF provide a great deal of transparency and access. Yet, participation in their activities and networks is very much more limited, and by invitation, especially in the case of ASEAN-ISIS. However, these case study networks are at the more open and observable edge of the global agora and may not be comparable to the vast majority of lesser-known and more technical or exclusive entities. Whilst transnational networks and global policy programmes are forging open new public spheres and spaces, the scope to be participative, cosmopolitan or democratic is an open question. The global agora is not made up of 'miniature democratic societies'; instead, it provides different spaces and opportunities for various 'political choreographies' (Laine, 2012: 53–54).

Networks are both structures *and* relational processes in the global agora. As processes, these networks are sites and venues – universities, think tanks, philanthropies, official commissions of inquiry and private initiative – for the construction of shared identities and problem definition, and for the flow of ideas and people. Within the capillaries of these networks, ideas have careers and are spread within and across nations. Ideas gain momentum, support and traction when they are repeated, translated, revised, reiterated, cross-referenced and disseminated through and beyond networks. Ideas are magnified by new collaborations, co-authoring, secondments, joint appointments, interlocking directorates and international advisory councils, whereby those in these networks write, speak and 'appear on platforms' at each other's events and contribute to in-house journals, magazines, web-sites and twitter campaigns (Ball and Exley, 2010: 155). These interpretative practices of consensus building create a unity and regularity of policy thinking, structuring the very terms of policy debate. But as constellations of interests and stakeholders, networks are conduits for the making of policy careers but also intersections for careers traversing university, NGO, private sector and public service. Knowledge networks are often composed of those who wish their worldview or scientific rationality to have authoritative force in their own right rather than mere influence with others who make or break policy. The knowledge actors and communities discussed here sought entry into transnational and national policy communities on the basis of their epistemic authority. Various types of networks have been one means of this engagement. Yet, as networking accelerates across policy sectors and proliferated globally, network mentalities, rationalities and techniques also become a mode of management. Networks accrue authority to steer social and economic processes, regulate behaviour and structure governance in the global agora.

Notes

1 The Global Agora: Privatising Policy Processes in Transnational Governance

1. The Athenian Agora Excavations: http://www.agathe.gr/introduction.html, date accessed 26 December 2012.
2. The Master of Global Policy Studies degree at the Lyndon B. Johnson School of Public Affairs claims to be 'path-breaking' and to go 'beyond traditional international affairs programs to offer a multidisciplinary approach to the complex economic, political, technological, and social issues of the 21st century and considers the full range of influences on contemporary global policy – governments, private industry, and non-governmental organizations': http://www.utexas.edu/lbj/degreeprograms/mgps, date accessed 26 December 2012.
3. University College London, MSc International Policy claims to be the first Masters programme of its type in the UK: http://www.ucl.ac.uk/spp/teaching/masters/msc-international-public-policy, date accessed 26 December 2012.
4. The School of Public Policy, Central European University: http://spp.ceu.hu/, date accessed 26 December 2012. SPP is built upon an existing Department of Public Policy that introduced graduate-level 'global policy studies' in 2004.
5. GAVI Partnership, previously known as the Global Alliance for Vaccines and Immunisation: www.gavialliance.org, date accessed 26 December 2012.
6. Global Water Partnership: www.gwpforum.org, date accessed 26 December 2012.
7. Lisa Anderson, Dean of Columbia University's School of International and Public Affairs – SIPA, quoted 19 September 2005. Likewise, Patrick Dunleavy, MPA Director at London School of Economics, commenting on the launch of the GPPN: 'In a globalised world we need to build much broader and deeper networks than we have had in the past, ones that integrate the partners in much more equitable, multi-polar ways, and that bridge more directly between research and advanced teaching': http://www.prnewswire.co.uk/cgi/news/release?id=154039, date accessed 26 December 2012.

2 Knowledge Networks/Policy Networks

1. International Network on Environmental Compliance and Enforcement, INECE: http://inece.org/, date accessed 26 December 2012.
2. The Evian Group: http://www.imd.org/research/centers/eviangroup/index.cfm, date accessed 26 December 2012. The Evian Group became a legal part of its host institution in 2012 and is now known officially as The Evian Group@ IMD. The International Institute for Management Development (IMD) is a business school based in Switzerland. Following on from the founder of the Evian Group, Jean-Pierre Lehman, the current director is Carlos A. Primo Braga, a former Vice-President (External Affairs) of the World Bank.

3. TRIPS is the WTOs 'Agreement on Trade Related Aspects of Intellectual Property Rights'; PRSPS are 'poverty reduction strategy papers' required by the IMF and World Bank in debt relief processes; GATS is the WTOs 'General Agreement on the Trade in Services' and GPGs are 'global public goods'.

3   Think Tank Thinking

1. Grattan Institute: http://grattan.edu.au/about-us, date accessed 26 December 2012.
2. CIDOB: http://www.cidob.org/en/cidob, date accessed 26 December 2012.
3. Institute of Public Affairs, Warsaw: http://www.isp.org.pl/about-isp,22.html, date accessed 26 December 2012.
4. Egyptian Center for Economic Studies: http://www.eces.org.eg/mission.asp, date accessed 26 December 2012.
5. Centre for European Reform: http://www.cer.org.uk/about, date accessed 26 December 2012.
6. C.D. Howe Institute: http://www.cdhowe.org/about-cd-howe, date accessed 26 December 2012.
7. Research Institute of the Finnish Economy: http://www.etla.fi/en/etla/, date accessed 26 December 2012.
8. Center for Global Development: http://www.cgdev.org/section/about/mission, date accessed 26 December 2012.
9. Chung-Hua Institution for Economic Research: http://www.cier.edu.tw/ct.asp?xItem=430&CtNode=25&mp=2, date accessed 26 December 2012.

4   RAPID Knowledge

1. Civil Societies and Partnership Programme at the Overseas Development Institute, funded by the UK Department for International Development: http://www.odi.org.uk/projects/2601-civil-society-partnerships-programme which evolved into the Evidence Based Policy in Development Network: http://www.ebpdn.org, date accessed 26 December 2012.
2. Author participation in meetings in 2006 and 2007.

5   Translating Foundation Ideas

1. Open Society Foundations 'Mission and Values': http://www.soros.org/about/mission-values, date accessed 19 June 2012.
2. OSF Experts: http://www.soros.org/about/experts, date accessed 19 June 2012.
3. Why INET? http://ineteconomics.org/about/why-inet, date accessed 19 June 2012.
4. Originally named Transparency International Research Institute (spun-off from Transparency International after a leadership dispute), the organisation prefers to be known as TIRI. It describes itself as one of 'a new generation of global policy network': http://www.tiri.org/, date accessed 19 June 2012.

5. Soros Joins Health Groups to Battle Drug-Resistant TB, HIV Explosion, 14 March, 2007: http://www.soros.org/initiatives/health/focus/phw/news/drugresistant_20070314, date accessed 12 December 2012.
6. The Vienna Declaration: A Global Call to Action for Science-Based Drug Policy, OSF Global Drug Policy Program, 1 July 2010: http://www.soros.org/initiatives/drugpolicy/news/vienna-declaration-20101701, date accessed 12 December 2012.
7. OSF Fellowship Guidelines: http://www.soros.org/sites/default/files/Open%20Society%20Fellowship%20Guidelines_0.pdf, date accessed 19 June 2012.
8. PASOS: http://pasos.org/about-pasos/, date accessed 12 December 2012.

6   Informal Diplomacy of the ASEAN-ISIS Network

1. ISIS Malaysia, Foreign Policy and Security Studies: http://www.isis.org.my/index.php?option=com_content&view=article&id=263&Itemid=186, date accessed 26 December 2012.
2. Membership of ARF includes the ASEAN states and dialogue partners – the USA, the EU, Australia, New Zealand, Canada, South Korea, Russia, China, Laos and Papua New Guinea.
3. *Dialogue and Research Monitor*: http://www.jcie.or.jp/drm/, date accessed 11 December 2012.
4. ASEAN Secretariat: http://www.aseansec.org/9545.htm, date accessed 3 February 2011.
5. CSCAP Member Committees: http://www.cscap.org/index.php?page=member-committees-page, date accessed 12 December 2012.
6. Shangri La Dialogue: http://www.iiss.org/conferences/the-shangri-la-dialogue/about/, date accessed 12 December 2012.

7   Bankrolling Knowledge Networks

1. The Development Grant Facility integrates the overall strategy, allocations and management of Bank grant-making activities funded from the Administrative Budget under a single umbrella mechanism. Since its inception in 1998, the DGF has supported some 183 priority programmes with a Bank contribution of US$2.1 billion, mobilising an estimated US$16.6 billion from other partners Most of these activities are 'global programmes', some of which were also mentioned in earlier chapters (for instance, the Global Facility for Disaster Reduction and Recovery) and will be subject of a future book. DGF: www.worldbank.org/dgf, date accessed 12 December 2012.
2. The AusAid 'Revitalising Indonesia's Knowledge Sector for Development Policy' programme will support the domestic supply of knowledge products to inform policy, as well as the ability of decision makers to use those products to inform their policy choices: http://www.ausaid.gov.au/publications/pages/6907_4230_9750_6366_1236.aspx, date accessed 12 December 2012.
3. Sheila Page, GDN Governance e-discussion, 9 February 2000. (URL no longer available. Author was the moderator of the World Bank e-discussion.)
4. GDNs Theory of Change: http://www.gdn.int/html/page8.php?MID=12&SID=35, date accessed 9 September 2012.

5. GDN Mission: http://cloud2.gdnet.org/cms.php?id=mission, date accessed 10 August 2012. The new strap-line of mission is 'The Global Research Capacity building Program': http://www.gdn.int/html/page8.php?MID=12&SID=35, date accessed 27 December 2012.
6. GDN Mission: https://researcher.gdnet.org/cms.php?id=mission, date accessed 10 August 2012.

Conclusion

1. UNESCO Chairs in university networking and twinning: http://www.unesco.org/en/unitwin/university-twinning-and-networking/, date accessed 30 May 2013.
2. AusAID: http://i2s.anu.edu.au/courses/bridging-the-research-policy-divide, date accessed 28 May 2012.
3. GR:EEN, which supports research on multilateralism, global governance and networks, is part sponsor of this volume: http://www2.warwick.ac.uk/fac/soc/csgr/green/. EU-GRASP focuses on EU peace and security interests to provide the required theoretical background for assessing the linkages between the EU's current security activities with multi-polarism, international law, regional integration processes and the UN system: http://www.eugrasp.eu/about-eu-grasp, date accessed 28 December 2012. Both are funded by the Seventh Framework Programme of the European Commission.
4. 'Mexican Presidency of the G20 holds the first Think20 Meeting',_G20 press release, 23 February 2012: http://g20mexico.org/en/press-releases/226-presidencia-mexicana-del-g20-celebrara-primera-reunion-del-think-20, date accessed 28 December 2012.
5. Sherpas are the personal representatives of the Heads of State and Government of the members of the Group of Twenty. They are also responsible for conducting all the necessary work prior to the G20 summits.
6. The World Bank's Global Gas Flaring Reduction public–private partnership was launched at the World Summit on Sustainable Development in Johannesburg in 2002. The gas flared annually is equivalent to 25 per cent of the US' gas consumption, 30 per cent of the EU's gas consumption or 75 per cent of Russia's gas exports. The gas flared yearly also represents more than the combined gas consumption of Central and South America. Gas flaring also contributes to climate change through 400 million tonnes of CO_2 emissions annually: http://go.worldbank.org/016TLXI7N0, date accessed 3 January 2013.

Appendix
Websites of Think Tank-Related Associations, Networks and Resource Banks

Accountability Principles for Research Organisations – One World Trust: http://www.oneworldtrust.org/aria/apro-programme

Asian Development Bank Institute, Think Tank Directory: http://www.adbi.org/partnership.think.tanks/

Association of South East Asian Nations Institutes of Strategic and International Studies – ASEAN-ISIS: http://www.isis.org.my/index.php?option=com_content&view=article&id=282&Itemid=127

Atlas Economic Research Foundation: http://atlasnetwork.org/

Council of Councils: http://www.cfr.org/projects/world/council-of-councils/pr1592

European Policy Institute Network – EPIN: http://www.epin.org/new/about

European Think-Tanks Group: http://worldpress.org/library/ngo.cfm

Europe's World: http://www.europesworld.org/NewEnglish/BottomMenu/ThinkTankEurope/tabid/958/Default.aspx

Evidence-Based Policy in Development Network: http://www.ebpdn.org/

Future World Association: http://www.futureworldfoundation.org/

Global Development Network – GDN: www.gdnet.org

International Relations and Security Network, Swiss Federal Institute of Technology, Zurich: http://www.isn.ethz.ch/

National Endowment for Democracy (NED) Network of Democracy Research Institutes: http://www.ndri.ned.org/

Network of East Asian Think Tanks – NEAT: www.neat.org.cn

NIRA's World Directory of Think Tanks (discontinued): http://www.nira.or.jp/past/ice/nwdtt/2005/

Observatoire des think tanks: http://www.oftt.eu/

OnThinkTanks: http://onthinktanks.org/about/

Policy Network: http://www.policy-network.net/

Prospect Think Tank of the Year Awards: http://www.thinktankawards.com/

Stockholm Network: http://www.stockholm-network.org/

Think Tank Fund of the Open Society Foundations Network: http://www.soros.org/initiatives/thinktank

Think Tank Initiative (co-ordinated by IDRC, Canada): http://www.idrc.ca/EN/Programs/Social_and_Economic_Policy/Think_Tank_Initiative/Pages/About.aspx

Think Tanks and Civil Societies Program (Global Go To Think Tanks): http://www.gotothinktank.com/

Think Tanks and Political Foundations – European Ideas Network: http://www.europeanideasnetwork.com/think-tanks

Think20: http://www.g20mexico.org/en/think20

Thinkl: http://thinkl.com/#!/pubs/all/

UNDP International Policy Centre for Inclusive Growth, Directory of Research Centres in Developing Countries: http://www.ipc-undp.org/PageNewSiteb.do?id=116&active=5

Worldpress.org: http://worldpress.org/library/ngo.cfm

References

Abelson, D. E. (2006) *A Capitol Idea: Think Tanks and US Foreign Policy* (Montreal: McGill-Queen's University Press).

Acharya, A. (2004) 'How Ideas Spread: Whose Norms Matter? Norm Localisation and Institutional Change in Asian Regionalism', *International Organisations*, 58 (Spring): 239–75.

Acharya, A. (2011) 'Engagement or Entrapment? Scholarship and Policymaking on Asian Regionalism', *International Studies Review*, 13 (1): 12–17.

Acharya, A. and Johnstone, A. I. Eds (2007) *Crafting Cooperation: Regional International Institutions in Comparative Perspective* (Cambridge: Cambridge University Press).

Adler, E. and Haas, P. M. (1992) 'Conclusion: Epistemic Communities, World Order and the Creation of a Reflective Research Agenda', *International Organisation*, 46 (1): 367–90.

Ahmed, M. (2005) 'Bridging Research and Policy', *Journal of International Development*, 17 (6): 765–69.

Alexander, C. and Pal, L. Eds (1998) *Digital Democracy, Policy and Politics in a Wired World* (Oxford: Oxford University Press).

Andjelkovic, B. (2003) 'A Limited Dialogue: Think Tanks and the Policy Making Process in Serbia', in United Nations Development Program (ed.) *Thinking the Unthinkable: From Thought to Policy. The Role of Think Tanks in Shaping Government Strategy; Experiences from Central and Eastern Europe* (Bratislava: UNDP Regional Bureau for Europe and the Commonwealth of Independent States).

Anonymous (2004) 'Editorial: Tracking Impact Case Studies on the Social Science-Policy Nexus', *International Social Science Journal*, 56 (179): 7–15.

Armitage, D. (2013) 'The International Turn in Intellectual History', in Macmahon, D. M. and Moyn, S. (eds) *Rethinking Modern European Intellectual History* (New York: Oxford University Press).

Arthurs, H. (2001) 'The Re-Constitution of the Public Domain', in Drache, D. (ed.) *The Market or the Public Domain* (London: Routledge).

Ball, D., Milner, A. and Taylor, B. (2006) 'Track 2 Security Dialogue in the Asia-Pacific: Reflections and Future Directions', *Asian Security* 2, (3): 174–88.

Ball, S. J. and Exley, S. (2010) 'Making Policy with "Good Ideas": Policy Networks and the "Intellectuals" of New Labour', *Journal of Education Policy*, 25 (2): 151–69.

Banjerjee, A., Deaton, A., Lustig, N., Rogoff, K. *et al.* (2006) 'An Evaluation of World Bank Research 1998–2005', http://siteresources.worldbank.org/DEC/Resources/84797-1109362238001/726454-1164121166494/RESEARCH-EVALUATION-2006-Main-Report.pdf, date accessed 5 December 2012.

Barani, L. and Sciortino, G. (2011) The Role of Think Tanks in the Articulation of the European Public Sphere, EUROSPHERE online working paper series, http://eurospheres.org/publications/workpackage-reports/, date accessed 21 December 2012.

Bassler, T. and Wisse-Smith, M. (1997) *Building Donor Partnerships* (New York: Open Society Institute).

Bauer, M. W. (2012) 'Tolerant, If Personal Goals Remain Unharmed: Explaining Supranational Bureaucrats' Attitudes to Organizational Change', *Governance*, 25: 485–510.

Bebbington, A., Guggenheim, S., Olson, E., and Woolcock, M. (2004) 'Exploring Social Capital Debates at the World Bank', *Journal of Development Studies*, 40(5): 33–64.

Beeson, M. and Stone, D. (2013) 'The Fortunes and Fallacies of the European Union Model of Regionalism', Paper for Public Policy in the Asian Century, University of Melbourne, 9th November.

Béland, D. and Cox, R. H. (2011) 'Introduction: Ideas and Politics', in Béland, D. and Cox, R. H. (eds) *Ideas and Politics in Social Science Research* (Oxford: Oxford University Press).

Bøås, M. and McNeill, D. (2004) *Global Institutions and Development: Framing the World?* (London: Routledge).

Bohle, D. and Nuenhöffer, G. (2005) 'Why Is There No Third Way? The Role of Neoliberal Ideology, Networks and Think Tanks in Combating Market Socialism and Shaping Transformation in Poland', in Plehwe, D., Walpen, B., and Neunhöffer, G. (eds) *Neoliberal Hegemony: A Global Critique* (London: Routledge).

Börzel, T. A. and Heard-Lauréote, K. (2009) 'Networks in EU Multilevel Governance: Concepts and Contributions', *Journal of Public Policy*, 29: 135–51.

Börzel, T. A. and Risse, T. (2012) 'From Europeanisation to Diffusion', *West European Politics*, 35 (1): 1–19.

Boucher, S. and Hobbs, B. (2004) 'Europe and Its Think Tanks: A Promise to Be Fulfilled. An Analysis of Think Tanks Specialised in European Policy Issues in the Enlarged European Union', *Notre Europe Studies and Research*, No. 35 (Paris: Notre Europe).

Braml, J. (2004) *Think Tanks Versus 'Denkfabriken'?: U.S. and German Policy Research Institutes' Coping with and Influencing Their Environments* (Baden-Baden: Nomos).

Brinkerhoff, J. M. (2002) 'Government-Nonprofit Partnership: A Defining Framework', *Public Administration and Development*, 22 (1): 19–30.

Broad, R. (2006) 'Research, Knowledge and the Art of "Paradigm Maintenance": The World Bank's Development Economics Vice-Presidency (DEC)', *Review of International Political Economy*, 13 (3): 387–419.

Brütsch, C. and Lehmkuhl, D. (2007) *Law and Legalisation in Transnational Relations* (London: Routledge).

Buldioski, G. (2009) 'Think Tanks in Central and Eastern Europe in Urgent Need of a Code of Ethics', *The International Journal of Non-Profit Law*, 11 (3): 42–52.

Buldioski, G. (2010) 'The Global "GO-TO THINK TANKS" and Why I Do Not Believe in It!' Goran's Musings', http://goranspolicy.com/ranking-think-tanks/, date accessed 6 December 2012.

Bull, B. and McNeill, D. Eds (2007) *Development Issues in Global Governance: Public Private Partnerships and Market Multilateralism* (London: Routledge).

Burton, P. (2006) 'Modernising the Policy Process: Making Policy Research More Significant', *Policy Studies*, 27 (3): 173–95.

Butcher, A. (2009) 'The Grand-Daddy of Track-Two Dialogues'. *The Interpreter*, July (Syndey: Lowy Institute).

Büthe, T. and Mattli, W. (2011) *The New Global Rulers: The Privatization of Regulation of the World Economy* (Princeton, NJ: Princeton University Press).

Caballero-Anthony, M. (2006) 'ASEAN ISIS and the ASEAN People's Assembly: Paving a Multi-Track Approach in Regional Community Building', in Soesastro, H., Joewonon, C., and Hernandez, C. G. (eds) *Twenty Two Years of ASEAN ISIS* (Jakarta: Centre for Strategis and International Studies).

Campbell, J. (2008) 'What Do We Know – or Not – about Ideas and Politics?' in Nedergaard, P. and Campbell, J. (eds) *Institutions and Politics* (Copenhagen: DJOF Publishing).

Campbell, J. and Pedersen, O. (2011) 'Knowledge Regimes and Comparative Political Economy' in Béland, D. and Cox, R. H. (eds) *Ideas and Politics in Social Science Research* (New York: Oxford University Press).

Capie, D. and Taylor, B. (2010) 'The Shangri-La Dialogue and the Institutionalisation of Defence Diplomacy in Asia', *Pacific Review*, 23 (3): 359–76.

Carothers, T. (1999) *Aiding Democracy Abroad: The Learning Curve* (Washington DC: Carnegie Endowment for International Peace).

———. (1996) 'Aiding Post-Communist Societies: A Better Way?' *Problems of Post-Communism*, 43 (5 September–October): 15–24.

Castells, M. (2008) 'The New Public Sphere: Global Civil Society, Communications Networks and Global Governance', *The ANNALS of the American Academy of Political and Social Science*, 616 (1): 78–93.

Cerny, P. (2010) *Rethinking World Politics: A Theory of Transnational Pluralism* (Oxford: Oxford University Press).

Chataway, C. (1998) 'Track II Diplomacy: From a Track I Perspective', *Negotiation Journal*, 14 (3): 269–87.

Clair, A. (2010) 'US Billionaires Club Together – To Give Away Half Their Fortunes to Good Causes', *The Guardian*, 4 August 2010.

Cohen, M. D. March, J. G. and Olsen, J. P. (1972) 'A Garbage Can Model of Organisational Choice', *Administrative Sciences Quarterly*, 17 (1): 1–25.

Coleman, W. D. (2012) 'Governance and Global Public Policy', in Levi-Faur, D. (ed.) *Oxford Handbook of Governance* (Oxford: Oxford University Press).

Collins, A. (2008) 'A People-Oriented ASEAN: A Door Ajar or Closed for Civil Society Organisations?' *Contemporary Southeast Asia: A Journal of International and Strategic Affairs*, 30 (2): 313–31.

Cooper, A. F. (2012) 'The G20 as the Global Focus Group: Beyond the Crisis Committee/Steering Committee Framework', G20 Information Centre, University of Toronto, http://www.g8.utoronto.ca/g20/analysis/120619-cooper-focusgroup.html, date accessed 6 December 2012.

Cooper, R. (2001) 'Financing International Public Goods', in Gerrar, C. D., Ferroni, M. and Mody, A. (eds) *Global Public Policies and Programs: Implications for Financing and Evaluation, Proceedings from a World Bank Workshop* (Washington DC: The World Bank).

Court, J. and Maxwell, S. (2006) 'Policy Entrepreneurship for Poverty Reduction: Bridging Research and Policy in International Development', in Court, J. and Maxwell, S. (eds) *Policy Entrepreneurship for Poverty Reduction: Bridging Research and Policy in International Development* (United Kingdom: the Overseas Development Institute and Practical Action Publishing).

Court, J., Hovland, I. and Young, J. (2005) 'Research and Policy in International Development: Introduction', in Court, J., Hoveland, I. and Young, J. (eds) *Bridging Research and Policy in Development: Evidence and the Change Process* (London: ITDG Publishing and the Overseas Development Institute).

Cox, R. W. (1981) 'Social Forces, States and World Orders: Beyond International Relations Theory', *Millennium: Journal of International Studies*, 10 (2): 126–55.

Crewe, E., Hovland, I. and Young, J. (2005) 'Context, Evidence, Links: A Conceptual Framework for Understanding Research Policy Processes', in Court, J., Hoveland, I. and Young, J. (eds) *Bridging Research and Policy in Development: Evidence and the Change Process* (London: ITDG Publishing and the Overseas Development Institute).

Danida (2001) *Partnerships at the Leading Edge: A Danish Version for Knowledge, Research and Development. Report of the Commission on Development-Related Research* (Copenhagen: Danida).

de Ridder, M. and Sánchez Díaz, P. (2012) 'Think20 a Weak Attempt of G20 to Achieve a Global Partnership for Development' (Den Haag: The Hague Center for Strategic Studies), http://www.hcss.nl/news/think-20-a-weak-attempt-of-g20-to-achieve-a-global-partnership-for-development/505/, date accessed 6 December 2012.

Deacon, B. (2007) *Global Social Policy and Governance* (London: Sage).

Denham, A. (1996) *Think Tanks of the New Right* (Dartmouth: Aldershot).

Denham, A. and Garnett, M. (2004) 'A Hollowed Out Tradition: British Think Tanks in the Twenty-First Century', in Stone, D. and Denham, A. (eds) *Think Tank Traditions: Policy Research and the Politics of Ideas* (Manchester: Manchester University Press).

Desker, B. (2010) 'CSCAP: Shaping the Future of the ASEAN Regional Forum', in Ball, D. and Guan, K. C. (eds) *Assessing Track 2 Diplomacy in the Asia-Pacific Region: A CSCAP Reader* (Australia and Singapore: Strategic and Defence Studies Centre and S. Rajaratnam School of International Studies).

Dethier, J. J. (2007) 'Producing Knowledge for Development: Research at the World Bank', *Global Governance*, 13 (4): 469–78.

Department for International Development(DfID) (2008) 'DfID's Response to the "Evaluation of DfID's Engineering Knowledge and Research (ENGKAR) Programme" Report', http://webarchive.nationalarchives.gov.uk/+/http://www.dfid.gov.uk/research/response-engkar-report.asp, date accessed 6 December 2012.

Diani, M. and McAdam, D. (2003) *Social Movements and Networks: Relational Approaches to Collective Action* (Oxford: Oxford University Press).

Djelic, M.-L. and Sahlin, K. (2012) 'Re-ordering the World – Transnational Governance and Its Challenges', in Levi-Faur, D. (ed.) *Oxford Handbook of Governance* (Oxford: Oxford University Press).

Drache, D. (2001) 'The Return of the Public Domain After the Triumph of Markets: Revisiting the Most Basic of Fundamentals', in Drache, D. (ed.) *The Market or the Public Domain* (London: Routledge).

Drori, G. S. Meyer, J. W. and Hwang, H. (2006) *Globalisation and Organisation: World Society and Organisational Change* (Oxford: Oxford University Press).

Dryzek, J. S. (2006) *Deliberative Global Politics* (Cambridge: Polity Press).

Dye, T. R. (1984) *Understanding Public Policy* (Englewood Cliffs, NJ: Prentice-Hall).

—— (1978) 'Oligarchic Tendencies in National Policy-Making: The Role of the Private Policy-Planning Organisations', *Journal of Politics*, 40 (2): 309–31.

Eckersley, R. (2007) 'Green Public Sphere in the WTO?: The *Amicus Curiae* Interventions in the Transatlantic Biotech Dispute', *European Journal of International Relations*, 13 (3): 329–56.

Eikenberry, A. (2006) 'Philanthropy and Governance', *Administrative Theory and Praxis*, 28 (4): 586–92.

Evans, M. (2009) *New Directions in the Study of Policy Transfer* (Oxford: Routledge/Taylor and Francis/Policy Studies).

Evans, P. (2006) 'Do Individuals Matter? Track Two Leadership with Southeast Asian Characteristics', in Soesastro, H., Joewono, C. and Hernandez, C. G. (eds) *Twenty Two Years of Asean ISIS* (Jakarta: Center for Strategic and International Studies).

Ferguson, J., Huysman, M. and Soekijad, M. (2010) 'Knowledge Management in Practice: Pitfalls and Potentials for Development', *World Development*, 38 (12): 1797–1810.

Fischer, F. (2003) *Reframing Public Policy: Discursive Politics and Deliberative Practices* (Oxford: Oxford University Press).

Fischer, R. (2006) 'Coordination between Track Two and Track One Diplomacy in Successful Cases of Prenegotiation', *International Negotiation*, 11 (1): 65–89.

Fraser, N. (2005) 'Transnationalising the Public Sphere', http://www.republicart.net/disc/publicum/fraser01_en.htm, date accessed 6 December 2012.

Freeman, R. (2009) 'What Is Translation?' *Evidence & Policy: A Journal of Research, Debate and Practice*, 5 (4): 429–47.

Future World Foundation (2013) 'Future World Foundation', http://www.futureworldfoundation.org/Home/Default.aspx, multiple pages accessed 1 January 2013.

Group of 20 (G20) (2008) 'Group of 20: A History', http://www.g8.utoronto.ca/g20/, date accessed 6 December 2012.

Global Development Network (GDN) (2001) 'Promotion of Research in All Social Sciences', memo from the GDN Governing Body (Washington DC: GDN).

Global Policy (2012) 'Editorial Statement and Background', *Global Policy*, http://www.globalpolicyjournal.com/about/background, date accessed 17 October 2012.

Grosse Stein, J. (2009) 'The Politics and Power of Networks: The Accountability of Humanitarian Organizations', in Kahler, M. (ed.) *Networked Politics: Agency, Power and Governance* (Ithaca, London: Cornell University Press).

Gross Stein, J., Stren, R., Fitzgibbon, J. and MacLean, M. (2001) *Networks of Knowledge: Collaborative Innovation in International Learning* (Toronto: University of Toronto Press).

Guilhot, N. (2007) 'Reforming the World: George Soros, Global Capitalism and the Philanthropic Management of the Social Sciences', *Critical Sociology*, 33: 447–79.

Haas, P. M. (1992) 'Introduction: Epistemic Communities and International Policy Coordination', *International Organisation* 46 (1): 1–35.

Habermas, J. (1989) *The Structural Transformation of the Public Sphere: An Inquiry into a Category of Bourgeois Society*, Thomas Burger (translator) (Cambridge, MA: The MIT Press).

Hajer, M. (1993) 'Discourse Coalitions and Institutionalisation of Practice: The Case of Acid Rain in Great Britain', in Fischer, F. and Forester, J. (eds) *The Argumentative Turn in Policy Analysis and Planning* (London: UCL Press).

Hajer, M. A. and Wagenaar, H. (2003) *Deliberative Policy Analysis: Understanding Governance in the Network Society* (Cambridge: Cambridge University Press).

Halfman, W. and Hoppe, R. (2004) 'Science/Policy Boundaries: A Changing Division of Labour in Dutch Expert Policy Advice', in Sabine Maasse and Peter Weingart (eds) *Scientific Expertise and Political Decision Making* (Dordrecht: Kluwer).

Hannay, A. (2005) *On The Public* (London: Routledge).

Hansen, H. K., Salskov-Iversen, D. and Bislev, S. (2002) 'Transnational Discourse Communities: Globalising Public Management', in Higgott, R. and Ougaard, M. (eds) *Understanding the Global Polity* (London: Routledge).

Herd, G. P. (2005) 'Colourful Revolutions and the CIS: "Manufactured" versus "Managed" Democracy', *Problems of Post-Communism*, 52 (2): 3–18.

Heydemann, D. C. and Hammack, S. (2009) *Globalization, Philanthropy, and Civil Society: Projecting Institutional Logics Abroad* (Bloomington, IN: Indiana University Press).

Higgott, R. and Erman, E. (2010) 'Deliberative Global Governance and the Question of Legitimacy: What Can We Learn from the WTO?' *Review of International Studies*, 36: 449–70.

Hird, J. (2005) 'Policy Analysis for What? The Effectiveness of Nonpartisan Policy Research Organizations', *The Policy Studies Journal*, 33 (1): 83–105.

Holten, R. (2008) *Global Networks* (Basingstoke, Palgrave Macmillan).

Hou, Y., Ya Ni, A., Poocharoen, O., Yang, K. and Zhao Z. J. (2011) 'The Case for Public Administration with a Global Perspective', *Journal of Public Administration Research and Theory*, 21 (suppl. 1): i45–i51.

Howell, J. Ed. (2012) *Global Matters for Non-Governmental Public Action* (Houndmills, Basingstoke: Palgrave Macmillan).

Hudson, A. (2007) 'Arms to Africa? Policy Coherence for Development and Power', http://www.odi.org.uk/opinion/4140-arms-africa-policy-coherence-development-power, date accessed 6 December 2012.

Huelshoff, M. and Kiel, C. (2012) 'Swan Song: Transnational Advocacy Networks and Environmental Policy in Chile – The Case of the Cisnes de Cuello Negro', *Interest Groups and Advocacy*, 1 (2): 260–278.

International Development Research Centre (IDRC) (2012) 'Think Tank Initiative', http://www.idrc.ca/EN/Programs/Social_and_Economic_Policy/Think_Tank_Initiative/Pages/default.aspx (home page), date accessed 6 December 2012.

Independent Evaluation Group (IEG) (2007) *Sourcebook for Evaluation Global and Regional Partnership Programs: Indicative Principles and Standards* (Washington DC: World Bank).

Ilcan, S. and Phillips, L. (2008) 'Governing through Global Networks: Knowledge Mobilities and Participatory Development', *Current Sociology*, 56 (5): 711–34.

Jacobsen, J. K. (1995), 'Much Ado about Ideas: The Cognitive Factor in Economic Policy', *World Politics* 47: 283–310.

Jacobson, N. (2007) 'Social Epistemology: Theory for the "Fourth Wave" of Knowledge Transfer and Exchange Research', *Science Communication*, 29 (1): 116–27.

Jay, M. (2006) 'Introduction: What's Next in International Development', *Annual Report* (London: Overseas Development Institute).

Jayasuriya, K. (1994) 'Singapore: The Politics of Regional Definition', *The Pacific Review* 7 (4): 411–20.

Job, B. (2003) 'Track 2 Diplomacy: Ideational Contribution to the Evolving Asian Security Order', in Alagappa, M. (ed.) *Asian Security Order: Instrumental and Normative Features* (Stanford: Stanford University Press).

Johnstone, I . (2005) 'The Power of Interpretive Communities' in Barnett, M. and Duvall, R. (eds) *Power in Global Governance* (Cambridge: Cambridge University Press).

Jones, B. (2011) 'Linking Research to Policy: The African Development Bank as Knowledge Broker', working paper Series N 131 (African Development Bank, Tunis, Tunisia).

Jones, H., Jones, N., Shaxson, L. and Walker, D. (2012) *Knowledge, Policy and Power in International Development: A Practical Guide* (Bristol: The Policy Press).

Jones, P. (2008) *Canada and Track Two Diplomacy* (Toronto: Canadian International Council).

Kahler, M. Ed. (2009) *Networked Politics: Agency, Power and Governance* (Ithaca, London: Cornell University Press).

Kanbur, R. (2001) 'Economic Policy, Distribution and Poverty: The Nature of Disagreements', *World Development*, 29 (6): 1083–94.

Kapur, D. (2006) 'The Knowledge Bank', in Birdsall, N. (ed.) *Rescuing the World Bank* (Washington DC: Centre for Global Development).

Kaul, I. (2005) 'Exploring the Policy Space between Markets and States: Global Public-Private Partnerships', in Kaul, I. and Conceição, P. (eds) *The New Public Finance: Responding to Global Challenges* (New York, NY: Oxford University Press and United Nations Development Programme).

—— (2001) 'Global Public Goods: What Role for Civil Society', *Non Profit and Voluntary Sector Quarterly*, 30 (3): 588–602.

Kaye, D. D. (2007) *Talking to the Enemy: Track Two Diplomacy in the Middle East and South Asia* (Santa Monica, CA: RAND Corporation).

Keck, M. and Sikkink, K. (1998) *Activists Beyond Borders: Advocacy Networks in International Politics* (Ithaca, New York: Cornell University Press).

Kennett, P. (2010) 'Global Perspective on Governance', in Osbourne, Stephen P. (ed.) *The New Public Governance: Emerging Perspectives on the Theory and Practice of Public Governance* (London: Routledge).

Keohane, R. O. and Nye, J. S. (1998) 'Power and Interdependence in the Information Age', *Foreign Affairs*, 77 (5): 81–94.

Kerr, P. (1994) 'The Security Dialogue in the Asia-Pacific', *The Pacific Review*, 7 (4): 397–409.

Keynes, J. M. (1936) *The General Theory of Employment, Interest, and Money* (New York: Harcourt, Brace & World).

Kim B. P. (2001) 'Asia's Informal Diplomacy: Track 2 Discussion and Regionalism, *Harvard International Review* 23 (1): 38–41.

Kingdon, J. (1995) *Agendas, Alternatives and Public Policies* (New York: Longman).

Kirton, J. (2012) 'Academics, Analysis and Accountability: Contributions to G20 Governance', paper presented at an international conference on 'Global Governance for the Next Generation: Building on the Los Cabos G20 Summit', Mexico City, http://www.g20.utoronto.ca/biblio/120425-kirton-itam.html, date accessed 6 December 2012.

Kjaer, P. and Pedersen, O. (2001) 'Translating Liberalisation', in Campbell, J. and Pedersen, O. (eds) *The Rise of Neoliberalism and Institutional Analysis* (Princeton and Oxford: Princeton University Press).

Kleinschmidt, J. and Strandsbjerg, J. (2010) 'After Critical Geopolitics: Why International Relation Theory Needs Even More Social Theory', Millennium Conference, 16–17 October, London School of Economics, http://millennium journal.files.wordpress.com/2010/09/kleinschmidt-strandsbjerg_after-critical-geopolitics_1-4.pdf, date accessed 21 December 2012.

Knutsen, K. and Sending, O. J. (2000) 'The Instrumentalisation of Development Knowledge', in Stone, D. (ed.) *Banking on Knowledge: The Genesis of the Global Development Network* (London: Routledge).

Koncz, K. (2006) *NGO Sustainability in Central Europe: Helping Civil Society Survive* (Budapest: LGI and Open Society Institute).

Kraft, H. (2002) 'Track Three Diplomacy and Human Rights in Southeast Asia: The Asia Pacific Coalition for East Timor', *Global Networks*, 2 (1): 49–63.

Krastev, I. (2000) 'Post-Communist Think Tanks: Making or Faking Influence', in Stone, D. (ed.) *Banking on Knowledge. The Genesis of the Global Development Network* (London: Routledge).

Krizsán, A. and Zentai, V. (2005) 'From Civil Society to Policy Research: The Case of the Soros Network and Its Roma Policies', in Stone, D. and Maxwell, S. (eds) *Global Knowledge Networks and International Development: Bridges across Boundaries* (London: Routledge).

Ladi, S. (2011a) 'Think Tanks, Discursive Institutionalism and Policy Change', in Papanagnou, G. (ed.) *Social Science and Policy Challenges: Democracy, Values and Capacities* (Paris: UNESCO).

Ladi, S. (2011b) 'Policy Change and Soft Europeanisation: The Transfer of the Ombudsman Institution to Greece, Cyprus and Malta', *Public Administration*, 89 (4): 1643–63.

Laine, S. (2012) *Young Actors in Transnational Agoras: Multi-Sited Ethnography of Cosmopolitan, Micropolitical Orientations*, Finnish Youth Research Society Publications 121 (Helsinki: Finnish Youth Research Network).

Leach, M., Scoones, I. and Wynne, B. (2005) *Science and Citizens: Globalisation and the Challenge of Engagement* (London: Zed Books).

Lee, C. (2009) 'Cross-Strait Participation in the Council for Security Cooperation in the Asia Pacific: A Case Study of a Multilateral Track Two Approach to Conflict Prevention', *Issues and Studies*, 45 (4): 189–215.

Lendvai, N. and Stubbs, P. (2007) 'Policies as Translation: Situation Transnational Social Policies', in Hodgson, S. M. and Iriving, Z. (eds) *Policy Reconsidered: Meanings, Politics and Practices* (Bristol: Policy Press).

Lloyd, G (2010) 'Intertwingled Work', posted 5 July, http://traction.traction softwar.com/traction/permalink/Blog1424, date accessed 6 December 2012.

Long, D. and Woolley, F. (2009) 'Global Public Goods: Critique of a UN Discourse', *Global Governance*, 15 (1): 107–22.

Lovitt, J. and Pajas, P. J. (2011) *How to Win Respect and Influence Policy Makers: Principles for Effective Quality Controls in the Work of Independent Think-Tanks* (Prague: PASOS).

Macdonald, K. and Macdonald, T. (2010) 'Democracy in a Pluralist Global Order: Corporate Power and Stakeholder Representation', *Ethics & International Affairs*, 24 (1): 19–43.

Manea, M. G. (2009) 'How and Why Interaction Matters: Asean's Regional Identity and Human Rights', *Cooperation and Conflict*, 44 (1): 27–49.

Marsh, D. and Sharman, J. C. (2009) 'Policy Diffusion and Policy Transfer', *Policy Studies* 30 (3): 269–88.

Maselli, D., Lys, J. A. and Schmid, J. (2004) *Improving Impacts of Research Partnerships* KFPE Swiss Comission for Research Partnerships with Developing Countries (Bern: Geographica Bernensia).

Maxwell, S. (2005a) 'Foreword', in Court, J., Hovland, I. and Young., J. (eds) *Bridging Research and Policy in Development: Evidence and the Change Process* (London: ITDG Publishing and the Overseas Development Institute).

Maxwell, Simon (2005b) 'Blogging international development – a new kind of conversation', Tuesday, June 14, 2005 3:40 PM at: http://blogs.odi.org.uk/blogs/main/archive/2005/06/14/3.aspx.

McGann, J. G. (2007) *Think Tanks and Policy Advice in the United States: Academics, Advisors and Advocates* (London: Routledge).

McGann, J. G. and Sabatini, R. (2011) *Global Think Tanks, Policy Networks and Governance* (London: Routledge).

McKewon, E. (2012) 'The Use of Neoliberal Think Tank Fantasy Themes to Delegitimise Scientific Knowledge of Climate Change in Australian Newspapers', *Environmental Journalism*, 13 (2): 277–297.

McLaughlin, L. (2004) 'Feminism and the Political Economy of Transnational Public Space', in Crossley, N. and Roberts, M. (eds) *After Habermas: New Perspectives on the Public Sphere* (Oxford: Blackwell).

McMichael, P. (2001) 'Revisiting the Question of the Transnational State', *Theory and Society*, 30: 201–210.

McNutt, K. and Pal, L. A. (2011) '"Modernizing Government": Mapping Global Public Policy Networks', *Governance*, 24: 439–67.

Medvetz, T. (2012) *The Rise of Think Tanks in America: Merchants of Policy and Power* (Chicago: University of Chicago Press).

Mexican Presidency of the G20 (2012) 'Think20 Infographic', http://www.sre.gob.mx/images/stories/infografias/think20/think20en.html, date accessed 6 December 2012.

Miller, C. (2007) 'Democratisation, International Knowledge Institutions and Global Governance', *Governance*, 20 (2): 325–57.

Milner, A. (2007) 'Reconciling Asean+3 and East Asia Summit', in Leong, S. (ed.) *Peace in the Pacific: Confronting the Issues* (Kuala Lumpur: ISIS Malaysia).

Mintrom, M. (2006) 'Policy Entrepreneurs, Think Tanks and Trusts', in Miller, R. (ed.) *New Zealand Government and Politics*, 4th edition (Oxford: Oxford University Press).

Misztal, B. A. (2012) 'Public Intellectuals and Think Tanks: A Free Market in Ideas?' *International Journal of Politics, Culture and Society*, 25 (4): 127–141.

Morrison, C. (2004) 'Track 1/Track 2 Symbiosis in Asia-Pacific Regionalism', *The Pacific Review*, 17 (4): 547–65.

Mosse, D. (2006) 'Anti-Social Anthropology: Objectivity, Objection, and the Ethnography of Public Policy and Professional Communities', *Journal of the Royal Anthropological Institute*, 12: 935–56.

Nan, S. A., Druckman, D. and El Hor, J. (2009) 'Unofficial International Conflict Resolution: Is There a Track 1-1/2? Are There Best Practices?' *Conflict Resolution Quarterly*, 27 (1): 65–82.

Nanz, P. and Steffek, J. (2004) 'Global Governance, Participation and the Public Sphere', *Government and Opposition*, 39 (2): 314–35.

Neier, A. (2011) 'Afterword', in Sudetic, C. *The Philanthropy of George Soros: Building Open Societies* (Philadelphia PA: Public Affairs).

Neilson, S. (2011) 'IDRC- Supported Research and Its Influence on Public Policy' (Canada: Evaluation Unit IDRC), http://idl-bnc.idrc.ca/dspace/handle/10625/31356, date accessed 12 December 2012.

Nelson, T. (1987) *Computer Lib/Dream Achines* (rev. ed.) (Redmond, WA: Tempus Books of Microsoft Press).

Nesadurai, H. (2011) 'The ASEAN People's Forum as Authentic Social Forum', in Beeson, M. and Stubbs, R. (eds) *Handbook of Asian Regionalism* (London: Routledge).

Newman, J. (2005) *Remaking Governance: Peoples, Politics and the Public Sphere* (Bristol: Policy Press).

Nowotny, H., Scott, P. and Gibbons, M. (2001). *Re-Thinking Science: Knowledge and the Public in an Age of Uncertainty*(Oxford, UK: Polity Press).

Overseas Development Council (ODC) (1999) 'Dialogue with Think Tanks: A Report of a Meeting with the United Nations Secretary General' (New York: United Nations Headquarters).

Overseas Development Institute (ODI) (2012) *Annual Review 2010–2011* (London: Overseas Development Institute).

———. (2011) 'Communications: Changing the Development Story', http://www.odi.org.uk/news/details.asp?id=337&title=communications-changing-development-story, date accessed 6 December 2012.

———. (2005) 'ODI Is the 2005 "Think-Tank to Watch"', posted 21 September, http://www.odi.org.uk/news/106-odi-2005-think-tank-watch, date accessed 6 December 2012.

———. (2006) 'What's Next in International Development' *Annual Report, ODI* (London: Overseas Development Institute).

———. (n.d.) ODI Milestones, http://www.odi.org.uk/about/50years/, date accessed 6 December 2012.

O'Neil, M. (2006) 'What Determines the Influence That Research Has on Policy Making', in Court, J. and Maxwell, S. (eds) *Policy Entrepreneurship for Poverty Reduction: Bridging Research and Policy in International Development* (United Kingdom: Overseas Development Institute and Practical Action Publishing).

Open Society Institute (OSI) (2009) *We Are ... Soros Foundations Network 2008 Report* (New York: Open Society Institute).

———. (2006) *Building Open Societies: Soros Foundations Network 2005 Report* (New York: Open Society Institute).

———. (2005) *Building Open societies: Soros Foundations Network 2004 Report* (New York, Open Society Institute).

———. (2004) *Building Open Societies: Soros Foundations Network 2003 Report* (New York: Open Society Institute).

Ottaway, M. (2001) 'Corporatism Goes Global: International Organisations, Nongovernmental Organisations Networks and Transnational Business', *Global Governance*, 7 (3): 265–92.

Ougaard, M. and Higgott, R. Eds (2002) *Towards a Global Polity* (London: Routledge).

Pajas, P. J. (2011) *Thinking Ethically: A Think-Tank Code of Good Governance* (Prague: PASOS).

Palley, T. (2003) 'The Open Institute and Global Social Policy', *Global Social Policy*, 3 (1): 17–18.

Papanagnou, G. (2010) 'Research, Discourses and Democracy. Innovating the Social, Science-Policy Nexus', *MOST-2 Policy Papers 20* (Paris: UNESCO).

Parmar, I. (2002) 'American Foundations and the Development of International Knowledge Networks', *Global Networks*, 2 (1): 13–30.

Pautz, H. (2011) 'Revisiting the Think-Tank Phenomenon', *Public Policy and Administration*, 26 (4): 19–435.

Peterson, M. J. (1992) 'Whalers, Cetologists, Environmentalists, and the International Management of Whaling', *International Organisations*, 46 (1): 147–86.

Plehwe, D. (2007) 'A Global Knowledge Bank? The World Bank and Bottom-Up Efforts to Reinforce the Neoliberal Developments Perspectives in the Post Washington Consensus Era', *Globalisations*, 4 (4): 514–28.

Popper, K. (1945) *The Open Society and Its Enemies* (London: Routledge).

Prince, R. (2011) 'Policy Transfer, Consultants and the Geographies of Governance', *Progress in Human Geography*, 36 (2): 188–203.

Prügl, E. (2004) 'International Institutions and Feminist Politics', *Brown Journal of World Affairs*, 10 (2): 69–84.

Raab, J. and Milward, H. B. (2003) 'Dark Networks as Problems', *Journal of Public Administration Research and Theory*, 13 (4): 413–39.

Rachman, G. (2008) How to Write about Pointless International Organisations', *Financial Times*, posted 11 July, http://www.thinktankwatch.com/2012/05/g20s-new-think-tank-think20.html, date accessed 6 December 2012.

Rai, S. (2005) 'Networking across Borders: South Asian Research Network (SARN) on Gender, Law and Governance', in Stone, D. and Maxwell, S. (eds) *Global Knowledge Networks and International Development: Bridges across Boundaries* (London: Routledge).

Rao, V. and Woolcock, M. (2007) 'The Disciplinary Monopoly in Development Research at the World Bank', *Global Governance*, 13: 479–84.

Ravallion, M., Gelb, A. and Harrison, A. (2012) 'Research for Development: A World Bank Perspective on Future Directions for Research', Policy Research Working Paper 5437 (Washington DC: World Bank).

Ravallion, Martin., Gelb, A. and Harrison, A. (2010) Research for Development: A World Bank Perspective on Future Directions for Research, Policy Research Working Paper 5437 (Washington DC: World Bank).

Reinicke, W. (1998) *Global Public Policy: Governing without Government* (Washington DC: Brookings Institution).

Reinicke, W., Deng, F. *et al.* (2000) *Critical Choices: The United Nations, Networks and the Future of Global Governance* (Ottawa: International Development Research Centre).

Rhodes, R. A. W. (2012) 'Waves of Governance', in Levi-Faur, D. (ed.) *Oxford Handbook of Governance* (Oxford: Oxford University Press).

Ricci, D. (1993) *The Transformation of American Politics: The New Washington and the Rise of Think Tanks* (New Haven: Yale University Press).

Rich, A. (2004) *Think Tanks, Public Policy, and the Politics of Expertise* (Cambridge: Cambridge University Press).

Ritzen, J. (2005) *A Chance for the World Bank* (London: Anthem Press).

Roelofs, J. (2003) *Foundations and Public Policy: The Mask of Pluralism* (Albany, New York: State University of New York Press).

Ronit, K. (2006) *Global Public Policy: Business and the Countervailing Powers of Civil Society* (London: Routledge).

Rouhana, N. N. (1995) 'Unofficial Third-Party Intervention in International Conflict: Between Legitimacy and Disarray', *Negotiation Journal*, 11 (3): 255–70.

Rüland, J. (2002) 'The Contribution of Track Two Dialogue Towards Crisis Prevention', *Asien*, 85 (October): 84–96.

Rushton, S. and Williams, O. D. (2012) 'Frames, Paradigms and Power: Global Health Policy-Making under Neoliberalism', *Global Society*, 26 (2): 147–67.

Ryan, J. and Garret, J. L. (2004) 'The Impact of Economic Policy Research: Lessons on Attribution and Evaluation from IFPRI', in Stone, D. and Maxwell, S. (eds) *Global Knowledge Networks and International Development: Bridges Across Boundaries* (London: Routledge).

Sabel, C. F. and Zeitlin, J. (2012) 'Experimentalist Governance', in Levi-Faur, D. (ed.) *Oxford Handbook of Governance* (Oxford: Oxford University Press).

Schäferhoff, M., Campe, S. and Kaane, C. (2009) 'Transnational Public-Private Partnerships in International Relations: Making Sense of Concepts, Research Frameworks, and Results', *International Studies Review*, 11 (3): 451–74.

Schatz, E. (2009) *Political Ethnography: What Immersion Contributes to the Study of Power* (Chicago: University of Chicago Press).

Schmidt, V. (2008) 'Discursive Institutionalism: The Explanatory Power of Ideas and Discourse', *Annual Review of Political Science*, 11 (1): 303–26.

Scott, J. (1999) 'Transnationalizing Democracy Promotion: The Role of Western Political Foundations and Think-Tanks', *Democratization*, 6 (3): 146–170.

Scott-Smith, G. and Baumgärtel, M. (2011) 'New Paradigms, Old Hierarchies? Problems and Possibilities of US Supremacy in a Networked World', *International Politics*, 48 (2–3): 271–89.

Seiler, C. and Wohlrabe, K. (2010) 'A Critique of the 2009 Global 'Go-to Think Tanks' Ranking', *CESifo DICE Report*, 8 (2): 60–63.

Sending, O. J. and Neumann, I. B. (2010) *Governing the Global Polity: Practice, Mentality, Rationality* (Ann Arbor, MI: University of Michigan Press).

Simon, S. (2010) 'Evaluating Track 2 Approaches to Security Dialogue in the Asia Pacific Region: The CSCAP experience', in Ball, D. and Guan K. C. (eds) *Assessing Track 2 Diplomacy in the Asia-Pacific Region: A CSCAP Reader* (Australia and Singapore: Strategic and Defence Studies Centre and S. Rajaratnam School of International Studies).

Sinclair, T. J. (2005) *The New Masters of Capital: American Bond Rating Agencies and the Politics of Creditworthiness* (Cornell: Cornell University Press).

———. (2000) 'Reinventing Authority: Embedded Knowledge Networks and the New Global Finance', *Environment and Planning C: Government and Policy*, 18 (4): 487–502.

Skogstad, G. (2011) *Policy Paradigms, Transnationalism and Domestic Politics* (Toronto: University of Toronto Press).

Slaughter, A. M. (2004) *A New World Order* (Princeton: Princeton University Press).

Smith, J. A. (1991) *The Idea Brokers: Think Tanks and the Rise of the New Policy Elite* (New York: The Free Press).

Soesastro, H., Joewono, C. and Hernandez, C. G. (2006) 'Introduction', in Soesastro, H., Joewono, C. and Hernandez, C. G. (eds) *Twenty Two Years of ASEAN ISIS* (Jakarta: Center for Strategic and International Studies).

Sørenson, E. and Torfing, J. (2007) *Theories of Democratic Network Governance* (Basingstoke: Palgrave Macmillan).

Soros, G. (1997) 'The Capitalist Threat', *Atlantic Monthly*, 279 (2): 45–58.

Soros, G. (2011) 'My Philanthropy', in Sudetic, C. (ed.) *The Philanthropy of George Soros: Building Open Societies* (Philadelphia PA: Public Affairs).

Squire, L. (2000) 'Why the World Bank Should Be Involved in Development Research', in Gilbert, C. L. and Vines, D. (eds) *The World Bank: Structure and Policies* (Cambridge: Cambridge University Press).

Steger, U., Amann, W. and Maznevski, M. Eds (2012) *Managing Complexity in Global Organisations* (Chichester, West Sussex: Wiley).

Stiglitz, J. (1999) 'Knowledge as a Global Public Good', in Kaul, I., Grunberg, I. and Stern, M. A. (eds) *Global Public Goods: International Cooperation in the 21st Century* (New York: Oxford University Press and UNDP).

———. (2000) 'Scan Globally, Reinvent Locally: Knowledge Infrastructure and the Localisation of Knowledge', in Stone, D. (ed.) *Banking on Knowledge: The Genesis of the Global Development Network* (London: Routledge).

Stone, D. (1996) *Capturing the Political Imagination: Think Tanks and the Policy Process* (London: Frank Cass).

Stone, D. (2007) 'Garbage Cans, Recycling Bins or Think Tanks? Three Myths about Policy Institutes', *Public Administration*, 85 (2): 259–278.

Stone, D. (2008) 'Global Public Policy, Transnational Policy Communities and Their Networks', *Policy Studies Journal*, 36 (10): 19–38.

Stone, D. (2009) 'RAPID Knowledge: 'Bridging Research and Policy in International Development at the Overseas Development Institute', *Public Administration and Development*, 29 (4): 303–15.

Stone, D. (2011) 'The ASEAN-ISIS Policy Network: Interpretative Communities, Informal Diplomacy and Discourses of Region', *Minerva*, 49 (2): 241–62.

Stone, D. (2012) 'Transfer and Translation of Policy', *Policy Studies*, 33 (4): 1–17.

Stone, D. and Maxwell, S. (2005) *Global Knowledge Networks and International Development: Bridges across Boundaries* (London: Routledge).

Stone, D. and Wright. C. Eds (2006) *The World Bank and Governance: A Decade of Reform and Reaction* (London: Routledge).

Struyk, R. J. (2007) *Managing Think Tanks: Practical Guidance for Maturing Organisations*, 2nd ed. (Budapest: Local Government and Public Service Reform Initiative, and Washington DC: Urban Institute).

Struyk, R. J. and Haddaway, S. R. (2012) 'Mentoring Policy Research Organizations: Project Evaluation Results', *Voluntas*, 23 (3): 636–660.

Struyk, R. J. and Miller, C. (2004) 'Policy Research in Bosnia and Herzegovina: The Role and Impact of Local Think Tanks', *Southeast European Politics*, 5 (1): 45–59.

Stubbs, P. (2005) 'Stretching Concepts Too Far? Multi-Level Governance, Policy Transfer and the Politics of Scale in South East Europe', *Southeast European Politics*, 6 (2): 66–87.

Stubbs, P. and Wedel, J. (2013) 'Policy flexians in Global Order', in Kaasch, A. and Martens, K. (eds) *Actors and Agency in Global Social Governance*, forthcoming.

Sturdy, A., Handley, K., Clark, T. and Fincham, R. (2008) 'Rethinking the Role of Management Consultants in Knowledge as Disseminators of Business Knowledge', in Scarborough, H. (ed.) *The Evolution of Business Knowledge* (Oxford: Oxford University Press).

Sukma, R. (2006) 'ASEAN ISIS and Political Security Cooperation in Asia Pacific', in Soestastro, H., Joewono, C. and Hernandez, C. G. (eds) *Twenty Two Years of ASEAN ISIS* (Jakarta: Center for Strategic and International Studies).

Sutton, R. (1999) 'The Policy Process: An Overview', *Overseas Development Institute Working Paper* No. 118. (London: Overseas Development Institute).

Tay, S. (2006) 'Challenges and Prospects for ASEAN ISIS', in Soesastro, H., Joewono, C. and Hernandez, C. G. (eds) *Twenty Two Years of Asean ISIS* (Jakarta: Center for Strategic and International Studies).

Taylor, M. (2005) 'Bridging Research and Policy: A UK Perspective', *Journal of International Development*, 17 (6): 747–55.

Taylore, P. (2012) Personal Communication and Invitation to Attend the Think Tank Funders' Forum in London; email sent September 24, 2012 12:16 AM.

The Conversation (2012) 'Who We Are', https://theconversation.edu.au/who_we_are, date accessed 6 December 2012.

The Royal Society (2011) *Knowledge, Networks and Nations: Global Scientific Collaboration in the 21st Century*, Policy Document 03/11 (London: Royal Society).

Think-20 Mexico (2012) Report to the G20 Sherpas, March, http://www.boell.org/downloads/FINAL_Think-20_Report_to_Sherpas.pdf, date accessed 26 December 2012.

Thirlwell, M. (2012) Think-20, the thinking person's G20', *The Interpreter*, posted 13 March 2012, http://www.lowyinterpreter.org/post/2012/03/13/Think-20-the-thinking-persons-G20.aspx, date accessed 6 December 2012.

Thompson, G. (2003) *Between Hierarchies and Markets: The Logic and Limits of Network Forms of Organisation* (Oxford: Oxford University Press).

Tickner, A. J. (2006) 'On the Frontlines or Sidelines of Knowledge and Power: Feminist Practices of Responsible Scholarship', *International Studies Review*, 8 (3): 383–95.

Torfing, J. (2012) 'Governance Networks', in Levi-Faur, D. (ed.) *Oxford Handbook of Governance* (Oxford: Oxford University Press).

Touaf, L. and Boutkhil, S. (2008) *The World as a Global Agora: Critical Perspectives on Public Space* (Newcastle-upon-Tyne: Cambridge Scholars Publishing).

Toye, J. and Toye, R. (2005) 'The World Bank as a Knowledge Agency', Overarching Concerns Programme Policy Paper 11 (Geneva: United Nations Research Institute on Sustainable Development), http://www.unrisd.org/unrisd/website/document.nsf/ab82a6805797760f80256b4f005da1ab/faef21fbef6af0c6c12570cb0030c5cc/$FILE/toye.pdf, date accessed 26 December 2012.

True, J. (2003) 'Mainstreaming Gender in Global Public Policy', *International Feminist Journal of Politics*, 5 (3): 368–96.

United Nations Development Program (UNDP) (2003) *Thinking the Unthinkable* (Bratislava: UNDP: Regional Bureau for Europe and the Commonwealth of Independent States).

United Nations Educational, Scientific and Cutlural Organization (UNESCO) (2008) 'Management of Social Transformations (MOST) Programme', http://www.unesco.org/new/en/social-and-human-sciences/themes/most-programme/, date accessed 26 December 2012.

United Nations Research Institute for Social Development (UNRISD) (2005) 'Improving Research and Knowledge on Social Development in International Organisations', http://www.unrisd.org/80256B3C005BB128/(httpProjects)/5CCCB80CEC61136380256B5D0045A6EF?OpenDocument, date accessed 12 December 2012.

Urbinati, N. (2000) 'Representation as Advocacy: A Study of Democratic Deliberation', *Political Theory*, 28 (6): 758–86.

Vogel, A. (2006) 'Who's Making Global Civil Society: Philanthropy and US Empire in World Society', *British Journal of Sociology*, 57 (4): 635–55.

Wacquant, L. (2004) 'Penal Truth Comes to Europe: Think Tanks and the "Washington Consensus on Crime and Punishment', in Gilligan, G. and Pratt, J. (eds) in *Crime, Truth and Justice: Official Inquiry, Discourse, Knowledge* (Cullompton: Willan Publishing).

Waddell, S. (2011) *Global Action Networks* (Basingstoke: Bocconi University Press and Palgrave Macmillan).

Walters, W. (2012) *Governmentality: Critical Encounters* (Abingdon, Oxon: Routledge).

Weaver, R. K. (1989) 'The Changing World of Think Tanks', *PS: Political Science and Politics*, 22 (3): 563–78.

Weidenbaum, M. (2011) *The Competition of Ideas: The World of Washington Think Tanks* (New Brunswick, NJ: Transaction Publishers).

Weiss, C. (1991) *Organisations for Policy Analysis: Helping Governments Think* (California: Sage).

Weiss, T. G. (1982) 'International Bureaucracy: The Myth and Reality of International Civil Service', *International Affairs*, 58 (2): 287–306.

Wendt, A. (1994) 'Collective Identity Formation and the International State', *American Political Science Review*, 88 (2): 384–96.

Weyrauch, V. (2007) *Weaving Global Networks. Handbook for Policy Influence* (Buenos Aires: Fundación CIPPEC).

Wheeler, G. (2009) 'Update on the Knowledge Agenda', World Bank/IFC/M.I.G.A. Office Memorandum to R. Zoellick EXC, 17 June. (Washington DC: World Bank).

Wildavsky, A. (1987) *Speaking Truth to Power: The Art and Craft of Policy Analysis* (Boston, Toronto: Little, Brown and Company).

World Bank (2012) Research Report. Research at Work: Assessing the Influence of World Bank Research, in Development Economics (DEC) (Washington DC: World Bank), http://documents.worldbank.org/curated/en/2012/04/16230169/research-report-2012-research-work-assessing-influence-world-bank-research.

World Bank, Operations Evaluation Department (2004) *Addressing the Challenges of Globalisation: An Independent Evaluation of the World Bank's Approach to Global Programs* (Washington DC: International Bank for Reconstruction and Development).

Wycherley, R. E. (1956) 'The Market of Athens: Topography and Monuments', *Greece and Rome*, 3 (1): 2–24.

———. (1942) 'The Ionian Agora', *The Journal of Hellenic Studies*, 62: 21–32.

Xu, Y. C. and Weller, P. (2008) 'To Be, but Not to Be Seen: Exploring the Impact of International Civil Servants', *Public Administration*, 86 (1): 35–51.

Yamamoto, T. and Hubbard, S. (1995) 'Conference Report', in Yamamoto, T. (ed.) *Emerging Civil Society in the Asia Pacific Community* (Singapore: Institute of Southeast Asian Studies and Japan Centre for International Exchange).

Young, J. (2005) 'Research, Policy and Practices: Why Developing Countries Are Different', *Journal of International Development*, 17 (6): 727–34.

Zhu, X. (2009) 'The Influence of Think Tanks in the Chinese Policy Process: Different Ways and Mechanisms', *Asian Survey*, 49 (2): 333–57.

Zhu, X. (2011) 'Government Advisors or Public Advocates? Roles of Think Tanks in China form the Perspective of Regional Variations', *The China Quarterly*, 207: 668–86.

Zonana, V. and Nayyar, A. (2009) *Policy Landscape and Think Tanks in India : Paradigms, Processes and Future Directions* (New Delhi: Bill & Melinda Gates Foundation).

Index

220 Index

Printed and bound by CPI Group (UK) Ltd, Croydon, CR0 4YY

CPI Antony Rowe

Chippenham, UK

2018-03-14 21:34